KT-519-576

Second Language Acquisition & Language Pedagogy

WITHDRAWN

Rod Ellis
Temple University Japan

MULTILINGUAL MATTERS LTD
Clevedon ● Philadelphia ● Adelaide

NAPIER UNIVERSITY LIBRARY

NAPIER UNIVERSITY LIBRARY

AC / /	ON 14007 48/5
LOC	SHMK S 418 · 007 ELL	SUP T·C·F.
CON	PR £16.95

Library of Congress Cataloging in Publication Data

Ellis, Rod
Second Language Acquisition and Language Pedagogy/Rod Ellis
(Multilingual Matters: 79)
Includes bibliographical references and index.
1. Second language acquisition. 2. Language and languages — Study and
teaching. I. Title. II. Series: Multilingual Matters (Series)
P118.2.E39   1991
418'.007   dc20

British Library Cataloguing in Publication Data

A CIP catalogue record for this book is available from the British Library.

ISBN 1-85359-136-X (hbk)
ISBN 1-85359-135-1 (pbk)

Multilingual Matters Ltd

UK: Frankfurt Lodge, Clevedon Hall, Victoria Road, Clevedon, Avon BS21 7SJ.
USA: 1900 Frost Road, Suite 101, Bristol, PA 19007, USA.
Australia: P.O. Box 6025, 83 Gilles Street, Adelaide, SA 5000, Australia.

Copyright © 1992 Rod Ellis.
First printing, 1992. Reprinted 1993.

All rights reserved. No part of this work may be reproduced in any form or by
any means without permission in writing from the publisher.

Printed and bound in Great Britain by the Cromwell Press, Melksham.

Contents

A Note on Terminology

1. The abbreviation 'SLA' is used to refer to second language acquisition as a *field* of study. In contrast, 'L2 acquisition' refers to the actual acquisition of a second language.

2. There is no consistency in the use of pronouns to refer generically to 'learner', 'native speaker', 'teacher' etc. This reflects my own changing practice in the use of these pronouns over the last decade. Whereas I initially opted for masculine pronouns I have more recently preferred feminine forms. I hope that, taken as a whole, the book offers reasonable balance between masculine and feminine pronouns and that, as a result, no serious offence to any reader will arise.

Section 1: Introduction

The last quarter of a decade has seen the birth of second language acquisition (SLA) as a field of study within applied linguistics. Although there were a few studies of how people acquired a second language (L2) before this period (see, for instance, Leopold's (1939) admirable study of the speech development of a bilingual child) it is certainly true that the growth in empirical work has been exponential since the late 1960s. This is reflected in a dramatic increase in the published journals that inform the field (*Applied Linguistics*, *Studies in Second Language Acquisition* and *Second Language Research*, for example, did not exist prior to 1980) and also in full-length books, providing both collections of conference papers and state-of-the-art reviews of the field. It is pertinent to ask three general questions:

(1) What motivated this growth in SLA studies?
(2) What developments in SLA have taken place over this 20-year period?
(3) What issues have SLA studies focused on?

Given that SLA has always been closely associated with proposals for language pedagogy — a theory of language learning together with a theory of language constituting the twin sources of the theoretical principles that give shape to particular instructional approaches (cf. Richards & Rogers, 1986) — it is also pertinent to ask a fourth question:

(4) In what ways have SLA studies informed L2 pedagogy?

This introduction will briefly examine each of these questions and in so doing provide a context in which to locate the papers that comprise this collection.

The Origins of SLA Studies

The sudden development in SLA studies which took place in the late 1960s was the result of a number of factors, which together conspired to interest researchers in how an L2 was acquired — in particular, in naturalistic surroundings. These factors were: (1) previous work in first language acquisition, (2) theoretical conflict as a result of competing views of how language is acquired, and (3) a growing disillusionment with contemporary approaches to the teaching of an L2.

The debt to L1 studies

The early 1960s saw a number of empirical studies of L1 acquisition. Roger Brown and associates at Harvard University conducted a longitudinal study of three children learning English. They collected spoken data of conversations between the children and their mothers in play situations, painstakingly transcribed them and then submitted them to a number of detailed analyses in order to investigate how the children gained control over the grammatical system of English. Similar studies were carried out by Dan Slobin and associates and by Lois Bloom. In each case the studies were longitudinal and the emphasis was on describing and accounting for the linguistic (in particular, grammatical) development that took place in young children.

De Villiers & de Villiers (1973) used a rather different approach. They collected data from a larger number of children but at a single point in time and then sought to determine the *accuracy* with which specific grammatical morphemes (e.g. plural -*s* and past tense -*ed*) were performed by the children, hypothesising that accuracy order and acquisition order would be closely related. In this way the cross-sectional study of acquisition could be used to provide information about L1 development.

These studies of L1 acquisition informed early work in L2 acquisition in a number of ways. First, they demonstrated that it was possible to investigate how a language was acquired in valid and reliable ways. Second, they offered a set of methodological procedures that could be used equally well in the study of L2 acquisition. Third, they provided a body of descriptive information about how children acquired English as their L1 which could serve as a baseline for investigating how learners acquired English as an L2. Fourth, they addressed key theoretical issues such as the extent to which L2 acquisition was influenced by environmental or innate factors.

SLA research has always owed much to the study of L1 acquisition. The early longitudinal studies (e.g. Ravem, 1968; Cazden *et al.*, 1975; Wode, 1976) borrowed extensively from the methods used by L1 researchers, relying on audio recordings and pencil-and-paper notes of naturally occurring speech. They also focused on the same set of gramatical features which had attracted attention in L1 studies (e.g. interrogation and negation), documenting the transitional rules that learners constructed on their way to target language competence. Similarly, cross-sectional studies (e.g. Dulay & Burt, 1973; Bailey, Madden & Krashen, 1974) calculated the accuracy order of the same set of grammatical morphemes that had figured in L1 studies. Somewhat later, as attention in L1 acquisition research switched to the role of input and interaction (cf. Cross, 1977), L2 researchers also became interested in such phenomena as foreigner talk and teacher talk and again made use of the methodological procedures developed for investigating caretaker talk.

Theoretical controversy

In the 1950s, the prevailing view of how an L2 was learnt was derived from behaviourist theories of learning. These emphasised the role of environmental factors. Learners learnt the L2 as a result of responding to stimuli and receiving feedback on the correctness of their productions. The principal mechanisms of learning were imitation, repetition and reinforcement. Successful learning occurred when the learner succeeded in forming new habits. Unsuccessful learning (which manifested itself in errors in learner production) was the result of negative transfer (interference) from the learner's L1.

This view of L2 learning was seriously challenged in the late 1960s. Drawing on the kinds of arguments with which Chomsky had challenged behaviourist accounts of language and on the growing body of information about the way children acquired their L1, applied linguists such as Newmark (1966), Corder (1967) and Selinker (1972) advanced theories of L2 learning that de-emphasised the role of the environment and gave greater recognition to learner-internal factors. The learner was credited with some kind of language learning mechanism (not necessarily identical with that which the child used to discover the rules of the L1). This mechanism accounted for the creative process by which learners constructed a mental grammar of the L2 — a process which manifested itself in errors of a uniquely developmental nature. These views were radically different from those advanced by the protagonists of audiolingual learning theory (Brooks, 1960; Lado, 1964) who drew heavily on behaviourist accounts of learning.

The controversy between behaviourist and mentalist theories of language learning stimulated some of the early empirical work in SLA. Researchers set out to use the techniques of error analysis to evaluate to what extent learner errors could be explained with reference to L1 transfer or to the process of creative construction. Such studies as Richards (1971) and Dulay & Burt (1974a) set out to test the rival claims by investigating corpora of learner errors. The results indicated that L1 transfer was far less prevalent than had previously been assumed, lending support to the mentalist position.[1]

Language teaching at the cross-roads

Language teaching in the 1950s and 1960s was dominated by the 'method' construct — the idea that it was possible to identify a set of procedures which, if executed correctly and efficiently, would result in successful language learning. During these decades the long-lived hegemony of the grammar-translation method, which emphasised the written medium and the study of explicit grammar rules, gave way to new methods based on scientific accounts of language and a well-established learning theory (i.e. behaviourism). In the USA audiolingualism was touted as the method which would make language learning accessible to all, including elementary school children. In Britain the oral method, derived from the practical teaching experience of a group of language educationalists (e.g. Palmer, West and Hornby), was promoted as a means of achieving real communicative skills. The audiolingual and the oral methods shared much in common, in particular the conviction that language was best taught inductively item by item through carefully controlled practice exercises.[2]

The claims advanced in the name of these methods, however, proved illfounded. Learners did not succeed in developing the kind of oral control over an L2 which they were expected to. Careful drilling did not succeed in avoiding or eliminating error. Even after hours of study, learners were often unable to hold even simple natural conversations. Furthermore, many learners found the intensive drilling and the insistence on formal correctness demotivating. The Foreign Languages in the Elementary School (FLES) movement in the USA, based on the audiolingual method, proved disappointing. Furthermore, large scale studies (e.g. Scherer & Wertheimer, 1964; Smith, 1970) conducted in the USA to test the efficacy of the audiolingual method in relation to more traditional, deductive methods failed to demonstrate its expected superiority. In general, it did not seem to matter what method was used.

This led to disillusionment with the 'method' construct, which in turn had two outcomes. First, it led to the advent of observational studies of actual classroom practice — a move from reliance on purely external accounts of how teaching should proceed to descriptions of what actually took place inside classrooms when particular techniques were used (e.g. Politzer, 1970). Second, it resulted in a strongly felt need to discover what kinds of conditions were needed to ensure that successful language learning took place. This motivated the study of L2 acquisition by learners in naturalistic settings, as this kind of acquisition was considered to be typically successful, especially in the case of children. Just about all the early studies of L2 acquisition were conducted with learners acquiring the L2 naturalistically and there was no serious attempt initially to study how languages were acquired in the classroom context, even though one of the motivating factors was a desire to improve language pedagogy.

These factors —the availability of research 'models' from L1 acquisition research, the rival claims of behaviourist and nativist theories of language learning and the desire to find out how successful, natural learning took place as a basis for improving language pedagogy — contributed to the emergence of SLA as a field of study in the late 1960s and early 1970s. They also helped to shape the kinds of enquiry that initially took place. The early studies investigated natural L2 acquisition. Work in error analysis set out to test whether errors could best be explained as the product of L1 transfer or of creative construction. Longitudinal and cross-sectional studies focused on a fairly limited set of morphological and syntactic features and sought to provide descriptive information about the developmental path that learners followed. From these beginnings, SLA has blossomed, so that now it is a rich and somewhat confusing field, encompassing a great range of research interests and employing a variety of research methods.

Developments in SLA Studies

It is possible to identify three broad trends in SLA research over the last 20 or so years: (1) a general move from *description* to *explanation* of L2 acquisition, (2) the widening of the frame of reference from the study of how learners acquire grammatical competence to how they acquire a knowledge of the pragmatic rules of an L2, and (3) the establishment of SLA as a relatively autonomous sub-discipline of applied linguistics and a concurrent lessening of interest in its application to language teaching.

From description to explanation

Lightbown (1984), summarising work done during the 1970s, comments that SLA researchers concentrated mainly on describing how L2 acquisition takes place. A number of studies produced evidence to suggest that learners with diverse language backgrounds appeared to follow more or less a standard route in the acquisition of grammatical morphemes and such areas of syntax as negation and interrogation. Other studies indicated that some variation in the order of development of these features could occur. Most of these studies, which made use of data obtained from naturally occurring interactions involving learners, were not theoretically motivated — rather they sought to provide information about how L2 acquisition took place, which could then be used to construct theories, a posteriori.

The 1980s, however, was a period when the concern for description and theory building gave way to the concern for explanation and theory-testing.

They began with the publication of Krashen's (1981a) *Second Language Acquisition and Second Language Learning* in which he advanced a theory (known initially as the Monitor Model) to account for how learners acquired the linguistic competence to communicate. This theory had a major impact on the field, producing a number of fiercely argued rebuttals (e.g. Gregg, 1984) as well as a number of empirical studies designed to test hypotheses derived from the theory (e.g. Pica, 1983). Krashen's theory, however, did not lend itself easily to hypothesis-testing research as many of its claims were not formulated in a way that made them falsifiable. In this respect, other theoretical positions that emerged during the 1980s were more promising. In Germany a group of researchers developed a theory based on a set of hierarchically ordered processing strategies to account for their findings relating to how L2 learners acquired German word order rules (cf. Meisel, Clahsen and Pienemann, 1981). This theory has motivated a number of classroom studies designed to test whether the predicted order of development occurred in the case of instructed learners (e.g. Pienemann, 1986). In the USA, and subsequently elsewhere, researchers turned to Universal Grammar (cf. Chomsky, 1980) which, tied as it was to descriptions of specific areas of syntax provided by Chomsky's Government and Binding Theory, afforded not only a set of very general constructs to explain acquisition but also precise hypotheses about the acquisition of particular grammatical features (see Chomsky, 1981). Many of the studies based on these theoretical positions have been experimental in nature and have made use of elicited rather than naturally occurring data (e.g. Flynn, 1987; White, 1989).

One way of characterising this general trend is of a movement away from a 'research then theory' approach towards a 'theory then research' approach (cf. Reynolds, 1971, cited in Long, 1985a). Of course, it is easy to overstate this trend, as much of the research conducted during the 1980s has continued to be descriptive in nature.

Going beyond linguistic competence

In the survey of SLA which I wrote in the early 1980s I had this to say:

Second language acquisition refers to all aspects of language that the language learner needs to master. However, the focus has been on how L2 learners acquire grammatical sub-systems . . . Research has tended to ignore other levels of language . . . SLA researchers have only recently turned their attention to how learners acquire the ability to communicate. (Ellis, 1985: 5)

There were initially very few studies of aspects of linguistic competence other than grammar — phonology and vocabulary acquisition were neglected. There were even fewer studies of how learners developed pragmatic competence — the knowledge of the 'rules of speaking' that govern how language is used in socially appropriate ways and how discourse is constructed. When studies did make reference to 'discourse' it was in the context of examining how interaction shaped the development of linguistic competence (e.g. Hatch, 1978a).

The position has now changed somewhat. There has been a growing interest in phonological and lexical acquisition (cf. Ioup & Weinberger (1987) and the collection of papers in *Studies in Second Language Acquisition*, Vol. 8. No. 2). Also, stimulated by models of communicative competence (e.g. Canale & Swain, 1980) and by both theoretical and descriptive work in discourse (e.g. Brown & Levinson, 1978; Sachs *et al.*, 1974), SLA researchers in the 1980s were much more concerned with documenting how learners develop pragmatic knowledge of an L2. On the one hand there has been a growing body of research which has studied how specific speech acts such as requests, apologies and refusals are performed by L2 learners in different social settings (e.g. Blum-Kulka, House & Kasper, 1989), while on the other there has been work done in how learners develop discourse skills by examining such issues as the repair of communication breakdown (e.g. Poulisse, 1989) and turn-taking (e.g. Lörscher, 1986).

Although it would be incorrect to claim that this work has been atheoretical in nature, it is the case that much of it has been descriptive rather than explanatory. Just as the early work on the acquisition of linguistic competence focused on documenting how this is acquired, so the early work on pragmatic competence has been primarily concerned with describing how learners perform pragmatically. Somewhat unfortunately, the bulk of the work completed to date has been cross-sectional in design and therefore provides only limited information about how L2 pragmatic knowledge develops over time.

Another feature of this area of SLA studies has been the use of data collected from within the L2 classroom. Ethnographic studies of the different types of interaction to be found in instructional settings have proved increasingly popular (e.g. Kasper, 1986; Van Lier, 1988). These have been motivated in part by the need to discover more about the processes that take place during L2 instruction — to find out how language lessons are accomplished, as it were — and as such reflect the drift away from large-scale comparative method studies, which has already been commented on. A second motivation has been the hope of discovering how interaction, 'the fundamental fact of language pedagogy' as Allwright (1984) calls it, contributes to acquisition. This branch of SLA links up with the work done in classroom observation during the 1980s. Increasingly, observational studies of the L2 classroom during this period have drawn on work done in SLA to provide a purpose and a focus for the development of observational frameworks (e.g. the Communicative Orientation in Language Teaching observation scheme developed by Allen *et al.*, 1984).

The break with language pedagogy

Many of the early studies of L2 acquisition were carried out by researchers with an explicit interest in language pedagogy. Indeed, as I have already argued, one of the primary motivations for investigating how learners acquired an L2 was to obtain insights which could be used to improve instructional practices. The articles published during this period, therefore, tended to follow a fairly defined format. First, the results of the study would be reported and discussed. Second, the findings would be related to language pedagogy in an 'applications' section. A good example of this is to be found in Dulay & Burt's (1973) article 'Should we teach children syntax?' After reporting the results of two studies designed to investigate the nature of the errors produced by a group of Spanish children acquiring L2 English and the accuracy order of grammatical morphemes in their speech, the authors conclude with a number of specific pedagogic proposals relating to the role of grammar teaching. The title of their article itself reflects the concern they had for teaching.

Increasingly, though, many SLA researchers have felt less of a need to apply their work to language teaching. Many of the studies reported in current issues of journals deal with purely theoretical questions. For many researchers SLA is now a sub-discipline of linguistics. They view data obtained from L2 learners as a means of testing alternative theories of language. For example, the extent to which language is a reflection of general cognitive abilities as opposed to a separate language faculty has been argued in relation to the data on German and Dutch word order acquisition (cf. Clahsen & Muysken, 1986). SLA data has also been used to test the validity of work on grammatical description carried out within the framework of Universal Grammar. Similarly much of the work done in the area of cross-cultural pragmatics has not included an applied aspect.

It would be untrue to say, however, that language pedagogy has ceased to be of interest to SLA researchers. Many researchers, myself included, have maintained a strong interest in teaching. What seems to have happened is that 'classroom SLA' has developed as a sub-field of SLA. Thus, whereas the early studies applied the results of studies of naturalistic acquisition, more recent studies have tried to examine how SLA takes place in a classroom environment. Krashen's Monitor Model, which was devised to address pedagogic issues, is essentially an extrapololation from studies of naturalistic acquisition — both first and second — carried out during the 1970s. In contrast, the 1980s were characterised by a number of projects specially set up to investigate how instructed L2 acquisition takes place (e.g. the Development of Bilingual Proficiency Project reported in Harley *et al.*, 1990).

It can be said that the 'applied' and the 'theoretical' concerns of SLA have come apart, pursued as separate strands, motivated by different research questions and often using different methodological procedures. SLA now faces in many directions, only one of which is language pedagogy.

There is always a danger in oversimplifying when trying to characterise the direction that a field of enquiry takes and to some extent the above account of SLA is guilty of this. Thus, there continues to be a substantial amount of work that is descriptive and theory building rather than explanatory and theory testing,[3] that focuses on linguistic rather than pragmatic competence and that seeks to apply results to language pedagogy rather than to address purely theoretical questions. The trends described above reflect the inevitable diversification of SLA rather than clear-cut changes.

Current Issues in SLA

It is not possible in the space of a short introduction to do justice to the full range of issues which are currently the subject of enquiry in SLA. However, a brief review of those issues which are reflected in the papers included in this collection will be provided.

Developmental sequences

The early interest in identifying the sequences of acquisition of different grammatical features has never completely disappeared and there continues to be a fair body of work devoted to describing the regularities of L2 development. The notion of 'sequence' refers to the idea that grammatical properties are acquired in a relatively fixed order such that feature z cannot be acquired before feature feature y has been acquired, which in turn is only learnable when x has been mastered etc. It is an extremely powerful notion, giving substance to the term 'interlanguage' and lending support to the claims that L2 acquisition is the product of innate factors that govern how and when different grammatical operations are mastered.

Strong evidence for the existence of developmental sequences has been provided by a series of studies investigating the acquisition of German and Dutch word order rules (e.g. the verb-end rule, which states that finite verbs are placed in clause final position in subordinate clauses). There has been a whole range of studies beginning in the late 1970s with the ZISA project (e.g. Meisel, Clahsen & Pienemann, 1981) which investigated adult and child learners with a romance language as their L1 and continuing up to the present moment with studies of learners from a greater range of language backgrounds (cf. Jordens, 1988).

It should be noted that, although there is a substantial body of research that testifies to the presence of developmental sequences in L2 acquisition, there is also counter-evidence to suggest that considerable variation in the order of acquisition can occur as a product of such factors as the learner's L1 and the context of learning. For some researchers the notion of developmental sequence remains a speculative one. In particular, it has been suggested that developmental sequences are only evident in spontaneous learner production and that the order in which L2 items enter the learner's abstract knowledge system is not so predetermined. Also, there is considerable disagreement regarding how developmental sequences are to be explained. Cognitive explanations based on speech processing strategies vie with linguistic explanations based on models of Universal Grammar.

The notion of developmental sequences is of particular interest to those researchers, such as myself, concerned with classroom L2 acquisition. Two key questions are, (1) is the developmental sequence found in naturalistic learners also found in instructed learners? and (2) is it possible to alter the natural developmental sequence through formal instruction? Two papers in this collection address these questions — one, 'Can syntax be taught?', is based on research which has shown that WH interrogatives follow a developmental route, while the other, 'Are classroom and naturalistic acquisition the same?', is based on research into German word-order rules.

Variability

The inherent variability of language-learner language has been commented on frequently and, not surprisingly, has attracted considerable attention from researchers (cf. Tarone (1988) for a survey of variability studies). Learners appear to go through stages when they alternate between two or more ways of expressing a given structure. For example, in the case of WH interrogatives they may sometimes say, 'What you are doing?', and sometimes, 'What are you doing?'. Similarly, they may sometimes produce sentences containing copula 'be': 'My name is Raza' and sometimes copula-less sentences: 'My name Raza.' In these examples, the variants consist of a target language form and an interlanguage forms.

Variability can be of two kinds. In some cases, the use of two or more forms may be in free variation. That is, the learner selects more or less haphazardly from her repertoire of forms for performing a given structure. In other cases, probably the majority, the use of alternative variants is systematic in the sense that it is possible to explain and perhaps even to predict when each variant will be used.

In order to explain systematic variability it is necessary to consider a number of factors (Ellis, 1989a). Some of these are sociolinguistic in nature — that is, they have to do with the social and discoursal context in which the utterance is produced. Some of them are linguistic — that is, they concern the nature of the linguistic environment in which the variant occurs. Also, some are psycholinguistic — they have to do with the processing conditions governing the production of utterances in different types of communication.

Variability can also be explained with reference to functional models of language, which seek to account for the relationships which hold between form and function. For example, a learner may use a No + verb negative structure for performing statements, e.g. 'Mariana no coming today' and a Don't + verb negative structure for commands, e.g. 'Mariana, don't come today.' Clearly, the process of acquiring an L2 involves learning which forms in the target language can be mapped on to which functions. Variability studies have provided a number of insights into how this mapping process takes place.

Once again, though, there is disagreement over both the significance of variability phenomena in the study of L2 acquisition and how best it can be explained. For example, Gregg's (1990) critique of the theoretical positions adopted by Tarone and Ellis and their responses to this critique show there is disagreement over whether variability is best viewed as an aspect of competence, as Tarone and Ellis argue, or whether it is merely a reflection of performance factors, as Gregg argues. Another area of controversy is free variation; Schachter (1986) disputes its existence.

Variability is an issue that is well-represented in this collection. 'Sources of variability in interlanguage' argues the case for a functional approach to variability. 'Interlanguage variability in narrative discourse' examines how planning time affects the use of past tense forms.

Input and interaction

Theories of L2 acquisition differ in the importance they attach to input and interaction. On the one hand nativist theories emphasise the insufficiency of input, arguing that 'the input underdetermines linguistic competence' (White, 1990: 121) in the sense that it can be shown that competent speakers of a language possess knowledge of their language that goes far beyond the actual sentences they could possibly have been exposed to. On the other hand, interaction has been viewed as a kind of crucible that forges knowledge of an L2 through the 'pouring back and forth' and 'gathering together and taking apart' (Brown, 1968: 287) which grammatical patterns are subjected to during the course of face-to-face communication.

The L2 classroom provides a convenient source of data for examining the nature of input and interaction. As we have already noted, there has been a number of classroom-based studies. Initially these focused on aspects of the teacher's language (e.g. the teacher's treatment of error or the modifications that teachers make to their input when they are addressing learners of different levels of proficiency). Subsequently, attention turned to the nature of the interactions that occur between teacher and learners (e.g. Ellis, 1984a) and among learners working in small groups (e.g. Bygate, 1988). These studies have provided detailed information about the kind of input and interaction that classroom learners may experience.

There have been few studies, however, that have investigated the effects of input and interaction on L2 acquisition. Strong claims have been made for the importance of comprehensible input (Krashen, 1985) and of opportunities for negotiating meaning when there is some kind of communication problem (Long, 1983a). There have also been arguments in favour of comprehensible output (i.e. providing opportunities for extended talk during which learners are encouraged to produce syntactically well-formed utterances — Swain, 1985). However, these claims have not been supported by studies which show that comprehensible input, meaning negotiation or comprehensible output results in acquisition. Indeed, in comparison with L1 acquisition research, SLA has not been very successful in examining this relationship, although there is a number of promising recent studies (e.g. Slimani, 1987).[4]

Two papers in this collection address input and interaction issues. 'Teacher–pupil interaction in second language development' is a longitudinal study of the nature of a teacher's input to two learners. This study also examines in a qualitative manner how interaction might contribute to acquisition. 'The classroom context — an acquisition-rich or an acquisition-poor environment?' is an unpublished paper which examines in a critical fashion the classroom research which has investigated the role of input and interaction to date.

Learning style

Whereas the SLA studies referred to so far have sought to establish ways in which learners are similar by focusing on the universal properties of L2 acquisition, there is also a rich tradition of research into individual learner differences. This has investigated a variety of factors that have been hypothesised to account for variation in the rate at which learners acquire an L2 and in the ultimate level of proficiency they reach. These factors include intelligence, language aptitude, motivation, personality traits such as extroversion–introversion and learning style (cf. Skehan, 1989, for a full survey of the research). Of these only learning style is dealt with in this volume.

Learning style refers to 'the totality of psychological functioning' evident in the way in which a learner approaches the task of learning the L2 (Willing, 1987). It is considered to be persistent and pervasive and is reflected in perceptual, cognitive and affective aspects of learning. Psychologists have identified a number of different styles. Bruner, Goodnew & Austin (1977), for instance, distinguish 'focusers' and 'scanners', while Pask (1976) identifies 'serialists' and 'holists'. The distinction which has attracted the most attention in SLA, however, is that of 'field independence' and 'field dependence' (Witkin et al., 1971). Field dependent learners tend to be strongly influenced by context and have difficulty in distinguishing the parts that make up a whole; they prefer an integrative approach to learning. Field independents are able to operate without being strongly influenced by context; they are analytic in approach. The distinction represents a continuum — that is, learners can be more or less field dependent/independent. A number of studies have been carried out to establish whether there is any relationship between measures of field independence/dependence (usually undertaken by means of a visual perception test known as the *Group Embedded Figures Test*) and measures of L2 proficiency. The results, as is often the case in individual difference studies, have been mixed, but on the whole lend some support to the claim that field independents achieve higher levels of proficiency.[5]

A different approach to the study of learning style entails the collection of questionnaire information regarding L2 learners' learning preferences (cf.

Reid, 1987; Willing, 1987). The responses of the learners can then be analysed using statistical techniques such as factor analysis in order to identify clusters of preferences that constitute a particular learning style. Willing used this procedure and discovered four learning styles, two pure (corresponding roughly to the field dependent/independent distinction) and two 'mixed', involving a second factor which he labelled passive/active.

It is probably true to say that the research into learning style is very exploratory at the moment. The concept itself is a somewhat vague one and so not surprisingly the research has not been able to produce very clear results. However, it is arguably an important one for language pedagogy, where the importance of learner-instruction matching has long been recognised. Two papers in this collection address the question of learning style. One — 'Individual learning styles in classroom second language development' — is quantitative and exploratory. The other — 'Classroom learning styles and their effect on second language acquisition' — is a more qualitative, case study of two foreign language learners.

SLA and Language Pedagogy

Here I want to consider in what ways SLA can contribute to language pedagogy. First, it is important to recognise that SLA serves as only one of several inputs that help shape pedagogic proposals. Stern (1983) identifies three sets of factors: (1) changing demands in education resulting from social, economic and political circumstances, (2) changes in theoretical orientation, and (3) the experience, intuitions and opinions of practising teachers. SLA relates to the second of these by offering theoretical accounts of how L2 learning takes place. It is probably true to say that whereas the development of traditional methods such as grammar translation and audiolingualism was influenced more by theories of language than of language learning, contemporary methods such as *Total Physical Response* (Asher, 1977) and the *Communicative Approach* (e.g. Brumfit & Johnson, 1979) have been influenced to a much greater extent by theories of language learning. This is almost certainly a direct reflection of the growth in SLA which has taken place. Nevertheless, SLA is not the sole source of inspiration in these methods.

We have seen that many of the early studies of L2 acquisition sought to 'apply' the results to language pedagogy by making specific proposals about what approach should be followed and even what methodological procedures should be used in the classroom. Subsequently there have been attempts to apply theories of SLA to pedagogy, as with the *Natural Approach* (Krashen & Terrell, 1983). This approach developed partly out of the practical teaching experiences of a teacher of Spanish (Terrell) but was shaped and refined to accord with the theoretical insights provided by Krashen's *Monitor Model*.

A number of researchers are more cautious about 'applying' the results of SLA in this way. Lightbown (1985a), for instance, has pointed out that there are few statements that can be made about L2 acquisition on the basis of research carried out to date about which we can be completely certain — there are no 'fundamental facts', even if some researchers proceed as if there were. Lightbown distinguishes teacher training and teacher education and argues that work in SLA is best used in the former than the latter. That is, it should be used to help teachers consider what learners are likely to do rather than to develop complete instructional programmes or even to suggest specific teaching techniques. Certainly attempts to apply the information about developmental sequences to syllabus design (e.g. Pienemann, 1985) have run into a number of objections based on both doubts about the validity of the research findings and also on the failure to take account of the practicalities of the classroom situation. There is a danger of being overcautious, of course. Teachers need to take instant decisions about how to proceed and cannot wait until more solid results and more robust theories are available. The papers in Section Six of this volume reflect an attempt to use SLA research as a basis for discussing central questions about the planning of L2 curricula and the choice of classroom methodology.

The alternative to 'applying' the results of research, which in many cases was not designed to address the issues that concern teachers, is to conduct studies that take as their starting point some pedagogic issue. Ellis (1988a) has argued that such an educational approach to SLA avoids many of the problems associated with the application of findings based on a psycholinguistic or linguistic approach. The educational approach seeks to illuminate language pedagogy through studies of what takes place in the name of instruction and how this affects acquisition. There have been an increasing number of SLA studies which have adopted this approach. These include studies of the effects of error treatment, of teachers' questions, of group work and of learner participation. The educational approach to SLA research is represented in this collection by 'The role of practice in classroom language learning', a survey of studies that have examined the effects of practice on L2 learning.

About This Collection

In the previous sections of this introduction, I have tried to characterise SLA, tracing it from its origins to its current state and identifying some of the issues which it has addressed. I have also considered the nature of the relationship between SLA and language pedagogy. In so doing, I have tried to show where specific papers in this collection belong, so that the reader can relate their contents to the field as a whole.

The papers are not entirely representative of SLA. Inevitably, they reflect my own interests and inclinations. The focus of the papers remains largely grammar (as opposed to other aspects of linguistic competence or pragmatic competence), which I now see as a limiting factor. The papers reflect my continuing interest in language pedagogy. Thus even the more theoretical ones (such as those in the first four sections) have a strong 'applied' orientation. It is for this reason, perhaps, that the number of SLA issues that they cover is somewhat limited — there are no papers dealing with such central issues in SLA as language transfer and linguistic universals, mainly because I am less convinced of the utility of these areas of enquiry to language teaching. In contrast, developmental sequences, input and interaction, variability and learning style strike me as issues of central importance to pedagogy.

I like to think that the papers 'belong' together in that they are all informed by my continuing interest in how an L2 is acquired in a classroom context and by my conviction that for language instruction to work it must be both learning and learner centred.

Notes

1. The role of transfer in L2 acquisition has continued to attract the attention of SLA researchers (cf. Gass & Selinker, 1983; Odlin, 1989). The current view is that transfer is a major factor but that various constraints govern when and where it occurs.
2. There were, of course, some notable differences between the oral and audiolingual methods. The oral method, for instance, placed considerable emphasis on teaching the meanings which different grammatical structures realised in communication, whereas the audiolingual method emphasised the purely formal characteristics of structural patterns.
3. A good example of recent descriptive research in SLA can be found in the publications arising out of the *Second Language Acquisition Project by Adult Immigrants* (cf. Klein & Perdue, 1988).
4. The main reason for the failure of SLA studies to establish a clear link between input/interaction and acquisition lies in the difficulty in controlling extraneous variables. In the classroom situation, for instance, it is difficult to decide what counts as input to the individual learner. In contrast, L1 acquisition researchers have fewer problems in obtaining reliable estimates of the input/interaction which children experience.
5. One of the problems facing research into field independence/dependence based on the GEFT is that this instrument only provides a measure of field independence — there is no independent measure of field dependence.

Section 2
Interaction and Second
Language Acquisition

One of the central questions in SLA concerns the relationship between interaction and acquisition. There have been a number of studies aimed at identifying what kinds of interaction are most facilitative of L2 acquisition. Many of them have taken place within the theoretical framework proposed by Long (1981; 1983a). According to this, acquisition is facilitated if learners have the opportunity to negotiate communication problems. Negotiation has been operationalised for purposes of empirical study as a set of interactional features through which conversational adjustements take place (c.f. Appendix A). However, as both the papers in this section make clear, there have been no studies which show a direct relationship between these interactional features and acquisition.

The first paper ('Teacher–Pupil Interaction in Second Language Development') was given at a conference in 1983 and subsequently published in Gass & Madden (1985). It was part of a larger investigation involving the longitudinal study of three L2 learners in a classroom environment. The paper draws on Long's interactional hypothesis, addressing the extent to which conversational adjustments are themselves developmental (i.e. vary according to the learner's overall stage of development). But the paper differs from other published work in a number of respects. First, the study is longitudinal rather cross-sectional in design. Second, the analyses go further than the set of features which Long has focused on by including measures of the teacher's treatment of task (e.g. the type of question used). Third, there is an attempt to examine how interaction contributes to acquisition by examining 'breakthrough points' (i.e. studying the nature of the interaction that occurs when learners produce utterances that give evidence of new grammatical structures). Among the results reported, two points now strike me as of particular interest. First, there is the observation that the contribution of conversational modifications may vary according to the characteristics of the individual learner — that personality differences in learners may result in preferences for different interactional styles. Second, there is the claim that when learners have control over the topic of conversation they are more likely to experience interaction that promotes acquisition.

The second paper was given at the conference on 'Text and Context; Cross-disciplinary and Cross-cultural Perspectives on Language Study' held at Cornell University in 1990. It aims to survey research that has addressed what factors contribute to an 'acquisition-rich' classroom. The paper is a rather bleak account of the failure to show empirically how interaction contributes to acquisition. It is critical of the general assumption that classroom L2 acquisition can be promoted most effectively by replicating the conditions of naturalistic learning and also of Long's interaction hypothesis (which is predicated on this assumption). Interestingly, of all the various aspects of classroom interaction examined (simplified input; interactional modifications; teachers' questions; topic control; learner participation; use of the L1) it is the issue of topic control which emerges as centrally important. In this sense, the second paper links up with the first.

It is probably true to say that the study of the relationship between interaction and L2 acquisition has produced few clear results. There has been a tendency to go for easily-conducted cross-sectional studies which lend themselves to quantitative analyses and statistical treatments. There is surely a case for more qualitative research based on longitudinal studies of individual learners.

1. Teacher–Pupil Interaction in Second Language Development

This chapter has two aims. The primary aim is to examine the relationship between the interactions that took place between one teacher and two pupils over a nine-month period and the process of second language development of the two children. The secondary aim is a methodological one. I want to argue that qualitative analyses as well as quantitative analyses of input data are essential if we are to increase our understanding of how input affects second language (L2) acquisition.

It has been hypothesised (e.g. Krashen, 1982; Long, 1983a) that L2 acquisition is dependent on the learner's obtaining 'comprehensible input'. One way that this may be achieved is through the adaptations — formal and interactional — that have been observed to occur in the speech that native speakers address to learners. Another way is through the learner's own use of communication strategies, which serve to help the learner overcome problems of communicating with limited second language resources. There are now several studies describing 'foreigner' or 'teacher talk' (e.g. Arthur *et al.*, 1980; Long, 1981; Gaies, 1977; Henzl, 1979) and several more examining the learner's communication strategies (e.g. Tarone 1977; 1981; Bialystok, 1983). These studies are largely taxonomic and quantitative. That is, they provide lists of categories of speech modifications or learner strategies and then count the frequencies of each category. In this way a picture has been built up of what the native speaker and the learner contribute to the task of making the input comprehensible.

One of the problems of this quantitative approach is that 'comprehensible input' is not really the result of the *separate* contributions of the native speaker and the learner but of their *joint* endeavours. The speech addressed to learners is the result of an ongoing interaction between learner and native speaker. In this process the interlocutors collaborate in establishing and maintaining a topic. This has been referred to as *negotiation* (e.g. Tarone, 1981). At the moment we do not have any effective categories of negotiation and have not been able to accurately count the interpersonal characteristics of negotiation.

One way that has been used to examine the process of negotiation is discourse analysis (e.g. Hatch, 1978a; Ellis, 1980). However, this has been used in qualitative rather than quantitative analyses of representative samples of native speaker–learner discourse. The advantage of discourse analysis is that it has provided us with information about the two-sided nature of the interactions that lead to comprehensible input.

Another problem with the quantitative approach is that it has not yet demonstrated whether there is any relationship between the observed speech modifications/strategies and L2 acquisition. The standard approach (e.g. Long, 1981, Scarcella & Higa, 1981) is to establish that quantitative differences exist between input addressed to native speakers and input addressed to non-native speakers and then to hypothesise how these differences are important for L2 acquisition. For example, Long (1981) demonstrates that these differences are more evident in what he calls 'interactional' features (e.g. expansions) than in 'input' features (e.g. average length of T units) and then suggests that the 'interactional' features are more important for L2 acquisition than the 'input' modifications. However, he does not offer any direct quantitative evidence to support this. Where the research design has been cross-sectional, as in Long's published work, it is not easy to examine the nature of the relationship between interaction and the process of development.[1] It is only possible to hypothesise that the relationship evident at a particular point in time is indicative of the relationship over time.

In order to examine the relationship between the types of interaction that result from native speaker speech adaptations and learner communication strategies on the one hand and L2 acquisition on the other, it is useful to ask three separate questions:

(1) What are the speech modifications and strategies that occur?
(2) Are the speech modifications and strategies developmental? That is, do they change according to the level of the learner's competence?
(3) Are the speech modifications and strategies related to the acquisition of new linguistic knowledge and/or the rate of acquisition, and, if so, how?

The first of these questions has been the primary concern of the research referred to above. The second question has received much less attention, but Henzl (1979) has shown that teachers' formal speech adjustments are sensitive to the general level of proficiency of the students being taught. The third question has become the central question in first language acquisition research, and a number of studies have addressed it (e.g. Ellis & Wells, 1980, Wells, 1981). It has received only speculative attention in L2 acquisition research, however.[2]

If we are to show that comprehensible input derived from interaction is important for L2 acquisition and how it is important, we need studies that consider questions (2) and (3). It is likely that this will require qualitative analyses based on longitudinal studies of L2 acquisition as well as quantitative analyses of cross-sectional data. The study reported in this chapter is an initial attempt to examine questions (2) and (3). It was part of a broader investigation into the relationship between the L2 acquisition of two children and their classroom environment. It will make use of both qualitative and quantitative analyses.

Method

The two children of the study, brother and sister, were R and T. They were aged 11 and 13, respectively, at the beginning of the study, and both spoke Punjabi as their mother tongue. R was illiterate to begin with and had had very little previous school experience. He was an extroverted child and rapidly made friends with other non-English-speaking children. He found it difficult to concentrate on any single activity for a long period of time and tended to prefer classroom tasks that he could perform easily. T had had more experience of school in Pakistan than her brother and could write a little. She was much quieter and had a greater attention span. She was able to work on classroom tasks for long periods of time without requiring the help of the teacher. Unlike her brother, she tended to make friends only with other Punjabi-speaking girls.

Both R and T were placed in a language unit specially set up to cope with children from overseas who had insufficient English to fit into the normal classroom of a secondary school. They were placed in a reception class which contained only other L2 learners, many of whom spoke Punjabi. English was used as the medium of instruction in the classroom and also served as the medium of communication among pupils with different first languages outside the classroom in the unit. For their first year R and T were almost entirely reliant on this environment for English input, as they received minimal exposure to English in the wider community. The English they were exposed to consisted of both the 'interlanguage' of other L2 learners and the standard language of native-speaking teachers.

The main study of their linguistic development was based on data collected from inside the classroom using audio recordings and pencil-and-paper records. This showed that they acquired English very slowly. By the end of their first school year (i.e. nine months from the start of the study), for instance, their interrogative utterances were still largely uninverted. There was no evidence of any ability to use the past tense in spontaneous speech and many of their utterances were propositionally reduced (see Ellis, 1982a). Their general progress was similar to that reported for Alberto (Schumann, 1978a).

The data for the analyses that follow were obtained from a series of 'interview' sessions between the two children and their regular class teacher. These took place in an empty room without the researcher being present and lasted approximately 15 minutes each. The teacher was asked to try to elicit speech from the two children. However, no attempt was made to elicit any specific structures. The idea was to 'hold a conversation' as far as this was possible. Each session involved the teacher asking questions about pictures with each child separately. The pictures were different in each session, but one set (*Learning Development Aids* 'What's Wrong Cards') was introduced on three separate occasions during the year. In addition to the talk centring around the pictures, there were attempts by the teacher to talk about events he knew the children had participated in and also to ask questions about their family and interests. These were more common in the sessions toward the end of the year. Altogether there were a total of 19 sessions for R and 18 for T.[3] The sessions took place at approximately two-week intervals over a nine-month period from November to July. Each session was audio-recorded and transcriptions prepared in normal orthography. These were shown to the teacher, who provided contextual information.

Analyses were carried out to investigate (1) to what extent the interactional features of each interview changed over time and (2) what role these features may have played in the children's L2 acquisition. These analyses are reported separately below.

The Developmental Nature of Selected Interactional Features

In order to investigate to what extent the nature of the teacher–pupil interactions changed over time, three different analyses were carried out. The first analysis considered developments in the teacher's use of a subset of 'interactional' features reported on in a study of native-speaker adjustments by Long (1983b). The second analysis concerned the teacher's treatment of the tasks he gave the pupils and also his response to communication breakdown. The third analysis concerned the pupils' contributions to the interactions. It examined their use of a number of communication strategies. Each analysis will be discussed separately.

The teacher's 'interactional' adjustments

The interactional features of the teacher's speech that were selected for investigation were a subset of those studied by Long (1983b). A description of these features can be found in Appendix A. Long found significant differences on six measures of the interactional structure of native-speaker speech addressed to non-native speakers in comparison with native-speaker speech addressed to other native speakers. To examine whether these differences would be reflected developmentally in the teacher–pupil (T–P) conversations, the first 100 turns in two of the early sessions (recordings 3 and 6) and two of the later sessions (recordings 15 and 18) were coded for each occurrence of the six interactional features.

Table 1.1 gives the number of occurrences of each feature and the extent to which the differences between the frequencies in the early and late recordings are significant, based on chi-squared scores. Taking 0.05 as the level of significance, two of the interactional features in the teacher's speech proved sensitive to both R's and T's level of development. Self-repetitions were *fewer* in the later recordings, whereas expansions were *more numerous*. In addition, the teacher used significantly more confirmation checks in the later sessions when conversing with R but not with T. None of the other features showed a significant difference from one time to the next.

TABLE 1.1 *A comparison of the interactional features of the teacher's input at different times*

Feature	R				T			
	n				n			
	T1	T2	$\chi^2(df=1)$	p	T1	T2	$\chi^2(df=1)$	p
1. Confirmation checks	3	11	4.57	0.05	3	7	1.60	ns
2. Comprehension checks	4	8	1.60	ns	3	1	1.00	ns
3. Clarification checks	8	10	1.00	ns	7	2	2.78	ns
4. Self-repetitions	17	5	6.55	0.02	10	2	5.33	0.05
5. Other repititions	12	8	0.80	ns	16	9	1.96	ns
6. Expansions	2	9	4.45	0.05	7	16	4.11	0.05

The teacher's treatment of task and communication breakdown

In addition to the comparison of the developmental nature of the six interactional features of the teacher's speech, an analysis of the type of task posed by the teacher's questions and an analysis of the teacher's approach to repairing communication breakdown were carried out. These analyses were based on conversations about five different pictures in the same four sessions as the previous analysis. However, as the length of the conversations varied substantially from session to session and from learner to learner, the scores obtained were weighted to correspond to the equivalent of 20 tasks, where a 'task' constituted an initial teacher question followed by whatever talk was required to resolve the demands set up by the question. The features investigated were:

(1) Type of task
  (a) Questions requiring object identification
      (e.g. 'What's this?')
  (b) Questions requiring some comment about the pictures
      (e.g. 'What's the man doing in the picture?' 'What's wrong with the picture?')
(2) Task establishment
  (a) Closed questions (i.e. questions for which the teacher had a preconceived response in mind)
  (b) Open questions (i.e. questions for which several possible answers would be acceptable to the teacher)[4]
(3) Response to communication breakdown
  (a) Teacher accepts (i.e. the teacher accepts a pupil response even though it is clearly not an appropriate response to the task)
  (b) Teacher repairs (i.e. the teacher seeks to elicit another response to the task either by repeating his initial question or by reformulating it or requesting clarification)
  (c) Teacher supplies (i.e. the teacher gives the solution to the task himself)

The results are shown in Table 1.2. In conversations with both R and T the teacher used far more questions requiring object identification in the early sessions than in the later ones. There were no significant differences involving either task establishment or the teacher's response to communication breakdown.

TABLE 1.2   *Comparison of teacher's treatment of task and response to communication breakdown at different times*

Feature	R				T			
	T1	*T2*	χ^2	*p*	*T1*	*T2*	χ^2	*p*
(1) Type of task								
(a) Object identification	22.5	8.5	13.31	0.001	25.8	8.0	28.9	0.001
(b) Comment required	17.3	31.5	(df = 1)		14.2	32.0	(df = 1)	
(2) Task establishment								
(a) Open Qs	6.8	13.2	1.88	ns	7.4	14.2	2.94	ns
(b) Closed Qs	32.2	26.8	(df = 1)		32.6	25.3	(df = 1)	
(3) Communication breakdown								
(a) Accept	9.2	1.4	5.51	ns	6.7	2.2	1.79	ns
(b) Repair	22.3	12.3	(df = 2)		12.7	15.7	(df = 2)	
(c) Supply	6.9	6.8			7.5	7.9		

The learners' communication strategies

The learners' contributions to the interview conversations were examined in terms of the distinction between 'reduction' and 'achievement' behaviour (Faerch & Kasper, 1980). Reduction behaviour was defined as the learner missing a turn by keeping silent, opting out of the task by the use of 'no' or 'I don't know', etc., topic switching (i.e. ignoring the task nominated by the teacher and substituting some other task in its place), or imitating (i.e. imitating part or the whole of the teacher's previous utterance irrespective of whether this was conversationally appropriate or not). Achievement behaviour was defined as using the first language, miming, requesting assistance, or guessing what response the teacher wanted. It was hypothesised that reduction behaviour would be more prevalent in the earlier sessions.

For the purposes of this analysis the same two early and two late recordings were examined. The basis was once again the weighted equivalent of 20 tasks in each session (see explanation above).

The results are shown in Table 1.3. R resorted to significantly more reduction-type behaviour in the early sessions, but T's behaviour did not change. Thus the hypothesis was confirmed for R but not for T.

TABLE 1.3 *Comparison of learners' communication behaviour at different times*

Feature	R				T			
	T1	T2	χ^2	p	T1	T2	χ^2	p
1. Reduction behaviour	22.0	6.1	9.94 (df = 1)	0.01	18.9	13.4	0.67 (df = 1)	ns
2. Achievement behaviour	16.4	24.7			9.5	9.7		

Discussion

The three analyses reported above were carried out in order to determine whether the T–P interactions changed as the ability of the two learners to use English grew. If, as has been claimed by Long (1983a) and Krashen (1982), L2 acquisition requires comprehensible input in order to proceed, it is to be expected that the conversational adjustments made by both the teacher and the learners will vary according to the stage of development of the learners. This is because the amount of adjustment required at an early stage of development will be greater than that required at a later stage (at least on some measures), in order to achieve comprehensible input.[5] The results of the analysis suggest that whereas some of the interactional features in the T–P conversations did change as a result of the learners' increased knowledge of English, other features did not change.

The features that proved developmentally sensitive included both teacher and pupil adjustments. On the teacher's side changes are evident in both 'strategies' for avoiding trouble and 'tactics' for repairing trouble (Long, 1983b). As regards 'strategies', the teacher favoured identification questions in the early sessions, presumably because they were simpler (Hatch, 1978a) and also because they served as a means of establishing intersubjectivity. In the later sessions the teacher switched to using more demanding questions. The teacher also used more self-repetition when the two learners possessed little competence in English. This served both to establish a task and to respond to breakdown. Where 'tactics' were concerned, the teacher produced more expansions in the later sessions, perhaps because he felt the two children possessed sufficient competence at this stage to benefit from the 'task' summaries which the expansions typically provided. On the pupils' side, only R's communicative behaviour changed with increased proficiency.

However, many of the features investigated did not change over time. On many of the features Long (1983b) found significant differences between native-speaker/non-native-speaker conversation and native-speaker/native-speaker conversation; no developmental effects were evident in the T–P conversations. The frequency of comprehension checks, clarification checks, and other repetitions did not change as the learners' competence grew. A number of possible explanations suggest themselves. One is that the results of this study reflect highly idiosyncratic interactional styles which would not be commonly found in a wider population. Another possibility is that the nature of the task affected the results. Show and tell pictures do not constitute a natural communicative task, and this may have restricted the occrrence of specific types of interactional behaviour. Another explanation is that some interactional features are only roughly tuned, whereas others are more finely tuned to the individual learner's stage of development. This has the support of mother-talk research (e.g. Ellis & Wells, 1980). If the latter explanation is correct, it might be expected that interactional differences will be more evident when the comparison involves stages of development more sidely separated than was the case with R and T, who, it will be remembered, did not progress very rapidly in the nine-month period the study covered.

It is also worthwhile drawing attention to the different interaction styles of the two children. Whereas R tried to cope with the communicative pressure posed in the early sessions by topic switching, T was more inclined to simply miss a turn or opt out. R's reduction behaviour had almost disappeared by the later sessions, but T continued to give up whenever the going got tough for her. This may partly explain why the teacher used more confirmation checks with R but not with T in the later sessions, as confirmation checks are contingent on the learner saying something. The point that I particularly wish to draw attention to, however, is that we should not necessarily expect the characteristics of interaction to be determined solely by the need to achieve comprehensible input. They can also be the result of personality. R's greater extroversion may account for why he was prepared to take greater communicative risks at an earlier stage than his sister.

The Role of Interactional Features in the Children's L2 Acquisition

Demonstrating that native speakers and learners make adjustments in order to achieve understanding and demonstrating that some of these adjustments change over time in accordance with the learner's knowledge of the L2 are not the same as showing that these adjustments facilitate L2 acquisition. To do this we need to show *if* and *how* interactional features contribute to the process by which learners develop an L2.

The SLA literature suggests that there are two ways in which the input may influence the route along which L2 learners pass.

(1) The input that results from the interlocutors' attempts to negotiate a shared topic results in specific syntactic forms being modelled more frequently than others. These are processed and acquired by the learner. Thus it is the basic rules of conversation which determine which forms are used frequently and so learned early. This view of the contribution of the input to L2 acquisition has been put forward by Hatch (1978a).

(2) The second way in which the input affects the course of development is through the use of what Wagner-Gough (1975) has called an 'incorporation strategy'. According to this view, conversations provide the learner with units of different sizes which can be incorporated into sentence structure. Thus the input controls which forms are processed by learners and also provides building blocks which they can use to construct new syntactic patterns, which otherwise lie outside the learner's competence.

In order to examine whether and in what way the T–P interactions contributed to R and T's acquisition of English, the transcripts of the first ten recordings were examined to identify utterances which featured 'new' syntactic knowledge. It cannot be claimed, of course, that these 'new' forms were actually in use for the very first time in these contexts, but it was felt that this approach would give an indication of the communicative conditions that appeared to facilitate the *use* of linguistic knowledge which had been recently acquired. As Faerch & Kasper (1980) point out, the automatisation of new items is just as much a part of L2 acquisition as their initial internalisation. Also it seems a reasonable hypothesis that those conditions that encouraged the use of new items were the same as those that facilitated their assimilation.

Only 'creative' speech was considered for this analysis. Imitations of previous teacher utterances were excluded.[6] The 'creative' utterances were then analysed in terms of their syntactic constituents in order to determine both the first instances of two-, three-, and four-constituent utterances and the first instances of new realisations of these utterances. Thus, for instance, it was possible to identify the first occasion in which single-constituent utterances (e.g. a noun phrase) were realised by two words as opposed to one word (e.g. 'blue umbrella' — adj. + N) and the first occasion on which two-constituent utterances (e.g. NP + verb) appeared in the speech of the two children.

Results

The pattern of development that emerged was very similar to that reported for the L2 acquisition of German by the children of migrant workers in Germany (see Pienemann, 1980). In the first two recordings both R and T were restricted to single-constituent utterances. In recording 3 they both produced the first instances of two-word realisations of single-constituent utterances:

R: Black/taes/(= tyres)
T: No water

and also the first instances of two-constituent utterances:

R: Man going.
T: A man wall.

For the next few sessions both R and T continued to operate with utterances consisting of one or two constituents, but they slowly expanded their syntactical range. The first clear instances of three-constituent utterances occurred in recording 7 for T:

T: This one is bigger.

and recording 8 for R:

R; The boy standing in the door.

T produced four-constituent utterances from recording 8 onward and R from recording 9:

R: Boot is open on car.
T: Boy is hold hand in the bus.

Thus syntactic development of the two children, as evidenced in the recording session, was systematically incremental. Various realisations of first one-, then later two-, three-, and four-constituent utterances were developed.

What contribution did the interactions between each of the two children and the teacher make at the 'breakthrough points'? In order to consider this question, selected interactions from the recordings will be analysed qualitatively to show the role played by negotiation. In the first example R and the teacher are looking at a What's Wrong Card depicting a bicycle with no pedals. The transcript of their conversation is as follows (see Appendix B for an explanation of the transcription conventions followed): R's first two-word utterance concluded this episode.

1. T: I want you to tell me what you
      can see in the picture or what's
      wrong with the picture.
2.   R: A/paik/(= bike)

3. **T:** A cycle, yes.
    But what's wrong?
4.   **R:** /ret/(= red)
5. **T:** It's red yes.
    What's wrong with it?
6.   **R:** Black
7. **T:** Black. Good
    Black what?
8.   **R:** Black/taes/(= tyres)

In this episode the task which the teacher began with in (1) was beyond R. He lacked the linguistic resources both to understand the teacher's demands and to respond to them. His two-word utterance in (8) was the result of a reduction strategy (i.e. topic switching) which the teacher accepted, and of an incorporation strategy based on the teacher's occasional question in (7).[7] Later on in recording 3, R produced another two-constituent utterance consisting of N + V, which again was the result of an incorporation strategy. R appeared to thrive when he was in control of the discourse topic and when he could 'lean' on the discourse to help him eke out his meager resources.

T's first two-constituent utterance was in recording 3 also. It also showed how important co-operation between the interlocutors was in the process of building utterances that lay outside or on the edges of the learner's competence. T and the teacher were looking at a What's Wrong Card depicting a man walking through the wall of a room.

1. **T:** Do you want to look at the
    next picture?
    Yeah? (.3.)
2.   **T:** Man
3. **T:** A man.
    And do you know what this is?
    (.4.)
    A wall.
4.   **T:** A wall
5. **T:** Like that one here. (pointing at
    picture)
    A wall.
6.   **T:** A wall, a wall
7. **T:** Yes.
    Now can you see what the man
    is doing?
8.   **T:** A man wall

9. T: He's going into the wall.

In this episode the major task that faced the learner was that of encoding the action process represented by the picture. Both R and T, however, were at a stage of development where their linguistic resources limited them to identifying objects. Like Yoshida's (1978) subject, their early vocabulary consisted almost entirely of nouns, and apart from the copula and 'have', they used very few verbs. The teacher helped T to get round this problem by breaking the task down into two parts. First, he and T identified the relevant objects in the picture — the man and the wall. Second, the teacher requested T to encode the action process (i.e. in (7)). T responded with a verbless utterance which juxtaposed the two previously practiced nouns. Her meaning was clear, however, and the teacher was able to conclude the episode with an expansion that provided a well-formed version of T's two-constituent utterance. Thus the success of this episode was the result of (1) the teacher breaking a complex task into parts (i.e. controlling the type of task the learner is faced with), (2) the teacher helping out with vocabulary, and (3) T's use of a juxtaposition strategy involving 'man' and 'wall'.

R's syntactic development also relied heavily on the discourse. His first three-constituent utterance occurred in recording 8:

1. **T:** What's the boy doing? (.2.)
2.   **R:** The boy (.)
3. **T:** Yeah, stand
4.   **R:** Standing in the door.
5. **T:** Standing in the door.
   Yes, standing by the door.
   By the door.

R responded to the teacher's initial request for action identification by imitating part of the question. The teacher started to supply R with the verb that he required (i.e. in (3)), but R was able to go on and complete the utterance himself in (4). The effect on the tape was of a more or less continuous utterance, with the teacher's prompt occurring at exactly the right moment to aid its completion. From this point onward, R produced plenty of three-constituent utterances.

Discussion

By identifying occasions when 'new' grammatical features appear in the speech of the two learners and then examining the discoursal context of these 'new' features, it is possible to shed light on how taking part in conversations contributes to L2 acquisition. This approach rests on a qualitative analysis of selected interactions. As such, it is not clear whether the discourse processes that appear to contribute to L2 acquisition are generalisable. Similar analyses of other learners in other learning situations are needed.

Where the T–P conversations examined in this study are concerned, a number of facilitating characteristics of the discourse can be identified:

(1) It appears that 'new' rules were most easily practiced when R and T were allowed to initiate the discourse topic. In this way the learners were able to establish intersubjectivity with the teacher without the difficulty of having to comprehend what the teacher wanted them to talk about. For example, in recording 9, R produced a total of seven three-constituent utterances and in each case the discourse showed R to be the initiator. The productive use of 'new' L2 forms required that the learners were given the freedom to establish what and how they will contribute to the discourse. In this way they were able to make the most of the English they already knew and the teacher was able to build on this.

(2) Reduction behaviour consisting of topic switching enabled the children to replace a teacher-nominated task, which they were not able to handle, with a topic, which they were able to handle. Topic switching which was accepted by the teacher was a device for establishing intersubjectivity.

(3) The teacher played an active role in helping R and T to stretch their resources and to build 'new' utterance types. One way he did this was by providing 'building blocks' which the learners could use as a basis for building 'vertical structures' of the type identified by Scollon (1976) in first language acquisition. That is, the children could incorporate part of a previous teacher utterance into one of their own utterances and so achieve a more complex utterance than they could have managed on their own.

(4) The teacher also gave feedback on the 'new' utterances produced by R and T. He did this principally through expansions which supplied the missing parts of utterances which the learners had struggled to produce and which, from a communicative point of view, had been successful.

In summary, it was apparent that R and T were most likely to produce 'new' forms when they were able to nominate the topic of conversation and when the teacher helped them by supplying crucial chunks of language at the right moment. Perhaps by providing feedback via expansions the teacher helped the learners to assimilate and further develop these 'new' forms.

Conclusion

It has been argued that comprehensible input is not simply the result of the speech adjustments made by native speakers but the product of interaction involving both the native speaker and the learner. In this interaction the native speaker makes certain formal and discourse adjustments to ensure understanding, while the learner employs certain communication strategies to overcome problems and to maximise existing resources. As Scarcella & Higa (1981) note, it may not be appropriate to talk of input facilitating L2 acquisition in terms of *simplification*. In a cross-sectional study they found that child learners received a simpler input than adolescent learners. They then asked why it was that child learners have been observed to learn more slowly than adolescent learners. They hypothesise that it is the *negotiation* that results from the adolescent learners' more active involvement that contributes to their faster development. This involvement is manifest in the strategies they use to obtain native speaker explanations for just those parts they do not understand and the extra work they do in sustaining discourse. Thus, if comprehensible input is a necessary condition for L2 acquisition, its provision needs to be understood in terms of the negotiation of mutuality of understanding between interactants rather than in terms of simplified input.

The analysis of the T–P interactions involving R and T lent some support to this viewpoint. The aspect of discourse that proved most sensitive to the children's level of development was the choice of topic. In the early stages topics involving object identification were preferred to topics involving comments about objects. Also the children were more likely to produce 'new' linguistic forms if they had sufficient control over the topic to make use of what they already possessed. The teacher's role in the successful exchanges was that of supplying those resources required by the learner to say what she or he wanted to say and of supplying feedback. The *negotiation* apparent in these exchanges was the product of both the search for intersubjectivity and the search for the linguistic forms necessary to establish, maintain, and develop this intersubjectivity.

Because comprehensive input is a negotiated rather than an absolute phenomenon, dependent on the learner's developing communicative proficiency, it may not be possible to specify a finite list of facilitative features. Different features may aid development at different times. For instance, in this study of T–P interactions teacher self-repetitions were more frequent at an early stage of development, and teacher expansions at a later stage. Also the context of activity in which interaction takes place is characterised by a dynamic, utterance-by-utterance adjustment by both partners in the conversation. Both the learner and the native speaker adjust their behaviour in the light of the continuous feedback about the success of the discourse with which they provide each other.

This suggests that simply counting native-speaker adjustments will not provide a complete picture of how input is made comprehensible and may, on occasions, be inaccurate. It is for this reason that the focus needs to be placed on how communication is negotiated. This can to some extent be achieved by examining selected interactional features, for, as Long (1983b) has pointed out, features such as confirmation checks involve taking into account the learner's contribution as well as the native speaker's. But the process of negotiation at the moment is probably best understood through qualitative analysis of selected interactions. This raises the question of which interactions to select for analysis. One possible answer — the one followed in this chapter — is to examine those interactions where the learner uses 'new' linguistic forms for the first time. This, of course, will require a longitudinal, case-study design.

The study of T–P interaction in this chapter was based on data collected outside the classroom. It is not possible to say, therefore, to what extent the patterns of negotiation that appeared to promote L2 acquisition are present in the everyday interactions of the classroom. One obvious constraint is the relative infrequency of one-to-one conversations in the classroom context. If negotiation of the type evident in the successful interview exchanges is the key to acquisition, it is important to discover how and to what extent this takes place in the ordinary classroom.

Appendix A

Description of six interactional features in the teacher's speech

The following description is closely based on Long (1983b).

(1) Confirmation checks, i.e. when the teacher repeats part or whole of learner's immediately preceding utterance and employs a rising intonation (e.g. A house?) or when the teacher repeats the utterance and adds a question tag. They are designed to elicit confirmation that the utterance has been correctly heard or understood.
(2) Comprehension checks, i.e. attempts by the teacher to establish that the learner is following what he is saying. Typical realisations are 'Right?' 'OK?' 'Do you follow?'
(3) Clarification requests. These differ from confirmation checks in that there is no presupposition that the teacher has understood or heard the learner's previous utterance. They can take the form of questions (e.g. 'Sorry?'), statements ('I can't hear.'), or imperatives ('Say it again.').

(4) Self-repetitions, i.e. when the teacher repeats part or the whole of his preceding utterance and also when the teacher paraphrases part or whole of his preceding utterance.
(5) Other repetitions, i.e. when the teacher repeats (but not paraphrases) part or the whole of the learner's preceding utterance without altering the intonation.
(6) Expansions, i.e. when the teacher expands a previous learner utterance whether by supplying missing formatives or by adding new semantic information.

Appendix B

Notational convention for transcripts

(1) The teacher's or researcher's utterances are given on the left-hand side of the page.
(2) The pupils' utterances are given on the right-hand side of the page.
(3) The teachers' utterances are labelled T and the pupils' utterances are labelled by their initials, T or R.
(4) Each 'utterance' is numbered for ease of reference in the discussions of the transcripts. An 'utterance' consists of a single-tone unit except where two-tone units are syntactically joined by means of a subordinator or other linking word or contrastive stress has been used to make what would 'normally' be a single-tone unit into more than one.
(5) Pauses are indicated in brackets:
(.) indicates a pause of a second or shorter.
(.3.) indicates a pause of 3 seconds, etc.
(6) Phonetic transcription (IPA) is used when the pupils' pronunciation is markedly different from the teacher's pronunciation and also when it was not possible to identify the English word the pupils were using.
(7) words are underlined in order to show:
overlapping speech between two speakers;
very heavily stressed words
(8) A limited amount of contextual information is given, where appropriate in brackets.

Notes

1. Long (1985a) proposes one solution to the problem that cross-sectional research faces in demonstrating a relationship between input features and SLA. He suggests that the role of the input can be assessed indirectly by (a) showing that linguistic/conversational adjustments promote comprehension, (b) showing that comprehensible input promotes acquisition and (c) deducing that linguistic/conversational adjustments promote acquisition.
2. Studies of the role played by motherese in first language acquisition have recognised the need to tackle all three questions listed and have also set about doing so empirically. SLA research in contrast has focused chiefly on the first of the questions, even though there has been tacit acceptance and general discussion of the importance of question (3).
3. In the first recording session the two children were 'interviewed' together in order to avoid creating unnecessary tension. T was absent from school on the date of the final recording.
4. Whether a question was coded as 'open' or 'closed' was determined by the subsequent discourse. That is, if the teacher conducted the subsequent discourse in a way which showed he did not accept the pupil's response to his question, it was coded as 'closed'. If the pupil's response was of the kind that suggested there was one and only one answer to the question, it was similarly coded. Otherwise the question was coded as 'open'.
5. Long (personal communication) has pointed out that the absence of significant changes in the teacher's discourse contribution from Time 1 to Time 2 is not unexpected. He argues that many of the discourse features will continue to reflect adjustment throughout the process of acquisition in order to disambiguate increasingly complex non-native speaker output. This is an interesting counter-argument to the one I am advancing, namely, that the frequency of adjustments will tend to reduce as the learner's proficiency grows. The available evidence from studies of motherese in first language acquisition indicates that at least some discourse features are developmental (e.g. Ellis & Wells, 1980), suggesting that this is also likely to be the case in L2 acquisition. It can be hypothesised that those discourse features which have a continued appropriateness throughout development will remain constant, while other features (such as expansions) are finely turned to the learner's level of development. If this is so, the research task is to identify which features are developmental and which ones are not.
6. It was not always easy to distinguish 'creative' and 'imitated' utterances. Many 'creative' utterances had, as one of their components, an imitation of the whole or part of the teacher's preceding utterance. The solution was to accept as 'creative' any utterance that was not wholly imitated.
7. An 'occasional question' is defined by Brown (1968) as a question that has declarative word order and substitutes the *wh-* pronoun for the sentence constituent required as a response to the question. Brown hypothesises that this type of question may aid first language acquisition.

2. The Classroom Context —
An Acquisition Rich or an
Acquisition Poor
Environment[1]

Introduction

The last thirty or so years have seen a major change in how we approach foreign language pedagogy. The starting point, which once was 'What does the target language consist of and how do I teach it?', has become 'How do learners acquire a second language and what do I have to do to facilitate it?' As Corder (1976) put it:

> Efficient foreign language teaching must work with rather than against natural processes, facilitate rather than impede learning. Teachers and teaching materials must adapt to the learner rather than vice-versa.

This change in perspective has led to researchers seeing the classroom not so much as a place where the language is taught but as one where opportunities for learning of various kinds are provided through the interactions which take place between the participants. One of the key questions has become 'What kinds of interaction promote L2 learning?'. In this paper I want to consider research which has examined a number of interactional features of language classrooms that bear on this question. I also want to examine critically the assumption that underlies much of this research, namely that acquisition is best promoted by providing opportunities for authentic communication and to give some consideration to the role formal instruction plays in helping to create an acquisition-rich classroom.

Classroom versus Naturalistic Discourse

Much of the research which has taken place has been motivated by the assumption that classroom L2 acquisition will be the most successful if the environmental conditions which are to be found in naturalistic acquisition prevail. According to this view, all that is needed to create an acquisition-rich environment is to stop interfering in the learning process (Newmark, 1966) and to create opportunities for learners to engage in interactions of the kind experienced by children acquiring their L1 or by child and adult learners acquiring an L2 naturalistically.

It is common to emphasise the differences that exist between pedagogic and naturalistic discourse. A good example of this is to be found in work on turn-taking. In ordinary conversations in English turn-taking is characterised by self-regulated competition and initiative (Sacks *et al.*, 1974), whereas in classroom discourse there is frequently a rigid allocation of turns. Who speaks to whom at what time about what topics is subject to strict control with the result that competition and individual learner initiative are discouraged. Lörscher (1986), for instance, found that English lessons involving learners aged between 11 and 18 in different types of German schools involved little opportunity for the negotiation of openings and closings. Turns were allocated by the teacher, the right to speak always returned to the teacher when a student turn was completed and the teacher had the right to stop and interrupt a student turn. These characteristics, Lörscher argues, are determined by the nature of the school as a public institution and by the teaching–learning process.

In general, the differences between pedagogic and naturalistic discourse are viewed negatively. Riley (1977), for instance, speaks of the 'falsification of behaviour' and 'distortion' that occurs in pedagogic discourse. Pedagogic discourse is seen as constituting an 'acquisition-poor' environment.

We need to examine such a conclusion critically, however. First, there is evidence to suggest that classroom discourse is not invariably different from naturalistic discourse. Van Lier (1988), for instance, reports that in the lessons he examined learners frequently do self-select and that 'schismatic talk' (i.e. talk that deviates from some pre-determined plan) occurs quite often. Faerch (1985) gives examples in classroom data of the same kind of vertical structures which have been reported in conversations with beginner learners in naturalistic settings. Mitchell (1988) provides evidence to show that classrooms can provide opportunities for real communication — as, for instance, when the L2 serves as the medium for classroom organisation. Classroom interaction is probably best viewed as a continuum, reflecting at one pole instructional discourse and at the other natural discourse (cf. Kramsch, 1985). The kind of discourse that arises will depend on the nature of the roles adopted by the teacher and learners, the teaching–learning tasks employed and whether the knowledge focus is on content and accuracy or on process and fluency.

Second, we need to consider the theoretical grounds for the claim that naturalistic discourse is necessary for an acquisition-rich environment. On what basis can we claim that having L2 learners communicate in a natural manner constitutes the most efficient way of promoting L2 acquisition? This is the central question, for we need to be certain that the kind of pedagogic discourse that results from traditional language teaching is not as restrictive as has been claimed. We will begin, then, by examining a number of features of classroom discourse which have attracted the attention of researchers on the grounds that they constitute the key to the relationship between communication and acquisition.

Interaction in the L2 Classroom and L2 Acquisition

Simplified input

The language which teachers address to language learners is often simplified. Furthermore, the degree of simplification that takes place relates to the learners' level of proficiency. Chaudron (1988), in a review of studies which have examined the rate of teachers' speech concluded 'the absolute values of speech to beginning learners are around 100 w.p.m' while intermediate and advanced learners receive speech that is 30–40 w.p.m. faster. Henzl (1979) and Kleifgen (1985), among others, found evidence of lexical simplifications, with lower type-token ratios with less proficient learners. Gaies (1977) and Håkansson (1986) have found marked differences in the syntactic complexity of speech which teachers address to learners as opposed to native speakers, although other researchers (e.g. Wesche & Ready, 1985) have failed to find any difference. In some instances, although rarely, teacher-talk can result in ungrammatical input (cf. Hatch, Shapira & Gough, 1978).

Teachers, it seems, do much the same as the caretakers of young children. Their speech is characteristically well-formed and they ensure that the general level of their language is tuned to their learners' level. There is, however, no clear evidence that these formal adjustments promote language acquisition. There have been no studies of L2 acquisition which have directly addressed the effect of simplified input on learning. L1 acquisition studies (e.g. Wells, 1985) report that all children get simplified input so the presence or absence of such input does not account for differences in the rate of acquisition by children.

It does not follow, however, that simplified input is unimportant. Indeed, it is almost certainly crucial in helping learners to segment the speech flow into phonological and grammatical units. Schmidt (1990) has argued that acquisition depends on learners being able to 'notice' linguistic features in the input. Access to simplified input may in fact be a necessary condition for 'noticing' to take place. As anyone who has tried to learn a language knows, acquisition depends on the ability to identify words and phrases and this is almost impossible in the early stages if the only source of input is 'authentic' native-speaker speech — one reason why listening to the radio or watching television is of little use in the early stages.

Teachers, then, need to simplify their speech but they do not need to be aware of the precise state of their students' L2 knowledge or to have an exact idea of gradations in linguistic complexity. All that is required is an intuitive feel for what makes input simple or complex for a given group of learners. Many teachers have an intuitive ability to simplify their speech, aiming perhaps at some hypothetical learner (Håkansson, 1986). They are able to establish a 'threshold level' by means of 'rough tuning' and so ensure that the majority of their learners receive input which they can process. Both Wong-Fillmore (1985) and Kleifgen (1985) characterise the expert teacher as one who is able to adjust her language in accordance with the feedback supplied by learners. But there are some teachers who, in my experience, do not possess this intuitive ability (or, alternatively, do not act on it) and whose input, as a result, is often pitched at an inappropriate level.

Interactional modifications

The *Interactional Hypothesis*, as propounded by Long (1983a), states that:

(1) interactional modifications which are directed at solving a communication difficulty help to make input comprehensible, and
(2) comprehensible input promotes acquisition.

According to the Interactional Hypothesis, an acquisition-rich environment is one that is characterised by high frequencies of such interpersonal functions as clarification requests, confirmation checks, comprehension checks, self- and other-repetitions. These constitute the overt signs of attempts to negotiate meaning. Long hypothesises that interactional modifications are much more important than input modifications of the kind examined in studies of teacher-talk.

There is some support for the first part of the hypothesis. Pica, Young &

Doughty (1987), for instance, compared the effects of pre-modified input in a lecturette with those of interactionally modified input that arose in two-way exchanges during a similar lecturette with no pre-modified input. They found that interactional modifications assisted comprehension, whereas the reduction of linguistic complexity in the pre-modified input had no such effect.

There is, however, very little evidence to support the second part of the hypothesis. I know of only one attempt to demonstrate that classroom discourse rich in interactional modifications results in accelerated L2 acquisition. Loschky (1989) studied the effects of premodified input (involving input modifications) and negotiated interaction (involving conversational modifications) on the acquisition of locative patterns by beginner learners of L2 Japanese. Loschky found that the group that experienced opportunities to negotiate meaning did better in comprehension of test sentences containing the locative patterns, but that there was no evidence of improved retention of the grammatical structure. In other words, Loschky's study provides support for the claim that negotiated interaction facilitates comprehension but not for the claim that it promotes acquisition.

The Interaction Hypothesis, despite the very limited empirical support it hs received, has motivated a number of classroom studies. Pica & Long (1986) compared the frequency of the kind of conversational adjustments involved in the negotiation of meaning in non-instructional and ESL classroom conversations and found a significant difference. Confirmation checks and clarification requests were much more frequent in non-instructional conversations, while comprehension checks were more frequent in the ESL classroom. They concluded that overall the amount of negotiation of meaning that occurs in the classroom setting is much smaller. Other studies have examined the effects of task type on the amount of modified interaction (e.g. Duff, 1986) and differences in the amount of negotiated interaction found in teacher-class lessons as opposed to small groups (e.g. Doughty & Pica, 1986). These studies have sought to identify the conditions under which maximum conversational modifications will occur.

The Interaction Hypothesis as currently stated, however, may be of limited value. First, there seems to be no clear empirical basis for the claim that negotiated interaction results in acquisition. Second, the theoretical rationale is of doubtful validity. Sato (1986), for instance, points out that conversational modifications may facilitate communicative performance without facilitating the acquisition of new linguistic features. Loschky comes to a similar conclusion, citing Sharwood-Smith's (1986) claim that the processes of using input for comprehsnion are different from those involved in using input for acquisition. Third, the categories used to measure modified interaction may be far less water-tight than the existing literature leads us to believe. Kitazawa (1990) attempted to replicate Doughty & Pica's study of interaction in small group work with conversations in L2 Japanese but found their classification system 'difficult and sometimes impossible to use'. The faith that has been placed in the identification of such a limited set of interactional features, on the grounds that these hold the secret to an acquisition-rich environment, seems unwarranted and, in retrospect, perhaps even a little naïve. It would be wrong to conclude, however, that interaction is not of central importance for acquisition. Roger Brown (1968: 287) is surely right when he commented:

> It may be as difficult to derive a grammar from unconnected sentences as it would be to derive the invariance of quantity and number from the simple look of liquids in containers and objects in space. The changes produced by pouring back and forth, by gathering together and spreading apart are the data that most strongly suggest the conservation of number and quantity.

We need to develop the tools to measure the 'pouring back and forth' and the 'gathering together and spreading apart' which takes place in interaction. It is doubtful whether the categories of modified interaction which Long & Pica have proposed achieve this. Far more promising is the kind of qualitative analysis which Bygate (1988) has undertaken. Bygate shows how oral communication in group work involves the learners in 'accessing chunks, constituting them correctly, combining them and modifying them efficiently' (Bygate, 1988: 65). His work shows how learners manipulate discourse, using it to negotiate their way to the construction of full clauses. Recent work undertaken by Pica and associates (cf. Pica, 1990) is also promising in that it attempts to show how particular kinds of interaction help to make semantic and structural relationships in the L2 more transparent and, therefore, more noticable by the learner.

Teachers' questions

Teachers — and, in particular, language teachers — ask large numbers of questions. There would appear to be two reasons for this. First, questions require responses and, therefore, they serve as a means of obliging learners to contribute to the interaction. Learners' responses also provide the teacher with feedback which can be used to adjust content and expression in subsequent teacher-talk. Second, questions serve as a device for controlling the progress of the interaction through which a lesson is enacted. It is for this reason that many teacher questions are of the display variety (i.e. designed to test and, therefore, have predetermined answers) rather than of the referential kind (i.e. truly information-seeking and, therefore, permit 'open' answers).

In language lessons where the focus is on form, display questions are likely to predominate. Long & Sato (1983) in a study of six ESL teachers found that 79% of their questions were display and pointed out that this contrasts with the use of questions in naturalistic discourse, where referential questions predominate. In lessons based on a content-based approach to teaching, display questions also predominate. Johnson (1990) found that 60% of the questions asked by three teachers in content classrooms were display. However, a careful study of the detailed results provided by both studies shows that there is considerable individual variation among teachers. Thus, in the Long & Sato study one teacher asked more referential than display questions, while in Johnson's study one teacher divided her questions more or less equally between referential and display. The teachers in these studies also varied greatly in the total number of questions they asked. Thus the predominance of display features is only a probable and not a necessary feature of language classrooms.

The general assumption underlying these studies of questioning behaviour is that display questions are less likely to contribute to an acquisition-rich environment than are referential questions. There would appear to be a number of grounds for such an assumption. First, educational arguments can be advanced for encouraging a less transmission oriented approach to teaching (Barnes, 1976). Referential questions allow the learner more opportunity to take part in her own learning. Second, referential questions are more compatible with a focus on meaning exchange (as opposed to form), which has been hypothesised to be necessary for acquisition to take place (Krashen, 1981a). Third, referential questions are more likely to result in extended learner responses. Brock (1986) found that learners' responses to referential questions were significantly longer and more syntactically complex and also contained more connectives than their responses to display questions. It should be noted once again, though, that a causative relationship between referential questions and acquisition has not been demonstrated. It may be that teacher questions of any kind are not especially facilitative in that they are topic-controlling (see below).

The questioning behaviour of teachers has proven amenable to change through training. Long et al. (1984) and Brock (1986) have shown that teachers can be successfully trained to increase the number of referential questions they ask and that the effects of such training appear to last. A simpler way to ensure questions that contribute to a more 'communicative' classroom environment, however, might be to have the learners ask the questions. Midorikawa (1990) found that when the responsibility for questioning was handed over to students, they invariably asked referential questions. When this occurs, the learner also achieves control of the topic.

Topic control

The issue of topic control has attracted somewhat less attention from L2 classroom researchers than other issues. This is surprising given that it has been shown to be a significant factor in naturalistic acquisition. Wells (1985) contrasts the interactional styles of mothers who are 'supportive' and who allow their children the opportunity to both initiate and control topics and those who are 'tutorial' in the sense that they control the discourse through the use of display questions and evaluative feedback. He argues that the supportive style results in faster L1 learning. Hatch (1978b) also provides evidence to show that allowing L2 learners the opportunity to nominate topics provides an effective basis for building conversations.

One study that has examined the effects of topic control in L2 classrooms is that of Slimani (1989). This study is also unique in that it seeks to establish a direct relationship between aspects of classroom interaction and acquisition. The method that Slimani used involved requesting students to record on 'uptake charts' any item they thought they had learned from a lesson and then checking through transcriptions of the lesson to identify where the items they listed occurred. Slimani found that 'whatever is topicalized by the learners rather than the teacher, has a better chance of being claimed to have been learnt'. Also, learners appeared to benefit from topics nominated by other learners rather than from topics they themselves had initiated. This suggests that learners might benefit more from listening to exchanges in which other students are involved than in participating themselves.

Topic control may be important for L2 acquisition in several ways. It is very likely that learners will be more motivated to attend to input if they are involved in choosing and developing the topics that are talked about. Having control over the topic is also one way of ensuring that the linguistic complexity of the input is tailored to the learner's own level. Better opportunities for negotiating meaning are likely to occur when a communication problem arises. Topic control may also stimulate more extensive and more complex production on the part of the learners.

It is no easy task to give learners control over the topics of conversation in large classrooms, however. One reason for the predominance of the tutorial style in the classroom, is the need to ensure that the interaction is orderly.

Another reason may be the teacher's felt need to cover the syllabus. In such situations — which are much more common than situations where classes are small and teachers are free to devise their own curriculum — handing over topic control to the students may seem methodologically very difficult and even undesirable. One way of ensuring at least some opportunities for learner topic control is through small group-work.

Learner participation

The role of learner participation in L2 acquisition is one of the more controversial issues. On the one hand there are those like Krashen (1985) who argue that 'speaking is the result of acquisition, not its cause'. On the other hand, a strong case has been made for learner output as a contributory factor to successful L2 acquisition. Swain (1985), for instance, has proposed the *Comprehensible Output Hypothesis*, as an addition rather than replacement for Krashen's Input Hypothesis. Swain argues that producing output that is precise, coherent and appropriate, encourages learners to develop the necessary grammatical resources, provides the learner with opportunities to test hypotheses and may force the learner to move from the kind of semantic processing which is possible in reception to the syntactic processing required in production.

According to Swain, it is not just any kind of output that is needed but rather 'pushed language use'. Allen *et al.* (1989) provide evidence to suggest that even in immersion classrooms, which might be expected to foster pushed language use there are, in fact, relatively few opportunities. Less than 15% of student turns in French immersion classrooms were 'sustained' (i.e. more than a clause in length). It is likely that the opportunities for pushed language use are even rarer in more traditional language classrooms.

Once again, however, there is an absence of clear, direct evidence to show that learner participation is crucial for successful L2 acquisition. Ellis (1988a) reviewed a number of studies that have investigated the relationship between learner participation and learning and showed that the results are very mixed. Some studies (e.g. Seliger, 1977; Naiman *et al.*, 1978) reported a positive correlation between measures of participation in class and learner proficiency, while others found no such relationship (e.g. Day, 1984). Even in those studies reporting a positive relationship it is not possible to claim that participation *causes* learning, for it is quite possible that learners with higher proficiency elect or are nominated to participate more frequently than those with lower proficiency. In other words, an 'acquisition–causes–participation' explanation is just as tenable if not more so than a 'participation–causes–acquisition' explanation.

Other evidence is available to cast doubts on the value of learner participation. Slimani, in the study referred to above, found that listening to other learners was most strongly related to uptake. Reiss (1985) found that 'silent speaking' (i.e. silently rehearsing answers to questions addressed to other learners) was one classroom strategy which good language learners used. Ellis & Rathbone (1987) found that some learners responded negatively when they were required to participate. Performing in 'public' in the classroom can result in a high level of learner anxiety.

These studies, however, have examined participation in general, not 'pushed language use'. Thus, they do not address the Comprehensible Output Hypothesis directly. Although they enable us to query the faith in learner production which underlies much language teaching, they do not provide a basis for rejecting learner participation as an important feature of an acquisition-rich classroom. It is likely that the relationship between learner participation and acquisition is a complex one depending on a host of factors to do with the personality of the learner, the learner's level of proficiency (participation may be much more important for more advanced learners than for beginners), whether the production is volunteered or requested, how sustained it is and to what extent learners need to express themselves precisely and coherently. The kind of participation needed to foster acquisition may be difficult to achieve in lockstep teaching. As Allen *et al.* (1989) suggest, the kind of talk needed may be best catered for through small group work.

Use of the L1

The extent to which the use of the L1 is desirable and the particular uses for which it is legitimate are issues of real importance to many foreign language teachers. Surprisingly, although there is no shortage of methodological advice, there has been little research which has addressed the use of the L1 and its effect on acquisition.

There is even a paucity of descriptive research informing us what use of the L1 teachers typically make. There are likely to be marked differences even in classrooms where the teacher knows the learners' L1. Kaneko (1990) found that in a classroom where both teacher and learners were Japanese nearly 40% of the total speaking time was conducted in the L1, whereas in a similar classroom where the teacher was an American who spoke fluent Japanese only 18% of the speaking time was in the learners' L1. The nature of the activity also affects what language is used. Thus, in Kaneko's study, the Japanese teacher was more likely to use English in interactions where there was an explicit pedagogic purpose than in interactions dealing with the organisational requirements of the lesson or in social interactions, where L1 Japanese predominated. In contrast, the America teacher used L2 English frequently in organisational and social interactions as well as pedagogic interactions. Mitchell (1988) found that teachers of elementary French in Scottish secondary schools also used the L2 in organisational instructions, but preferred the L1 when it came to giving instructions relating to the performance of a pedagogic activity.

When it comes to the relationship between L1 use and acquisition we know even less. Wong-Fillmore (1985) in a study of classrooms in American schools containing children with limited proficiency in English argues that a clear separation of languages is desirable. She comments: 'In the bilingual classes that worked well for learning, the two languages of instruction were kept quite separate.' Translation obviated the need for students to figure out what was being said. Also if teaching took place in both languages, the L2 version was unlikely to contain the necessary modifications to aid comprehension and the students tuned out. Kaneko examined the effects of language use on learner uptake (using Slimani's method of measuring this). She found that students reported learning L2 items which occurred in topic sequences conducted entirely or mainly in the L2 to a much greater extent than they did in topic sequences conducted mainly or entirely in the L1. This proved to be the case in the lessons conducted by both the Japanese and American teachers.

There is little information on which to base any firm conclusions regarding the use of the L1. Clearly learners learn from L2 input and if they have little of this they will not learn much. Some methodologists (e.g. Prabhu, 1987) have rejected extensive use of small group work in monolingual classrooms on the grounds that the learners will communicate together using their shared L1 and opportunities for uptake will be reduced. But there may be some legitimate uses of the L1 — such as translating unknown lexical items or explaining grammar rules.

Conclusion

Hatch (1986) has characterised the task of applied linguistics as that of discovering the links between experience and learning. The problem is that we still know very little about the relationship between experience and acquisition — a point that Hatch herself acknowledges and which is clear from the research reviewed in the previous section.

We do know that learners — first and second — can acquire a language successfully without the benefit of formal instruction. L2 learners, both children and adults, are able to use the experiences provided by participating in face-to-face interaction with native speakers or other learners to build a knowledge structure of the L2. One way of creating an acquisition-rich environment in the classroom, therefore, is by replicating these natural learning experiences. As Hatch (1986: 20) has put it:

> For both the teacher and the teacher trainer, the task is to find those experiences that contribute most to learning and to work out ways to bring reasonable copies of those experiences, and the ways of dealing with them, into the classroom.

The following are some of the features which we examined earlier and which have been hypothesised important for creating the kind of naturalistic environment which is believed to contribute to successful language acquisition:

(1) Teacher talk is simplified to a level that makes it possible for the learners to process input for comprehension.
(2) Classroom interaction provides opportunities for learners to observe the way utterances are constructed in the process of building discourse and to manipulate chunks of language in the expression of meaning content.
(3) Referential questions which encourage learners to express their own content in their own way in extended responses are used.
(4) Learners have opportunity to nominate their own topics and to control the development of these topics.
(5) Learners are given opportunities to participate actively in the classroom communication but are not required to produce until they are ready to do so. Advanced learners may need opportunities for extended production.
(6) The use of the L2 is not restricted to pedagogic functions but is also used for organisational and social functions.

It is probably true to say that most L2 classrooms do not manifest these characteristics and, therefore, might be said to constitute acquisition-poor environments. One reason for this is what Edmondson (1985: 162) has called 'the teacher's paradox'. This states:

> We seek in the classroom to teach people how to talk when they are not being taught.

The paradox results in a tension between discourse appropriate to pedagogic goals and discourse appropriate to pedagogic settings. The classroom affords 'coexisting discourse worlds', depending on whether the participants are engaged in trying to learn or trying to communicate. In many classrooms, pedagogic discourse is predominant.

The question we need to ask is whether classrooms that offer only pedagogic discourse constitute acquisition-poor environments. Clearly, if a strong 'natural learning' position is adopted, the answer is 'yes'. This is Krashen's position and, somewhat less clearly, also Long's. The thrust of their theoretical and empirical work and their advice to teachers is that classrooms should concentrate on creating the conditions needed for authentic communication to take place. However, if, like Edmondson, we take up a less absolutist position and accept that formal language instruction can contribute to learning, we will also have to accept that pedagogic discourse, even though it displays very different characteristics from those listed above, can provide experiences that contribute to learning.

There is sufficient evidence now available to refute a strong natural learning position (cf. Long (1988a) and Ellis (1990) for detailed reviews of research which has investigated the effects of formal instruction on L2 acquisition). Although there are clear restrictions which govern whether formal instruction directed at a specific linguistic feature results in its acquisition, learners who receive formal instruction do appear to learn more rapidly and to develop higher levels of proficiency. Also, some adult naturalistic learners such as the Japanese painter, Wes, that Schmidt (1983) investigated fail to develop much in the way of linguistic competence even though their overall communicative abilities develop considerably. One explanation which Schmidt provides for this is that Wes did not receive any formal instruction. It would seem, therefore, that activities that require the learner to behave as a 'learner' rather than as a 'communicator' may be desirable.

An acquisition-rich classroom, therefore, is best characterised as one which provides both those experiences associated with communicating in natural discourse and those experiences derived from cognitive activities designed to raise the learner's consciousness about the formal properties of the L2 and their function in language use. Spada (1987) in a comparative study of learner groups exposed to different types of instruction found that 'attention to both form and meaning works best' and that both are required in the development of oral communication skills. This is, of course, nothing new. The need for some kind of mixture of opportunities for communicating and learning has long been recognised and is reflected in mainstream language pedagogy. There are still important questions to be answered, however. One concerns the nature of relationship between the two discourse-worlds that result from attempts at communicating and at learning. To what extent can these worlds be interlinked through activities that require the learner to transfer what has been studied formally into authentic language behaviour? Are the worlds so incompatible that trying to integrate them is like mixing oil and water? What are the ideal proportions of the two types of discourse in an instructional programme?

Finally, we need to acknowledge the difficulties that teachers in many parts of the world face in creating the conditions in which genuinely communicative experiences can occur in a classroom context. Creating an acquisition-rich communicative environment in the classroom represents a major challenge. It involves not only access to the methodological techniques of a communicative methodology but also, more crucially, the attitudes of both teacher and learners. In many teaching contexts, the target language continues to be viewed as an object to be studied rather than as a tool for communication. If the focus of attention in the last decade has been on how to create opportunities for communicative experiences in the classroom, this is surely because these have often been missing. Thus, even though we still know very little about how communication shapes acquisition, this focus is probably the right one, providing that it does not result in the exclusion of opportunities for formal learning.

Notes

1. This paper was read at an Ivy League Consortium Conference held at Cornell University on 12–14 October, 1991; it is also part of a volume entitled *Text and Context: Cross-Disciplinary Perspectives on Language Study* published by D.C. Heath and Company in their series on Foreign Language Acquisition Research and Instruction.

Section 3
Formal Instruction and Second Language Instruction

The papers in this section address the role of formal instruction in promoting L2 acquisition. The term 'formal instruction' refers to attempts to induce classroom learners to acquire specific L2 properties — in this case, grammatical properties.

There have been an increasing number of studies which have investigated the effect of formal instruction on L2 acquisition. This is an issue which is important for both general theories of L2 acquisition and for language pedagogy. In the case of the former, studies of formal instruction provide a means of testing hypotheses about the role of input (as opposed to learner-internal factors) in determining acquisition. If it can be shown that formal instruction is unable to affect the developmental sequences which have been reported in studies of naturalistic acquisition, then mentalistic theories will receive strong support. In the case of language pedagogy, studies of formal instruction inform the ongoing debate regarding the extent to which teaching should try to intervene directly in the learning process or allow learners to develop naturally through participating in communicative activities. The papers that follow are concerned chiefly with language pedagogy, although general theoretical questions are also addressed.

A number of 'themes' emerges from the three papers:

(1) There is a clear commitment to the existence of developmental sequences on my part. Thus the first paper in this section draws on research which has shown that WH interrogatives are acquired in a relatively fixed sequence, while the second paper refers to studies which demonstrate a natural sequence for German word order rules. The reader might like to bear in mind that this commitment is not shared by all researchers.
(2) There are clearly constraints that affect whether the instruction is successful. Learners do not appear able to use the instruction they receive to develop their interlanguages unless they have reached the requisite stage of development.

(3) It does not follow that formal instruction is of no pedagogic value — even if it is not timed to match the learner's developmental stage. It may facilitate subsequent development by raising the learner's consciousness. In other words, the real value of formal instruction may rest in a delayed rather than immediate effect. In this way, formal instruction may speed up learning and, perhaps, prevent fossilisation, even if it does not affect the route that learners follow.

(4) Formal instruction needs to be viewed as general 'input', which may be used in ways quite unintended by the instruction, as well as deliberate attempts to teach specific grammatical structures.

(5) Formal instruction is best viewed as a particular kind of classroom interaction which is negotiated by the participants. As such it constitutes a social event, subject to influence by a host of factors, such as the learner's learning preferences and the teacher's views about how a teacher should behave.

The general picture that I think emerges from these papers is of the complex nature of formal instruction. This picture is in sharp contrast to both the view taken by some SLA researchers and language teaching experts, which tend to simplify the issues involved. It follows that we need more qualitative studies of what transpires when formal instruction takes place. Only in this way will we develop sufficient knowledge of the variables at work and so be better equipped to design quantitative and experimental studies.

'Can syntax be taught? A study of the effects of formal instruction on the acquisition of WH questions by children' (*Applied Linguistics* 5, 138–55) reports on an experimental study that was carried out as part of the longitudinal study of three ESL learners referred to in Section 2. 'Are classroom and naturalistic acquisition the same? A study of the classroom acquisition of German word order rules' (*Studies in Second Language Acquisition* 11, 305–28) is a quantitative but non-experimental study of 39 foreign language learners. 'The role of practice in classroom learning' was first published in *Teanga* 8, 1–25 and subsequently in *AILA Review* 5.20–39. It constitutes an attempt to illustrate the 'educational approach' referred to in this Volume's Introduction by examining the pedagogic construct of 'practice' in the light of SLA research.

3. Can Syntax be Taught? A Study of the Effects of Formal Instruction on the Acquisition of WH Questions by Children

Introduction

In 1973 Dulay & Burt published an article entitled 'Should we teach children syntax?'. The answer they gave was that syntax should not be taught to children. If children were exposed to a natural communication situation the 'natural processes' responsible for second language (L2) acquisition would be activated and a resulting 'natural order' of development occur. In the decade that followed the publication of this study, the conviction among SLA researchers that formal instruction was not the best way to learn a second language grew, Krashen (1982), in particular, has argued that because there is no 'interface' between 'acquired' and 'learnt' knowledge, because there are constraints on the nature and number of rules that can be 'learnt', and because utterances are initiated only with 'acquired' knowledge, little time should be spent in teaching grammar. Krashen's position is not only that syntax *should* not be taught (to any great extent) but also that it *cannot* be taught.

However, it is a huge leap from advising against formal instruction for children, on the grounds that there is a better way to encourage L2 acquisition, to rejecting formal instruction for both children and adults on the grounds that it does not work. It runs contrary to the intuitions of many language teachers who operate on the basis that 'skill getting' precedes 'skill using' (Rivers & Temperley, 1978). According to this view, formal instruction may not be instantly successful, but it may act as an 'acquisition facilitator' (Seliger, 1979) by sensitising the learner to a specific form which can then be fully acquired and more easily used later on. This is one version of the 'interface hypothesis', which states that knowledge derived from formal study can be utilised in everyday conversation if not sooner, then later. Protagonists of the 'interface' position (e.g. Bialystok & Fröhlich, 1977; Sharwood-Smith, 1981) argue that explicit (or 'learnt') knowledge can become converted into implicit (or 'acquired') knowledge, providing the learner has the opportunity and motivation to automatise new rules through practice. Even if formal instruction does not result in a different acquisitional route (and there is no agreement about this), it is still desirable, because it can speed up development. 'Acquisition' is a slow process; the provision of carefully selected and graded input that is thoroughly practised may accelerate it.

The 'interface' debate is conducted largely in theoretical and speculative terms. There is little in the way of hard empirical evidence. Krashen (1981b), responding to Sharwood-Smith's (1981) arguments in favour of consciousness-raising, reviews his reasons for denying any seepage from 'learnt' to 'acquired' knowledge. There are learners like 'P' who are strongly motivated to practise, but who still do not 'acquire' rules like the third person singular of the present simple tense. 'Self-report' data do not support the view that rules are 'learnt before they become automatised. The evidence for the 'natural order' is very strong, suggesting that learners cannot beat it. Finally, if development occurs via comprehension (as opposed to production), then it is unlikely that practice of formally presented language items will contribute to 'acquisition'. In Krashen's opinion the interface position consists of nothing but appeals to intuition.

Those empirical studies that have investigated the effectiveness of formal instruction have typically done so either by comparing learners who have received language teaching with those who have not (e.g. Fathman, 1975), or by correlational studies involving measures of target language proficiency (e.g. Krashen et al., 1978). Krashen (1982: 34 ff.) reviews seven studies of the first type. He concludes that formal instruction can help, but only to the extent to which it provides 'comprehensible input'. He suggests that it is most successful in foreign language teaching situations, where the students are not exposed to the target language outside the classroom. In this interpretation, therefore, it is not consciousness-raising or practice that aids development, but simply exposure to input pitched at the appropriate level to facilitate 'acquisition'. However, Krashen et al. (1978) found that the proficiency of 116 ESL students correlated more strongly with the number of years of formal English study than with the number of years they had spent in an English-speaking environment. The conclusion they reached is in striking contrast to the view formulated in Krashen (1982): 'What may be inferred from the results is that formal instruction is a more efficient way of learning English for adults than trying to learn it "in the streets" ' (p. 260). The apparent contradiction can be resolved only by distinguishing 'exposure' and 'instructional' variables in language teaching; is it the 'comprehensible input' or the 'consciousness-raising' that occurs in language teaching which contributes to development? This is a vital question, but the answer cannot be determined from studies that do not examine the nature of the classroom interactions that take place in the name of language teaching.[1]

Some of the strongest evidence in favour of the non-interface position comes from studies that have investigated the relationship between explicit knowledge of grammatical rules and actual performance. Seliger (1979), for instance, found that there was no relationship between his subjects' ability to use 'a' and 'an' before a noun and their ability to state the rule involved. If this finding generalises to a large number of other rules, it would appear that conscious knowledge of a rule is of little use in spontaneous communication. However, as Seliger recognises, this does not mean that instruction is without value, as it may ease the way for later acquisition. His study does suggest that the processes responsible for learning about a rule are not those responsible for using it in ordinary conversation.

Rather surprisingly, however, the interface issue has not been subjected to the most penetrating form of empirical investigation, i.e. the study of the effects of formal instruction in *specific* grammatical rules on students' abilities to use these rules in informal contexts. An exception is the investigation by Lightbown *et al.* (1980). They studied the effects of classroom teaching on 175 French-speaking students' use of the [s] inflection, the copula in equational clauses, and locative prepositions of motion. They observed that scores on a grammatical judgement test improved on average 11% in comparison to a 3% improvement in a control group who received no instruction, although scores fell back to an intermediate level in a later administration of the test. This study suggests that formal instruction can have some effect in improving the general accuracy of learners' speech, but the grammatical judgement test may measure 'learning' rather than 'acquisition'; it gives no indication of whether formal instruction leads to an improved ability to use the target structures in ordinary conversation.

The kind of investigation undertaken by Lightbown *et al.* is problematic as a result of the difficulty in both identifying and controlling for the independent variables that may influence the success of formal instruction. There is a host of potential instructional variables. As Sharwood-Smith (1981) points out, 'consciousness-raising' can take place in varying degrees, depending on the level of elaboration and explicitness with which the rule is presented. Practice can vary in both amount and type. Some grammatical rules may be amenable to formal instruction and others might not — Krashen (1982) suggests that the third person singular is an example of the former, and WH interrogatives an example of the latter. It may also prove to be the case that whereas formal instruction is of little use where rules are concerned, it can prove very effective for formulaic speech (Ellis, 1984). In either instance, however, the student must be prepared to treat the formal instruction as a means of developing a knowledge of the target language and not as a problem-solving task, otherwise it is likely that instead of 'interlanguage competence' developing, all that will result is 'reproductive competence' (Felix, 1977).

In addition to the above instructional variables, there is also a host of learner variables that may influence the success of formal instruction. The student's stage of development may be crucial. Vygotsky (1962) pointed out that for training to be effective, it must occur at the learner's 'zone of proximal development'. Also, beginners may be able to benefit more from instruction than advanced learners, or perhaps vice versa.[2] The importance of taking into account the age of the student in planning formal instruction is generally recognised; students who have reached the Piagetian stage of Formal Operations are likely to be better equipped to benefit from grammar teaching than those who have not. The attitudes and motivation of the students are likely also to be crucial. For example, students who *expect* language teaching to consist of formal instruction may be more receptive to it than others. A host of other variables could be considered — personality, cognitive style, the student's mother tongue, whether the student is literate or not in his mother tongue, the student's relationship with his teacher, etc. In general very little is known about how learner variables influence classroom language learning.

The difficulty of controlling for these (and other) instructional and learner variables is probably the major reason why there have been so few empirical studies of the direct effects of formal instruction on the acquisition of specific rules. Nevertheless, it is arguably time to lend support to theorising and speculating about whether syntax can or cannot be taught by beginning the difficult process of submitting the arguments to empirical study. It is unlikely that any single study will resolve the issue, but the accumulative evidence of many studies may help to answer what has become the major question of applied SLA research — can syntax be taught?

The study that is reported in the subsequent sections of this paper has two major aims. The first is to make a start on examining empirically how the teaching of specific structures contributes to their acquisition, and the second is to identify a number of methodological issues that future studies will need to take into consideration. It must be emphasised that because of the difficulty of identifying and controlling for learner and situational variables that can influence acquisition, the study is to be viewed as exploratory, rather than rigidly experimental.

The Design of the Study

The study was designed to investigate the effects of approximately three hours of teaching on the ability of 13 children to ask WH questions that were semantically appropriate and that displayed subject-verb inversion.

The subjects

The 13 children were aged between 11 and 15 years. They were full-time ESL pupils at a Language Unit in London. They differed in the amount of time they had been resident in Britain, the mean being approximately one year. All the children were exposed to English outside the classroom, particularly in the Language Unit, where English functioned as a lingua franca among teachers and pupils. The extent to which they used English outside the Unit is less certain. In many cases the pupils were socially 'distanced' from an English-speaking community, and in one or two cases probably did not use English at all. However, the possibility of acquisition occurring as a result of outside contacts cannot be excluded and should be borne in mind in evaluating the results.[3] The children varied considerably with regard to age, first language (Punjabi, Mandarin Chinese, Arabic), time spent at the Unit, and mother tongue literacy. There were also differences apparent on other variables such as personality and learning-style. They were in many ways typical of the motley collection of 'first stage' learners found in Language Units throughout Britain.

Two of the children in the study, R and T, were the subjects of a longitudinal study of classroom SLA. This study showed that at the time of the WH interrogative investigation, the two children had begun to use WH questions in spontaneous classroom speech, but that their development was by no means complete. Table 3.1 shows their development of questions in terms of four aspects at the time of this study. Both children typically relied on intonation rather than WH or inverted yes/no questions. Only about half of their total interrogative utterances contained a verb; only R used subject–verb inversion in his interrogatives, and many of these consisted of formulas (e.g. 'What's this?'). Table 3.1 is based on the spontaneous utterances the children produced in the classroom in the four weeks preceding this study.

TABLE 3.1   *Development of interrogatives in two of the children at the time of the WH interrogative investigation*

Aspect of development	R	T
1 Per cent of intonation questions in total interrogatives	53.3	68.8
2 Per cent of interrogatives containing a verb	56.7	50.0
3 Per cent of WH interrogatives in total interrogatives	36.7	31.3
4 Per cent of interrogative utterances with subject–verb inversion	33.3	0

These two children, R and T, were at the lower end of proficiency in the class as a whole. This is reflected in their 'when' development score (see below for an account of this); R had a score of twenty-five and T of nought (see Table 3.3). Therefore, given that both children were using WH questions in their spontaneous speech at the time of this study, it would seem reasonable to assume that WH interrogatives were within most of the 13 children's 'zones of proximal development'. Indeed, WH interrogatives were carefully chosen with this point in mind.

The formal instruction

The children were used to a fairly eclectic teaching style. Any formal language work that normally took place was of the audiolingual type. There was little in the way of grammatical explanation, probably because this was considered difficult for this kind of child to grasp. It was decided, therefore, to base the formal teaching of WH interrogatives on an audiolingual approach.

The formal instruction consisted of three lessons, each lasting about one hour and taught on three consecutive days in the morning between break and lunchtime. A total of three hours of teaching is very little, so it was not expected that the children would have 'acquired' either the ability to use WH pronouns correctly or the ability to invert the subject and verb in the sense of reaching a 90% criterion level of success. It was felt, however, that three hours of teaching was sufficient to examine whether formal instruction had any impact on acquisition of the kind noted by Lightbown *et al.*

The aim of the first lesson was to ensure an understanding of the different meanings of four WH pronouns — 'who', 'what', 'where', and 'when'. In this lesson the teacher did not pay much attention to whether the children's interrogatives were inverted. The second and third lessons sought to actively teach subject–verb inversion. The plan of each of the lessons is sketched out below:

Lesson 1

The teacher grouped the children around a wall frieze displaying events taking place in a High Street. He began by asking a series of WH questions using first 'who' and 'what' and afterwards 'where' and 'when', and inviting individual pupils to respond. He corrected only when their responses were semantically inappropriate. For written practice the pupils were given a matching exercise — a series of questions about the frieze and jumbled answers.

Lesson 2

The teacher began by going over the written exercise of Lesson 1. He then again used the wall frieze to ask WH questions — this time with only 'who' and 'where' — but on this occasion corrected formal errors in the pupils' responses, in particular failure to invert questions. The pupils were then divided into groups and shown pictures to prompt 'who' and 'where' questions. Each pupil took it in turn to make a question, and another pupil to respond.

Lesson 3

The teacher revised questions with 'who' and 'where' by firing questions at the pupils. There then followed another session around the frieze during which the teacher asked 'what' and 'when' questions, concentrating on the latter, which posed the greater difficulty. Group work followed on the same pattern as in the previous lesson.

These lessons were taught by the children's normal class teacher. They were devised jointly by the researcher and the teacher, who was made aware of the purpose of the investigation. Each lesson was audio-recorded and transcriptions in normal orthography prepared.

The elicitation instrument

The elicitation instrument used to obtain a corpus of WH interrogatives from the children was an adaptation of the technique used by Beebe (1980a): This required the children to make up WH questions about a picture of a classroom scene. To ensure that they produced a variety of WH questions, they were given cue cards for 'who', 'what', 'where', and 'when', and asked to produce an appropriate question for each card they took from the pile. There were also blank cards, when the children could use any question word they liked. A blank card was inserted after every fourth card.

To diminish tension created by the elicidation procedure, and also to provide a more natural conversational framework, the pupils performed in pairs (except for the thirteenth child, who performed alone with the researcher) and were awarded points for each question they were able to ask and which their partner accepted as sensible. In this way the sessions were turned into a game. The scoring of points, however, did not contribute to the subsequent analyses.

The elicitation instrument was administered in an empty classroom with only a pair of children and the researcher present. It was used on the day before the first lesson was taught and three days after the last lesson (i.e. a weekend intervened between the last lesson and the second elicitation session). Both elicitation sessions were audio-recorded and transcripts in normal orthography prepared.

Results

The 13 children were asked to make ten WH questions each in the first elicitation session. These were made up of two questions each for the four WH pronouns and two other questions of their own choice. In the second session the children were asked to make 15 WH questions, three questions for each of the four WH pronouns, and three others of their own choice.

Each question produced by the children was scored as follows:

(1) According to whether it was meaningful irrespective or whether or not it was well-formed.
(2) According to whether it displayed subject–verb inversion. For this analysis, only those questions that were semantically acceptable were considered, as some pupils treated 'where' and 'when' as free variants of 'what' and inverted them through extension of the 'what + s' pattern. A question was counted as inverted irrespective of whether a second auxiliary was incorrectly used after the main verb (e.g. 'When does she's eating?').
(3) According to whether it contained an auxiliary verb. The longitudinal study of two of the children showed that early interrogative utterances may omit the auxiliary verb. Thus an increase in the proportion of WH questions containing an auxiliary, irrespective of whether subject–verb inversion occurred, might be considered evidence of development. Questions which were suspected of being formulas were excluded from this analysis.
(4) According to whether it contained a main verb. The longitudinal study also showed that an early feature of interrogatives is the omission of the main

verb. Thus an increase in WH interrogatives containing a main verb might also be considered evidence of development.

The scores that were obtained by the 13 pupils in both elicitation sessions are given in the Appendix. A two-tailed t-test (Robson, 1973: 78–9) was used to establish to what extent the difference in the scores between Time 1 and Time 2 was significant. The level of significance did not reach the 0.05 level on any of the measures. However, as Table 3.2 indicates, the mean scores at Time 2 were in each instance greater than at Time 1. Although the improvement in performance was not spread evenly across the 13 pupils, there was a marked improvement in a number of the children.

TABLE 3.2   *Mean percentage scores at Times 1 and 2 and overall increase in scores*

	Meaningful WH questions	Subject– verb inversion	Use of auxiliary	Use of main verb
Time 1	71.8	56.8	13	24.4
Time 2	81.4	66.7	20	28.7
Overall increase	9.6	9.9	7	3.7

An interesting feature of the results for the individual children is that a clear accuracy profile emerges. The accuracy order for the meaningful use of different WH pronouns correlates closely with that for subject inversion in the different WH questions. 'What' questions are easiest, closely followed by 'who'. 'Where' questions are substantially more difficult, and 'when' most difficult of all. The application of the subject inversion rule is more likely in WH questions that employ WH pronouns whose meaning the learner has a clear understanding of. Thus the individual scores for meaningful use of the WH pronouns always exceed those for correct application of the subject–verb inversion rule. It would seem that learners first develop functional use of a WH question and then later develop the formal rules of usage. Figure 3.1 illustrates the accuracy profile that emerged at Time 1.

The developmental order reflected in the accuracy orders at Time 1 mirrors that found in the longitudinal study of two of the children.[4] It would seem, therefore, that progress along this route may be facilitated by teaching, but that the effects are not general. Whereas some children benefit to a considerable degree from formal instruction, others do not benefit at all. Why is this so? The answer may lie in individual learner differences, but it may also lie in the nature of the classroom interactions in which individual children took part. In order to pursue the second possibility, it is necessary to peer inside the 'black box' itself.

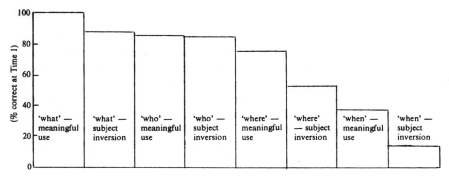

FIGURE 3.1   *Developmental order for WH interrogatives based on accuracy orders at Time 1*

The investigation of the relationship between the teaching and the acquisition of WH interrogatives was restricted to 'when' questions. Whereas many of the children had already achieved full competence with regard to 'who', 'what', and to a lesser extent 'where' questions, only one pupil had done so with 'when'. The hypothesis that was examined was that development of the subject–verb inversion rule for 'when' questions could be explained by the number of opportunities given to individual pupils either to comprehend or to produce a 'when' question in the lesson. Seliger (1977) suggested that 'high input generators' acquire an L2 more successfully and more rapidly than 'low input generators'. Seliger measured the amount of interaction that individual students participated in by counting every speech act that was performed in the classroom. However, because of the disorderliness of many of the interactions that took place in the 'when' lesson, an identical approach was not possible in this study. An alternative was to count the number of occasions when each individual pupil was nominated by the teacher either to produce or to answer a 'when' question. The advantage of this method was that such occasions could be readily and reliably identified from the transcript of the lesson and also that such occasions were representative of the mainstream 'instruction' offered by the teacher, and so were invariably supplied with feedback. The disadvantage was that every 'nominated' opportunity to use a 'when' question was also 'public', in the sense that any pupil could choose to attend to it if he or she wished and even to volunteer an unsolicited response which might or might not receive feedback.

A 'when' development score was calculated by awarding one point for each semantically appropriate 'when' question and a further one point if the question was inverted, converting the scores to percentages and then subtracting the difference between each pupil's percentage score for the first elicitation game from that for the second. The pupil whose 'when' questions appeared to be fully developed at Time 1 was not included in this analysis.

Table 3.3 shows the number of nominated 'when' exchanges that each pupil took part in, the total number of turns produced by the nominated pupils in these exchanges, and the 'when' development scores. The *Fisher Exact Probability Test* (Siegel, 1956) was used to establish the extent of any relationship between nominated opportunities for using 'when' questions and the development that took place between the two elicitation sessions. The twelve pupils were divided into two groups, labelled 'high interactors' and 'low interactors' in accordance with the number of 'when' exchanges they participated in, with the dividing line at three exchanges or more. The number of high and low interactors who showed a positive 'when' development score was then calculated. The result was quite startling; the expected relationship between high interaction and 'when' development did not emerge. In fact it was the slow developers who typically engaged in high interaction, and the fast developers who were typically low interactors ($p > 0.05$).

The results of the study can be summarised as follows:

(1) For the group of 13 children as a whole, there was no significant increase in their ability to use semantically appropriate and grammatically well-informed WH questions as a result of three hours of teaching.
(2) Individual children showed a marked improvement in the ability to use semantically appropriate and grammatically well-informed WH questions.

TABLE 3.3 *Nominated 'when' exchanges, pupil turns, and 'when' development scores for each pupil*

Pupil	No. of exchanges	No. of pupil turns	'when' development score
1	2	4	58
2	5	17	0
3	3	5	0
4	4	3	0
5	2	3	0
6	1	3	100
7	4	14	0
8	0	0	50
9	1	13	50
10	3	11	25
11	3	7	0
12	1	7	0

(3) An accuracy order based on the use of semantically appropriate and inverted 'what', 'who', 'where', and 'when' questions at Time 1 reflects a clear developmental progression which matches that observed in the longitudinal study of two of the children.
(4) With regard to development in the ability to use semantically appropriate and grammatically well-formed 'when' questions, it was the low interactors, rather than high interactors, who progressed.

Discussion

Formal instruction can influence second language acquisition in two rather different ways. It can result in a different developmental *route*, or it can increase the *rate* at which learners pass along a standard route. The results of the three hours of teaching of WH questions show that there were no effects on the route. The pattern of development that was observed cross-sectionally and from one elicitation session to the other was that observed in a longitudinal study of two of the children. It should be noted that the teaching did not completely follow the 'natural' order of development. The 'natural' order is (1) 'who' and 'what', (2) 'where', and (3) 'when'; whereas the teaching order was (1) 'who' and 'where', and (2) 'what' and 'when', although all four pronouns were presented together in the first lesson. It is difficult to conclude from this study that teaching does or does not influence the route of development. The results do suggest, though, that teaching does not lead to the dramatic appearance of 'new' rules but to a gradual improvement in the appropriateness and accuracy with which specific rules are developed and also to a slow accretion of syntactical complexity of utterances to which rules in the process of being developed are applied. Such an account is in accordance with current accounts of interlanguage as a variable system (e.g. Dickerson, 1975; Huebner, 1979).

It is also difficult from this study to decide whether teaching WH questions to the 13 children helped the rate of development. It has been shown that some of the children made conspicuous improvement, but this improvement does not appear to be related to the amount of direct teaching specifically addressed to the children. The opportunity for plentiful practice did not lead to rapid development. This does suggest that practice of the kind provided in the three hours of teaching is not effective in aiding development. As has already been pointed out, however, there are innumerable instructional variables that can have a potential effect on the degree of success. Perhaps the teaching provided was of the wrong kind. Perhaps it is not active participation in practice, but listening to the attempts of other pupils that aids development.

The failure to find any significant effect for the amount of practice afforded individual children contradicts the results of Seliger's (1977) study. He found a significant correlation between the amount of interaction students took part in and their performance on achievement tests administered at the end of the course. What explanations are there for this contradiction? Seliger's subjects were adults, whereas in this study they were children. Seliger considered every utterance the students produced, whereas this study considered only nominated exchanges. Also Seliger speculated that his results were best explained by the fact that high interaction inside the classroom was matched by high interaction outside, and that 'active learners' were successful because they made use of all language environments. The high interactors in this study were those selected by the teacher. It is possible that the teacher distributed opportunities for using 'when' to those pupils whom he considered most in need of formal instruction and that these were the pupils who were maximally socially 'distant' from an English-speaking community and thus the least likely to be high interactors outside the classroom. If this is the case, however, it would seem that formal instruction is not able to compensate for lack of general exposure to the target language.

The results raise an interesting and important question: why did those children who received the least practice improve the most? One possibility is that put forward by Allwright (1980) in his discussion of one high interactor. Allwright speculates that even if high interactors do not themselves benefit from using the language, their classmates might well benefit in a listening role. Another possibility is that it is not the quantity of interaction that counts, but the quality. One hypothesis might be that development is fostered by consistency and accuracy of teacher feedback. Another hypothesis, one that is in tune with much current thinking on both first and second language development, is that communicatively rich interaction which affords opportunities for the negotiation of meaning may aid development where more structured forms of interaction do not. In order to examine these 'quality' hypotheses, the transcript of the 'when' lesson was analysed.

There is little support for the first hypothesis. There are clear cases of pupils who were submitted to rigorous correction but who registered no improvement, and also of pupils who were allowed to get away with incorrect questions but who showed substantial development. Here are two examples;[5] (1) involves a zero developer, and (2) a fast developer.

(1)   P7: When does her cooking?
                                                 P2: When does the mother . . .

    T: When does she cook the
       dinner?

P7: When does she cooks the dinner?

T: When does she cook the dinner?

P7: When does she cook the dinner? (exasperated)

T: All right. OK. When does she cook the dinner?

(2) T: Can you ask a 'when' question? When.

P1: When does she's she's going shopping?

T: When does she go shopping? Again.

P1: When does she goes shopping?

T: Right.

The second hypothesis looks more promising. Although there were obviously relatively few communicatively rich exchanges in a lesson designed to drill the use of 'when' questions, a number of occasions for more spontaneous conversation did arise and these always involved a pupil from the group that showed some development. Protocol (3) is an example of such an occasion.

(3) T: Gurinder, would you like to ask a question?

P9: Who?

T: When. When does.

P10: In the park?
P?: Ssh!
P9: In the park?

T: No, I think from the High Street I think.

P9: Oh.
P?: Yes, come on.

T: I know. I'm going to help him a little bit.

Ps?: No. No.

T: Ask me ask then a when question — the postman deliver.

T: Ssh!

P?: When does . . .

P9: When does the postman
deliver . . . What?

Ps?: No. No.

P9: I know. What when does
the postman . . .

T: Deliver.

P9: Deliver/kl/

P?: Letter.

P?: Letter.

P9: Letter?

T: Letters. Good. Stand up.
Stand up. Silence. Say it
again, please. Look at the
class. Say it again

P9: When does the postman.

T: Deliver.

P: Deliver collect a letter.

T: No. Deliver.

P9: Deliver.

T: Letters.

P9: Letters.

T: Right. Who do you want to
answer?

P9: Raljip. (= name of postman)

T: No. Anyone.

P9: Eh?

T: Anyone. You pick someone.

P?: What Sir?

P?: Oh!

T: When does the postman
deliver letters?

P2: In the morning.

Ps?: (noise) In the morning.

T: In the morning.

This episode, which consists of 41 turns, is the longest in the lesson. Its length is the product of the need to negotiate the task in a variety of ways. First, the pupil (P9) needs to establish what WH pronoun he is supposed to use. Then he needs to establish the content of the question (i.e. whether it should be about the pictures of the park or of the High Street). Later he requires specific help with the lexical content of the question (e.g. 'deliver'). Finally, he misunderstands the teacher's instruction about choosing a pupil to answer his question and instead answers it himself — wrongly in fact, as he treats it as a 'who' question. The task is clearly a difficult one for this pupil, but there is no doubting his determination to succeed. The task itself serves to guide rather than dictate the structure of the episode. There is a lot of conversational work taking place just to stay on task, so it is not always clear where the cognitive focus lies. In the sequence dealing with the word 'deliver', for instance, the principal goal (constructing a 'when' question) appears to become of secondary importance. Arguably this is what occurs in natural conversations (see Schwartz, 1980). The exchange structure frequently departs from the three-phase patterns of most classroom interactions with the focus on drilling a linguistic rule. It involves more of the topic-incorporation devices that characterise certain kinds of mother — child interaction and which have been found facilitative (see Wells, 1980). It is of course not possible to say what the pupil learnt from this exchange, but it is possible that the respite from the focus on form and the opportunity to negotiate an understanding did help him to achieve a better understanding of 'when' questions.

If this rather speculative argument has any legitimacy, it would seem that 'exposure' — for that is what it is suggested protocol (3) illustrates — is far more important than 'instruction' as represented in protocols (1) and (2). In other words, it is not focusing on the form of 'when' questions that helped some of the children to develop, but the opportunity to negotiate a communicative task.

An extension of this argument is that the development that took place between the two elicitation sessions was not only the product of the exposure provided in the classroom, but also of that occurring in the elicitation sessions themselves. As Faerch (1980) has commented, interlanguage development may be the result of 'research internal' exposure just as much as 'research external' exposure.

An inspection of the transcript prepared from the second elicitation game lends some support to the view that the exposure in the sessions aided development. A good example is Pupil 10, who was one of the two children studied longitudinally. This pupil succeeded in producing a semantically appropriate 'when' question only on his final turn in the second elicitation game. Earlier, however, his partner, Pupil 9, had modelled 'when' questions for him. Also Pupil 10 appeared to seek out opportunities to practise 'when' questions by opting for 'when' on drawing a blank card. This contrasted with other pupils who typically chose an easy WH pronoun such as 'what' or 'who'. Protocol (4) is an example of the kind of practice that he constructed.

(4) **R:** Blank. Any question you
     like, R . . .

        P10: When is his (.) talking to
              him?
        P9: What?
        P10: When does his talking to
              him?
        P9: Because he's happy.
        P10: Happy?

    R: Is that right, R . . .?

        P10: No.

    R: What's the answer?

        P10: (.1.) Yes, right.

    R: All right.

Although this exchange is not a successful one, it (and other attempts like it) may have enabled thepupil to experiment with a new form in a more or less communicative manner. Pupil 10's attempt in protocol (4) seems to reflect a genuine effort to use 'when' meaningfully. As such it stands in marked contrast to the drill-like practice he took part in in the classroom, where Pupil 10 responded not so much by using language as with language-like behaviour.

The argument that is being tentatively put forward is that 'language teaching' involves both 'formal instruction' and 'exposure', and that for ESL children of the type investigated in this study, it is 'exposure' rather than 'instruction' that facilitates the development of WH questions. The illustrative evidence seems to indicate that when conditions are right (e.g. the learner is motivated and focused on meaning rather than form; the target rule is within the learner's 'zone of proximal development') acquisition can take place. In contrast, the statistical evidence indicates that the opportunity to practise the target rule in drill-like sequences does not aid acquisition. Implicit in this argument is the view that the L2 acquisition of English follows a uniform route in children learning English as a second language and that classroom teaching will influence only the rate of development. It must be emphasised, however, that this is a speculative interpretation.

Conclusion

The stated aims of the study of the 13 ESL children were to make a start on directly examining how the teaching of specific structures contributes to their acqusition, and to identify a number of methodological issues important for this kind of research.

The effects of teaching on the acquisition of syntax

The study reported in the previous section cannot be said to have proved that teaching does not aid the acquisiton of syntax for children. It indicated that for all the children the teaching did not subvert the 'natural' order of development, but then the teaching that was provided was not intended to achieve this. If the teaching had focused exclusively on 'when' questions and similar results achieved, then a strong case could have been made out for the failure of teaching to influence the developmental order. This may be a profitable line for future enquiry.

The study showed that the opportunity to take part in nominated teacher exchanges did not help acquisition of WH interrogatives. It is possible only to speculate on why this was the case. A number of possibilities can be put forward:

(1) It is not production but comprehension that aids development, as argued by Krashen (1982). The low interactors had the chance to learn by attending to interactions involving the high interactors.
(2) It is not the quantity of interaction, but the quality, that ensures acquisition. Some illustrative evidence has been put forward to suggest that when the learner has the chance to negotiate meaningfully, acquisition may be facilitated. This suggests that the instruction worked when it provided the right type of interaction.
(3) The kind of instruction provided worked for those who had already begun the process of acquiring 'when' questions, but not for those who had not. In other words, WH interrogatives (the 'when' type in particular) were not within the 'zones of proximal development' of all the children. Slender evidence for this can be found in the fact that R, who was more advanced at the time of the study, out-developed T, whose 'when' score was zero.

This study, however, was not tuned finely enough to be able to distinguish among these possibilities.

What light can this study shed on current theories concerning the role of instruction in the acquisition of syntax? I shall conclude by attempting to relate the findings to two different positions — the 'interface' and the 'non-interface' position.

The 'interface' position

The 'interface' position states that formal instruction can contribute to development by providing the learner with the opportunity to practise and so to automatise new rules (Sharwood-Smith, 1981; Stevick, 1980). It is through practice that 'explicit' knowledge, which is non-automatic, becomes 'implicit' knowledge, which is automatic. Instruction can both provide explicit knowledge and help to convert it into implicit knowledge.

This study does not appear to support the interface position. Producing exemplars of a pattern in a drill does not foster their use in spontaneous communication (if that was what the elicitation session was) involving children of the type investigated. This study does not, of course, disprove the interface position. The instruction provided may have been of the wrong type, in insufficient quantities, at the wrong time, etc. It would be necessary to replicate this study several times with different structures and different learners before the interface position could seriously be challenged.

The 'non-interface' position

The main protaganist of the 'non-interface' position is Krashen. Briefly, Krashen argues that 'acquired' knowledge, which is internalised through participating in authentic communication, is stored separately from 'learnt' knowledge, which is the result of conscious study. Not only are the knowledge stores separate, but 'learnt' knowledge cannot be converted into 'acquired' knowledge. The findings of the interrogatives study is entirely compatible with Krashen's theory. The lessons provided two types of input: input where the focus was on form and input where the focus was on meaning. In the discussion of the study these have been referred to as 'instruction' and 'exposure'. The study provided no evidence that 'instruction' aided the ability of the learners to perform in the elicitation game, which (presumably) required the use of 'acquired' knowledge. However, 'exposure' in certain types of interaction, in both the lessons and the elicitation games, may have served to facilitate development. One difference between Krashen's position and that taken up in the discussion of the interrogatives study is that whereas Krashen talks of 'comprehensible input', this paper emphasises 'meaningful interaction'. In other words, it may not just be a question of listening with understanding, but also of productive use of new structures that aids development.

It should be pointed out, however, that the findings of the interrogatives study are also compatible with other theories of SLA. Bialystok (1982), for instance, has proposed that L2 knowledge be characterised in terms of an *analysed* factor as well as an *automatic* factor. The analysed factor concerns the degree to which the learner is able to form a 'propositional representation' of target language knowledge. Bialystok suggests that four basic types of knowledge can be identified by permuting the presence or absence of the two factors, i.e. (1) −automatic, −analysed; (2) +automatic, −analysed; (3) −automatic, +analysed; and (4) +automatic, +analysed. This framework can account for what may have happened in the drills practising WH interrogatives; the pupils developed Type (4) knowledge. However, if spontaneous communication calls on knowledge that is unanalysed (i.e. Types (1) and (2)), then Type (4) knowledge would be of little use in the elicitation game. Furthermore, the ESL pupils may not be motivated to develop analysed knowledge if they intuitively recognise that it is of little use in unplanned discourse. The 'exposure' to target language forms which the pupils received in both some of the lesson interactions and also in the elicitation games themselves may aid the development of unanalysed knowledge in varying degrees of automaticity, depending on the amount and the quality of exposure available. Language drilling, in contrast, serves only to automatise analysed knowledge.

This study cannot be used, therefore, to decide in favour of Krashen's or Bialystok's theory. Krashen claims that 'learnt' knowledge can be used only in highly restricted circumstances and that 'acquired' knowledge is primary in that it is used to initiate utterances. Bialystok claims that different kinds of knowledge are involved in the performance of different tasks. Future studies, therefore, might use several elicitation instruments in order to discover whether the kind of knowledge that children internalise from 'instruction' can be used in certain kinds of task but not in others.

Methodological issues

The methodological implications of the study are somewhat clearer than the theoretical conclusions. They are:

(1) A single study cannot hope to prove or disprove any specific theoretical position. The only solution to the problem of identifying confounding variables is a 'shot-gun' approach. Multiple studies that provide similar results will enable these variables and their effects to be more clearly identified, and a 'general' position regarding the role played by instruction with different kinds of learners to be established.

(2) It is important to take into account the 'zone of proximal development'. One way to achieve this is to relate studies of classroom instruction to longitudinal studies of specific learners, as attempted in this study.

(3) One of the major faults of the comparative methodology studies of the 1960s was their failure to examine what went on in the 'black box'. This study has shown that the nature of 'language teaching' cannot be taken for granted, no matter how apparently prescribed the method is. All teaching provides both 'instruction' and 'exposure'. It is necessary, therefore, to examine the actual interactions that take place.

(4) 'Research internal' exposure may be a crucial variable in 'treatment'

studies that use some eliciting or testing device before and after the treatment. This variable can be handled by treating the elicitation sessions as 'exposure' (i.e. by recording and preparing full transcripts), as was undertaken in this study. Ideally it should also be handled through the use of control groups. If a control group had been used in this study, it might have been possible to determine more accurately what was gained from the instruction itself.

How instruction affects the route and rate of L2 acquisition is a crucial issue for ESL provision (and for language teaching in general). It has been the subject of much speculation. This paper is an attempt to begin the task of relating argumentation to empirical study.

Notes

1. Krashen (1981a) does in fact seek to explain the apparent success of the classroom in fostering development in terms of 'comprehensible input'; i.e. it is 'exposure' to an appropriate level of input, rather than 'instruction', that aids development. In none of his published work, however, does Krashen examine actual samples of classroom interaction in order to identify what constitutes 'exposure' and what constitutes instruction'.
2. There are opposing arguments here. A common argument put by language teachers is that students need to be given some knowledge of the TL before they can begin to 'acquire' through natural communication. In this view, beginners need formal instruction more than advanced students. On the other hand, it can be argued that a basic knowledge of the TL can be 'picked up', but more complex knowledge (e.g. embedding and thematising devices) requires formal explanations. In this view, formal instruction is best suited to advanced students who have 'fossilised'.
3. As the experiment was conducted within the space of a single week, the chance of acquisition occurring as a result of outside contacts with English is reduced.
4. The order of development is also very similar to that reported in studies of WH interrogatives in naturalistic SLA.
5. The following are the notational conventions used in the transcripts:
   — the teacher's or researcher's utterances are given on the left-hand side of the page;
   — the pupils' utterances are given on the right-hand side of the page;
   — the teacher's utterances are labelled 'T'; the researcher's utterances 'R'; the pupils' utterances are labelled P1, P2 etc., if indentifiable, and 'P?' if not identifiable;
   — pauses are indicated in brackets:
      (.) indicates a pause of shorter than a second
      (.1.) indicates a pause of one second duration.

Appendix

Scores obtained by the 13 children in the two elicitation sessions.

TABLE 3.4   *Proportion of different WH questions that were (a) semantically appropriate and (b) inverted for the whole group at Times 1 and 2*

	Semantically appropriate				Subject–verb inversion			
	What	*Who*	*Where*	*When*	*What*	*Who*	*Where*	*When*
Time 1	1.00	0.83	0.69	0.35	0.85	0.84	0.50	0.09
Time 2	1.00	0.85	0.82	0.59	0.92	0.80	0.68	0.26

TABLE 3.5   *Proportion of WH questions that (a) contained an auxiliary verb and (b) contained a main verb for each pupil at Times 1 and 2*

Pupil	Auxiliary		Main verb	
	Time 1	*Time 2*	*Time 1*	*Time 2*
1	0.10	0.13	0.30	0.33
2	0.40	0.60	0.60	0.60
3	0.20	0.40	0.40	0.53
4	0.00	0.07	0.40	0.27
5	0.11	0.00	0.25	0.27
6	0.00	0.00	0.00	0.20
7	0.00	0.33	0.00	0.33
8	0.00	0.07	0.00	0.07
9	0.20	0.33	0.22	0.33
10	0.10	0.33	0.50	0.33
11	0.00	0.00	0.00	0.00
12	0.00	0.20	0.00	0.07
13	0.50	0.27	0.50	0.40

4. Are Classroom and Naturalistic Acquisition the Same? A Study of the Classroom Acquisition of German Word Order Rules

The study of classroom second language acquisition (SLA) has both a theoretical and an applied purpose. The theoretical purpose derives from interest in the role that input plays in the acquisition of a second language. Language instruction consists of the external manipulation of input; the learner is confronted with data specially contrived to provide exemplars of the linguistic feature that is the target of instruction. It is possible, therefore, to test hypotheses relating to the effect that exposing the learner to data rich in specific linguistic features has on their acquisition. The applied purpose concerns the relevance and efficiency of particular kinds of language instruction. Currently, language teaching methodologists are interested in whether classroom L2 acquisition can be best promoted by meaning-focused or form-focused instruction. They are also interested in establishing the best order for presenting grammatical items to the learner.

The study reported in this paper was designed to contribute to both the theoretical understanding of the nature of L2 acquisition and also to language pedagogy. The general question the research addresses is 'Is the sequence of acquisition of grammatical structures the same or different in naturalistic and classroom L2 acquisition?' This question is of theoretical interest because it relates to the ongoing debate regarding the role of input in L2 acquisition (cf. White, 1987). It is of applied interest because it informs about the utility of form-focused instruction.

The comparison of acquisitional sequences in naturalistic and classroom L2 acquisition is one of two principal ways in which researchers have tried to investigate whether formal instruction can alter the 'natural' route of acquisition. Much of this research has relied on the methodology provided by the morpheme studies. The procedure followed by these studies involved collecting samples of learner language, identifying the obligatory occasions for the use of those grammatical morphemes that were the focus of the research, and establishing their degree of accuracy. The rank order of accuracy was then equated with the order of acquisition. The early 1970s saw a number of morpheme studies of naturalistic and mixed language learners (e.g. Bailey, Madden & Krashen, 1974; Dulay & Burt, 1973; Larsen-Freeman, 1976). In the late 1970s and early 1980s, a number of morpheme studies of classroom learners were carried out (e.g. Fathman, 1978; Krashen, Sferlazza, Feldman, & Fathman, 1976; Makino, 19780; Pica, 1983; Sajavaara, 1981; Turner, 1979). In general, these studies lend support to the hypothesis that the order of morpheme acquisition is the same in formal and informal settings. It should be noted, however, that some of the studies have reported differences in the naturalistic and classroom orders (e.g. Sajavaara, 1981), while other studies have found that some structures (such as third person and plural -s) are performed more accurately by instructed learners, even though the difference was not sufficient to produce variations in the morpheme order. Also, the types of errors produced by the two kinds of learners have been shown to differ in some cases.

The morpheme studies have attracted considerable criticism (cf. Hatch, 1978b) and are no longer fashionable. There are grounds for believing that accuracy and acquisitional orders cannot be equated. The method of determining the accuracy of individual morphemes is suspect because it ignores the functions performed by the morphemes. Rank orders and rank order correlations (the principal means of comparing orders produced by naturalistic and classroom learners) conceal facts about the acquisition of specific features that may be significant. Also, there seems to be no theoretical basis for comparing the acquisition of one feature (e.g. articles) with another (e.g. aux—be) which comes from a totally separate sub-system of the grammar of the language. The morpheme studies have not been motivated by any well-defined theory of grammar or by a theory of language learning. For many researchers, the results provided by the morpheme studies are of little theoretical or practical interest.

More recent comparisons of naturalistic and classroom L2 acquisition have tried to overcome these problems by:

(1) carrying out longitudinal, rather than cross-sectional, investigations; and
(2) focusing on particular grammatical subsystems such as negatives or interrogatives or by carrying out indepth analyses of individual grammatical morphemes.

Studies by Lightbown (1983), Ellis (1984b), Pienemann (1986), and

Weinert (1987) have shown that, at least for some grammatical structures, the route of acquisition does not vary in any significant way from one setting to another. They support the claim that the effects of instruction are highly constrained. Weinert (1987), for instance, found that Scottish secondary school students manifested structures and processes in the classroom acquisition of L2 German negatives similar to those reported in naturalistic acquisition. Far from facilitating learning, the traditional instruction these learners received appeared to inhibit the processes of interlanguage construction by providing them with ready-made formulaic negatives that obviated the need for active processing of input. This and other studies suggest that the same acquisitional mechanisms operate, irrespective of setting.

The other way that researchers have tried to examine the effects of instruction on the sequence of acquisition is by means of experimental or pseudo-experimental studies (e.g. Ellis, 1984a; Pienemann, 1984; Schumann, 1978a). These studies involve a standard pre-test/post-test design with the intervening treatment consisting of instruction in some grammatical feature. The purpose of the studies is to establish whether the treatment helps the learner to 'beat' the natural order of acquisition or whether it can push the learner from some pidgin-like, transitional stage in the acquisition of a grammatical structure to the target language form. In these studies, the choice of grammatical structure is an informed one; it is based either on a longitudinal study of the subjects or is motivated by a linguistic theory. The results suggest that instruction does not result in the acquisition of new grammatical properties unless the learner is developmentally ready to acquire them.

The study reported here is intended to further test the hypothesis that formal instruction does not affect the sequence of acquisition. The specific hypothesis tested is as follows: the route of acquisition of German word order rules apparent in the elicited speech of 39 adult classroom learners does not differ from that reported for naturalistic learners.

The study can be considered a strong test of the hypothesis on a number of grounds. First, the naturalistic acquisition of the target structure (German word order rules) has been the subject of intensive research that has demonstrated the existence of a robust acquisitional sequence. This research provides a solid basis for comparison. Second, the subjects of the study were totally reliant on the classroom for L2 input. They were foreign, rather than second, L2 learners and, therefore, were not 'contaminated' with naturalistic learning, as was the case with the subjects of several of the studies referred to earlier. Third, the subjects were all adult successful language learners with substantial experience of classroom foreign language learning. Thus, they were well-equipped — cognitively and in experience — to benefit from formal instruction.

I shall begin by describing the German word order rules that are the focus of the study and then will go on to review previous research that has investigated the naturalistic and classroom acquisition of these rules. There then follows an account of the classroom study. Finally, I shall consider the implications of the results of the study for both SLA theory and language pedagogy.

German Word Order Rules

German has a number of word order rules. Their surface representation can be described as follows:

1. *Subject–verb–object*
   The word order that many linguists consider canonical is subject–verb–object,
   e.g. Ich trank ein Glas Milch.
        'I drank a glass of milk.'
2. *Adverb preposing*
   In German, adverbs can be shifted from sentence internal or final positions to sentence initial position,
   e.g. Gestern trank ich ein Glas Milch.
        'Yesterday drank I a glass of milk.'
   Adverb-preposing requires inversion — see (4). The movement of the adverb is considered a separate rule, however.
3. *Particle*
   This rule states that non-finite verbal elements are moved to clause-final position. It applies in a number of linguistic contexts. For example, when the VP consists of modal + V infin,
   e.g. Ich möchte heute abend ins Kino gehen.
        'I would like tomorrow evening to the cinema go.'
   when the VP consists of aux + Ven,
   e.g. Ich bin gestern abend ins Kino gegangen.
        'I am yesterday evening to the cinema gone.'
   and when the VP consists of a particle + V.
   e.g. Ich rufe sie morgen abend noch einmal an.
        'I call you tomorrow evening once more up.'
4. *Inversion*
   This rule states that a finite verb form precedes the subject of its clause in certain linguistic contexts, such as when adverb-preposing occurs — see (2) — and after a sentence-initial direct object,

e.g. Fleisch esse ich nicht.
   'Meat eat I not.'
In both cases inversion is the result of the requirement that the verb comes second in main clauses.
Inversion also occurs in WH interrogatives,
e.g. Wann gehen wir ins Kino?
   'When go we into the cinema?'
5. *Verb-end*
Finite verbs are placed in final position in all embedded clauses,
e.g. Ich trank das Glas Milch, während ich den Brief schrieb.
   'I drank the glass of milk while I the letter wrote.'

The research reported in this article investigated three of these rules: (3), (4), and (5). Rules (1) and (2) were not studied because of the difficulty of determining obligatory occasions for their use.

Previous Research into the Acquisition of German Word Order Rules

Naturalistic acquisition

The following account of the naturalistic acquisition of German word order rules is based primarily on the results of the ZISA (Zweispracherwerb italienischer, spanischer, and portugiesischer Arbeiter) project carried out in West Germany and reported in a series of publications (Clahsen, 1980; 1984; 1985; Meisel, 1983; Meisel, Clahsen & Pienemann, 1981; Pienemann, 1980). The project set out to describe and explain the acquisition of German by adult migrant workers with Romance language backgrounds and their children. Both cross-sectional and longitudinal studies were carried out using natural language data from informal interviews and free conversations. In addition, information relating to such factors as the learners' origins, education, jobs, contact with Germans and other foreigners, neighbourhood, and use of mass media was collected in order to determine the learners' attitudes towards learning German. The particular analysis that concerns us here focused on the acquisition of syntactic features and, in particular, word order. *Acquisition* was defined by the ZISA researchers as the first appearance of a word order rule in a nonformulaic utterance.

The results of the various studies indicate that for L2 learners with Romance backgrounds there is:

(1) a definite developmental sequence for the three word order rules; and
(2) individual learner variation within each stage of development.

In the first developmental stage, learners use a basic subject–verb–object word order irrespective of the linguistic context. That is, they show no control of the optional adverb-preposing rule or of the obligatory particle, inversion, and verb-end rules. These rules are acquired sequentially. Adverb-preposing is acquired first, particle second, inversion third, and verb-end last. The sequence of acquisition comprises an implicational scale:

Verb-end > Inversion > Particle > Adverb-preposing.

Thus, the acquisition of any one rule implies the acquisition of other rules further down the scale, but not those higher up. For example, a learner who has acquired verb-end would also have acquired the other three word order rules, but a learner who has acquired adverb-preposing would not necessarily have acquired any other rule.

Each word order rule applies to a number of different linguistic contexts (see above). One possibility, then, is that learners will not only acquire each rule sequentially, but also learn to apply each rule across contexts incrementally. That is, there would be a developmental ordering for the acquisition of the different linguistic contexts. However, this does not appear to happen. Within each stage of development there is considerable individual variation, and no ordering of contexts is apparent. Some learners (dubbed 'error-avoiders') seek to master a rule across a full range of contexts before moving on to the next rule. Other learners (dubbed 'communicators') display control of a rule in only one or two contexts before moving on along the scale.

Table 4.1 is based on Meisel (1983). It displays cross-sectional data for nine naturalistic learners. Three word order rules (the obligatory ones) are printed in italics, with the contexts for each rule beneath it. The figures represent the proportion of correct suppliance of each rule, both overall and in different contexts, by the nine learners, X denotes that no obligatory occasions for the application of a particular rule were present in the data, while (0) shows that although there were obligatory occasions, there were fewer than five. The most advanced learner is learner 1, who has categorical control over all three word order rules. The least advanced is learner 9, who has not acquired any of the rules. Other learners are at various stages of development, displaying variable or categorical use of one or more of the rules.

There have been a number of other studies of the naturalistic acquisition of these word order rules in German and also Dutch and Afrikaans, which have a similar set of rules (see Jordens (1988) for a review). This research covers learners with different language backgrounds — Turkish (Clahsen &

Muysken, 1986), Moroccan (Coenen & Van Hout, 1987), and English (Duplessis, Solin, Travis & White, 1987). There is some disagreement about the interpretation of the results obtained and evidence to suggest that the learners' L1 interacts with input in the process of acquisition. However, clear regularities emerge. As Jordens shows, all learners cope with the problem of identifying L2 word order rules in similar ways and manifest a very similar sequence of acquisition to that reported by the ZISA researchers.

TABLE 4.1 *Implication scale for German word order rules in naturalistic SLA* (based on Meisel, 1983)

	Learners								
Rules	*1*	*2*	*3*	*4*	*5*	*6*	*7*	*8*	*9*
Verb-end	1.0	0.56	0	(0.5)	X	0	0	0	X
Comp	1.0	0.67	0	0	X	0	0	0	X
Wh	1.0	0.67	X	X	X	0	0	X	X
Rel	1.0	0	0	(1.0)	X	X	0	X	X
Inversion	1.0	0.91	0.85	1.0	0.83	0.46	0	0	X
Wh	1.0	1.0	1.0	(1.0)	0	(1.0)	X	X	X
Adverb	1.0	1.0	0.70	1.0	1.0	0.40	0	0	x
Do	1.0	1.0	(1.0)	(1.0)	X	X	X	X	X
Comp	1.0	0	1.0	(1.0)	X	X	0	0	X
Particle	1.0	0.82	(0.93)	1.0	1.0	1.0	0.71	0.10	X
Mod + V	1.0	0.77	1.0	(1.0)	(1.0)	1.0	(1.0)	(0.50)	X
Aux + V	1.0	0.71	1.0	1.0	1.0	1.0	0.70	X	X
P + V	1.0	1.0	(1.0)	(1.0)	(1.0)	X	X	0	X
Vcomp	1.0	1.0	0.67	(1.0)	X	1.0	(1.0)	X	X

Classroom acquisition

There are a growing number of empirical studies of the acquisition of German word order rules in instructional settings. These have doubtlessly been stimulated by the strength of evidence demonstrating the presence of a natural sequence of acquisition in this area of grammar.

In an experimental study involving ten children (ages 7–9), Pienemann (1984) found that instruction in inversion only resulted in the acquisition of this word order rule if the learners had already acquired the rule immediately preceding it in the sequence (i.e. particle). This led Pienemann to formulate the *Learnability Hypothesis* (Pienemann, 1985), which states that developmental features such as German word order rules can only be learned if the learner is psycholinguistically ready. Furthermore, Pienemann provides some evidence to suggest that premature instruction can have a negative effect. Two of the children he investigated regressed in the application of the adverb-preposing rule as a result of instruction in inversion, possibly because the learners sought to avoid a structure that required inversion. Pienemann's study is an important one. It is, however, based on a very small sample, so care must be taken in generalising from it. Also, the subjects were young children who might be predicted not to benefit greatly from formal instruction.

In a subsequent longitudinal study, however, Pienemann (1986) investigated three adult classroom learners of L2 German in Australia. All three were complete beginners. He documents when specific word order rules were introduced and shows that the instruction only resulted in the acquisition of a new word order rule if the learners were developmentally primed. For example, the particle rule was explicitly taught in week 7 of the course, but was not acquired until weeks 15 and 17 by two of the learners, and not at all by the third learner. Pienemann also documents how the instruction resulted in avoidance behaviour; the learners were taught the complexities of the perfect tense at an early stage, but because they were unable to handle the necessary processing operations, they tended to avoid using this form altogether.

Two other studies have investigated the effects of instruction on German word order rules. Daniel (1983; cited in Pienemann, 1986) carried out a cross-sectional study of adult beginners at a university in Australia. Her results revealed the same implicational order of acquisition as that reported for naturalistic learners. Finally, Westmoreland's (1983) cross-sectional study, which involved similar types of learners, showed the same developmental sequence.

The empirical study of the classroom acquisition of German word order rules, therefore, supports these claims:

(1) The sequence of acquisition of these rules is the same in classroom and naturalistic settings.
(2) Premature instruction can cause learners to regress by avoiding transitional rules that they know, resulting in ungrammatical utterances.

It should be noted that (1) holds true for adults as well as children. Even adults who are well equipped in terms of experience and intelligence to benefit from formal instruction follow the natural sequence.

The Study

In this section, I will describe the study carried out to examine the effects of instruction on three of the word order rules: particle, inversion, and verb-end. As already stated, the study was restricted to these rules because they are obligatory and their presence or absence in data can be clearly determined.

Subjects

The subjects were 39 students taking *ab initio* courses in L2 German as part of their first-year degree programmes. They were taught in two separate institutions of higher education in London and were divided into groups ranging in size from six to nine.

The subjects were administered a questionnaire at the beginning of their study in order to obtain general background information. This questionnaire revealed that there were 27 female and 12 male learners. The mean age of the learners was 20.95 years, the eldest being 41 years and the youngest 18 years. The L1 backgrounds of the learners were varied: Spanish, English, French, Mauritian Creole, and Arabic.

All the 39 learners can be considered successful language learners in that they needed passes in the General Certificate of Education (GCE) A Level or an equivalent examination in at least one foreign language in order to gain entry to the degree programme. The learners differed in the extent and nature of their L2 experiences: 17 had knowledge of three L2s, 21 had knowledge of two L2s, and 1 student had knowledge of only one L2. All the learners had acquired at least one of their L2s in a classroom setting, but several of the subjects had acquired one or more of their other L2s naturalistically. The subjects, therefore, comprised a group of experienced and sophisticated language learners.

Although the course was designed for complete beginners, 14 of the subjects had some previous knowledge of German. This varied from a few months of classroom study in school to contact with native speakers in Germany. The subjects with previous experience were learners 5, 6, 8, 17, 21, 22, 23, 24, 26, 27, 28, 35, and 36.

The subjects differed in one other way. Some of them were committed to continuing the study of German beyond the *ab initio* course in order to fulfil the requirements of their degree programme. Others, however, had the option of abandoning German at the end of the year. This factor proved significant in determining the levels of achievement of individual students.

Type of instruction

As the subjects were divided into five different groups taught by different teachers, there was no uniformity in the instruction they received. Classroom observations of individual lessons that were carried out on a regular basis over two academic terms (22 weeks) revealed, however, that the similarities in instructional practices outweighed the differences.

The teaching received by Groups A, B, C, and D consisted of formal language instruction throughout and regional studies in the second term (this involved lectures and readings on social, economic, and political issues). The formal instruction was based on the Grundkurs Deutsch Course (Schapers, Luscher & Glück, 1980). This is a traditional, structurally graded text book that emphasises formal grammar study. The students also had the opportunity to work in language and microcomputer laboratories 1 or 2 hours a week. This resulted in further work that was essentially form-focused. Groups A and C received 12 hours of instruction, while Groups B and D received only nine hours. Also, greater emphasis was placed on grammatical accuracy in Groups A and C. The nature of the instructional activities in all four groups was broadly similar, however. The instruction was text-based, involved frequent translation into English, teacher explanation of new grammatical points (often in English), and pattern practice exercises. There was little opportunity for real communication and hardly any small group work.

Group E was taught in a separate institution. The instruction was based on *Themen* (Aufderstrasse, Bock, Gerdes & Muller, 1983). This is a notional-functional course. The students also spent one hour per week using video materials from the television series *Deutsch Direkt*. The general instructional style, however, followed a very similar pattern to that evident in the lessons experienced by the other groups. An analysis of the amount of time spent in meaning-focused (as opposed to form-focused) activity and in student-centred (as opposed to teacher-centred) work revealed no significant differences between Group E and the other groups. Altogether, this group received six hours of instruction per week, which was less than the other groups, although this was largely compensated for by an intensive 40-hour induction programme.

Instruction in the word order rules

None of the groups received specific instruction in the three obligatory word order rules. Instead, formal instruction was provided in the various grammatical structures that require the application of the rules. Thus, for example, no attempt was made to teach particle, but this rule was indirectly taught in lessons dealing with modal + Vinfin and auxiliary + Ven. The presentation of the word order rules, therefore, did not conform to the process of acquisition observed in naturalistic settings.

The two text books used by the learners together with the teachers' records of work and the students' homework records were examined in order to determine (a) the order in which the three rules were introduced in the five instructional groups, and (b) the instructional emphasis given to each of the three rules over the 22 weeks of the study.

Table 4.2 shows the order of introduction of particle, inversion, and verb-end. It also shows the date when a structure requiring each rule was formally presented for the first time. All five groups experienced the same instructional order. That is, inversion was presented first, followed by particle and verb-end. In Groups A, B, C and D, structures involving the three rules were introduced over a six-week period and were evenly spaced. In Group E, structures involving inversion and particle were introduced more or less together, with verb-end appearing some six weeks later. In all the groups, verb-end — the most difficult of the rules — was the last to be introduced.

TABLE 4.2 *Order of introduction of the three word order rules in the instruction*

Word order rule	Groups A, B, C, D	Group E
1 Inversion	Lesson 3 (mid-Oct.)	Lesson 1, Bk. 1 (mid-Sept.)
2 Particle	Lesson 7 (early Nov.)	Lesson 2, Bk. 1 (late Sept.)
3 Verb-end	Lesson 9 (late Nov.)	Lesson 2, Bk. 2 (mid-Dec.)

Table 4.3 shows the instructional emphasis given to each structure. This was calculated by ascertaining the number of explicit references to structures requiring each of the three word order rules in the text books, teachers' records, and homework records. The number of references are shown in brackets. There were differences in the order of emphasis between Groups A and B on the one hand and Groups C, D, and E on the other. Verb-end received the most attention in Groups A and B, while particle was the

TABLE 4.3 *Instructional emphasis given to each word order rule*

Order	Groups A and B	Groups C and D	Group E
1	Verb-end (27)	Particle (33)	Particle (24)
2	Particle (22)	Verb-end (24)	Verb-end (15)
3	Inversion (6)	Inversion (13)	Inversion (7)

principal focus of instruction in the other groups. In all five groups, inversion received the least attention.

From this analysis, we can make the following conclusions:

(1) The order of introduction of the three word order rules did not correspond to the naturalistic order of acquisition reported by the ZISA project in any of the five groups of learners. The difference between the order of introduction and order of acquisition was least evident in Group E.
(2) The order of emphasis given to the three word order rules in the instruction did not correspond to the degree of difficulty in their acquisition in a naturalistic setting. The mismatch between emphasis and difficulty was least evident in Groups A and B.

Hypotheses

In order to address the research question regarding whether classroom and naturalistic acquisition are the same, this study investigated the general hypothesis that adult classroom learners of L2 German would manifest the same sequence of acquisition of word order rules as that reported for naturalistic learners. Three operational hypotheses were tested:

(1) The sequence of acquisition of three obligatory German word order rules would match the order reported for naturalistic learners by the ZISA researchers rather than the order in which the rules were first formally taught in the classroom.
(2) The order of accuracy of three obligatory German word order rules would correspond to the order of acquisition reported for naturalistic learners by the ZISA researchers rather than to the degree of emphasis in the instruction given to the rules.
(3) The order of accuracy of three obligatory German word order rules obtained by each of the five instructional groups would correspond to the order of acquisition reported for naturalistic learners by the ZISA researchers. A corollary of this hypothesis is that there would be no differences in the order of accuracy of the rules among the different groups despite the fact that there were differences in both the order and emphasis of instruction.

Procedure

Data were collected from the 39 learners by means of a speech elicitation task. In this task the learners worked in pairs. A picture composition was cut up and two pictures given to each learner. Each learner was asked to describe his or her pictures in German without showing them to their partner so that they could jointly work out the story. This is an example of a two-way communication task, which Long (1983a) has claimed is the kind of task most likely to stimulate conversation containing plenty of interactional adjustments. In this case, the task ended with one of the learners being asked to tell the complete story in German (i.e. to produce an oral monologue). Each pair repeated the task three times, using different sets of pictures. The first time was treated as a warm-up and was intended to familiarise the subjects with the procedure. The second and third times required first one and then the other member of each pair to perform the oral monologue at the end of the task. The learners performed the task in a language laboratory large enough to seat two students at a booth. They were audio-recorded after they had completed the warm-up task.

The speech elicitation task was administered on two occasions — at the end of the first term (i.e. after 11 weeks of instruction) and at the end of the second term (i.e. after 22 weeks of instruction).

Transcriptions of the audio tapes were prepared in normal orthography. As the elicitation task had been designed to tap unmonitored, informal language use in order to afford comparisons with the ZISA research, which was based upon this kind of data, the transcripts were examined for evidence of monitoring of the word order rules. Evidence of monitoring would suggest that the learners were attempting to apply explicit knowledge of the rules. A problem would then arise, as the naturalistic learners could be assumed to have used implicit knowledge. In seeking to compare classroom and naturalistic acquisition, it is essential to ensure that the data used to make the comparison are indeed comparable.

Table 4.4 gives the number and type of linguistic corrections performed by the seven learners who produced the highest number of corrections at Time 2. It shows that although the students did monitor their output, their efforts were directed at morphological features of German (e.g. articles and verb tense morphemes) rather than syntax. Only learner 19 self-corrected a word order rule (verb-end) and only on one occasion:

einer Polizist erm (.2.) der ist erm der angekommt ist
'a policeman who is who arrived is'

It would seem, therefore, that the learners did not appear to pay conscious attention to the correct production of the three rules. In other words, the data produced by the speech elicitation task were comparable with those obtained by the ZISA researchers.

TABLE 4.4   *The linguistic corrections performed by seven learners at Time 2*

Learner	Focus of Linguistic Correction		
	Morphology	*Syntax*	*Other*
4	5	0	1
8	4	0	0
19	3	1	0
22	5	0	0
23	4	0	0
28	7	0	0
38	3	0	1
Totals	31	1	2

Obligatory occasions for the three word order rules in the data collected from each learner at Times 1 and 2 were identified. The proportion of accurate suppliance of each rule was then calculated. Also, incidences of overuse of each rule were recorded. It should be noted that not all the learners produced sufficient obligatory occasions for each rule. For this reason, the results for some of the analyses reported here relate to subsets of the population for the learners studied.

Results

Three sets of results will be presented, in accordance with the operational hypotheses described earlier. First, the order of acquisition of the three rules in individual learners is examined. Second, the level of accuracy of the rules achieved by the sample as a whole is indicated, and third, the results for the different instructional groups are presented.

Order of acquisition

In order to establish the order of acquisition of the three word order rules, two analyses were carried out. First, an implicational scale was drawn up for those learners at Time 1 who produced three or more obligatory occasions for each word order rule. Second, the development that occurred between Time 1 and Time 2 was investigated.

As mentioned earlier, many of the learners failed to produce an adequate number of obligatory occasions for one or more of the word order rules. This is not surprising, as avoidance of 'difficult' structures is a familiar phenomenon in SLA. It conforms with similar results reported by the ZISA researchers for many of their subjects. It does, however, pose problems for the researcher. In particular, a decision has to be taken as to what constitutes a satisfactory number of occasions on which to base a judgement as to whether a particular rule has been acquired. In this case, the minimum number was set at three. This is rather meagre, but to have set a higher number would have reduced the sample size to an unacceptably low number. The individual learners' raw scores for the number of obligatory occasions, the number of correct suppliances, and the frequency of overuse are provided in the Appendix.

Table 4.5 presents the implicational scale for the 17 learners who produced three or more obligatory occasions at Time 2. The learners have been scaled on the basis that a suppliance level of 0.75 or above for a particular rule constitutes acquisition of that rule. Hatch & Farhady (1982) rightly argue

TABLE 4.5 *Implicational scale for 17 learners at Time 2*

Learners	Word Order Rules		
	Particle	*Inversion*	*Verb-end*
8	1.0	0.89	0.78
4	0.83	0.85	0.75
14	1.0	0.77	0.15
23	0.88	0.86	0.50
10	1.0	0.66	0.63
38	1.0	0.66	0.60
22	1.0	0.60	0.50
16	1.0	0.46	0.40
25	1.0	0.33	0.20
35	1.0	0.33	0.20
12	1.0	0.29	0.74
17	1.0	0.25	0.00
2	0.88	0.64	0.00
15	0.80	0.44	0.13
36	0.77	0.60	0.00
9	0.75	0.33	0.20
11	0.25	0.17	0.18

Note: Coefficient of reproducibility = 1.0; minimal marginal reproducibility = .43; % improvement in reproducibility = .57; coefficient of scalability = 1.0.

that the choice of criterion level must be justified. The 0.75 level was chosen on the grounds that if learners are able to supply a feature in three out of four instances, this constitutes sufficient evidence that a feature has been internalised. In contrast, two out of three instances is less convincing evidence. Using this criterion, the results show a perfect scaling (i.e. the Coefficient of Scalability = 1). In other words, there is no learner who has acquired verb-end who has not also acquired the other two rules, and no learner who has acquired inversion who has not also acquired particle. Of the 17 learners, 16 demonstrated acquisition of particle, 4 of inversion, and 2 of verb-end. The three rules can be implicationally ordered as follows: Verb-end > Inversion > Particle.

The implicational scale presented in Table 4.5 provides a cross-sectional analysis of the data. The study was also designed to allow for a longitudinal analysis of development of word order rules from Time 1 to Time 2. Table 4.6 presents the results of this analysis, based on nine learners who produced three or more obligatory occasions for each rule on both occasions. Once again, the criterion level for acquisition was fixed at 0.75. Of these learners, three (learners 10, 17, and 23) displayed development from Time 1 to Time 2. That is, they progressed by adding the acquisition of a new word order rule. In each case, the process of acquisition conformed to the expected sequence. For example, learner 10 displayed zero acquisition of all three rules at Time 1 but had acquired particle at Time 2: learner 23 had already acquired particle at Time 1 and added inversion at Time 2. However, not all the learners progressed. Learners 25 and 38 stayed at the same stage of acquisition. Learners 18, 22, and 27 took backward steps (i.e. displayed loss of an already

TABLE 4.6   *The acquisition of the three word order rules by nine learners at Times 1 and 2*

Learner	Time 1			Time 2		
	Particle	Inversion	Verb-end	Particle	Inversion	Verb-end
10	—	—	—	+	—	—
14	—	+	—	+	+	—
17	—	—	—	+	—	—
18	+	—	—	—	—	—
22	+	+	—	+	—	—
23	+	—	—	+	+	—
25	+	—	—	+	—	—
27	+	+	—	+	—	—
38	+	—	—	+	—	—

acquired rule). In these cases, the loss reversed the natural sequence for acquisition. For example, learner 22 provided evidence of having acquired both particle and inversion at Time 1, but only particle at Time 2; in other words, he 'lost' the more difficult of the two rules. Only one learner, learner 14, showed an unexpected pattern, as at Time 1 she appeared to have acquired inversion, but not particle; however, by Time 2 she had acquired particle. None of the nine learners had acquired verb-end, even by Time 2.

Level of accuracy in the whole group

Next, we consider the level of accuracy in the performance of each word order rule in the group as a whole.

Table 4.7 gives the proportions of accurate suppliance of the word order rules at Times 1 and 2 for the entire 39 learners. It can be seen that particle is performed more accurately than inversion, which in turn is performed more accurately than verb-end on both occasions. The accuracy order, therefore, is: (1) particle; (2) inversion; (3) verb-end. Particle is conspicuously easier than the other two rules; the difference between the accurate suppliance of inversion and verb-end is relatively small. The gain in accuracy in these two structures from Time 1 to Time 2 is noticeably greater than that for particle (0.14 for both inversion and verb-end but only 0.08 for particle). This is largely explained by the high level of accuracy of particle at Time 1.

TABLE 4.7   *Proportions of accurate suppliance of the three word order rules by 39 learners*

	Time 1			Time 2		
Word order Rule	Accurate suppliance	Obligatory occasions	Proportion	Accurate suppliance	Obligatory occasions	Proportion
Particle	150	192	0.78	175	203	0.86
Inversion	63	168	0.38	99	192	0.52
Verb-end	38	119	0.32	96	209	0.46

Level of accuracy in the five instructional groups

Turning to the performance of the five groups at Time 2 (Table 4.8), it is evident that particle is performed with a high level of accuracy by all of them. There are, however, differences with regard to inversion. Group A achieves a high level of acquisition of this rule; Groups B, C and E achieve average levels; but Group D shows no acquisition at all, although the learners in this group produced very few obligatory occasions for inversion. Differences are also apparent with regard to verb-end. Groups A and D manifest higher levels of acquisition than Groups B and C, with Group E showing the lowest level. In general, the different groups' accuracy orders mirror the natural order of acquisition, the only exception being Group D.

TABLE 4.8   *Levels of accuracy (Time 2) of the three word order rules in the different instructional groups*

	Obligatory occasions	Accurate suppliance	Proportion
Group A			
Particle	31	27	0.87
Inversion	69	57	0.83
Verb-end	46	31	0.68
Group B			
Particle	37	32	0.86
Inversion	59	27	0.46
Verb-end	79	31	0.39
Group C			
Particle	53	47	0.89
Inversion	27	16	0.59
Verb-end	46	17	0.37
Group D			
Particle	42	33	0.79
Inversion	6	0	0.00
Verb-end	18	12	0.67
Group E			
Particle	40	35	0.88
Inversion	21	9	0.43
Verb-end	20	5	0.25

Discussion

It was possible to show that, although some lerners did monitor extensively, they did not pay explicit attention to word order rules. Instead, they focused on morphological difficulties. This is not surprising, given that the instruction they had received focused primarily on morphological rather than syntactical features. The learners were, therefore, probably much more conscious of the need to produce articles, pronouns, and tenses correctly than word order rules. The absence of linguistic corrections targeted at these rules suggests that they were performed more or less spontaneously, although it is possible that some planning took place prior to production. In general, however, there are reasonable grounds for claiming that the word order data obtained from the communication task are comparable to the natural data obtained by the ZISA researchers.

The first hypothesis was that the instruction received by the 39 learners would not lead to a different order of acquisition from that reported for naturalistic learners. The results reported in the previous section lend support to this hypothesis. Implicational scaling of 17 learners (who produced three obligatory occasions for each word order rule) at Time 2 showed an identical order of acquisition. Also, an analysis of the development of nine learners who produced three obligatory occasions for each rule at Time 1 and Time 2 revealed that progress consisted of the incremental acquisition of rules in accordance with the sequence found in naturalistic learners. Learners who regressed from Time 1 to Time 2 moved backwards along the sequence. It should be noted that the order of acquisition in these learners differed from the order in which the rules were introduced in the instruction. All five groups were introduced to inversion first. However, acquisition of particle far outstripped the acquisition of inversion in all the learners. It would seem, therefore, that learners have their own 'syllabus' for the acquisition of German word order rules and that this syllabus is the same for both tutored and untutored learners.

The second hypothesis was that the level of accuracy achieved in the production of the three word order rules by the 39 learners would correspond to the order of acquisition reported for naturalistic learners. The overall levels of accuracy of the three rules achieved by the whole sample at Time 2 matched the order of acquisition found in naturalistic learners by the ZISA researchers. Thus, particle was produced most accurately, followed by inversion, with verb-end last. Particle was, in fact, performed much more accurately than the other two rules. In contrast, the order of instructional emphasis experienced by any of the 39 learners is insufficient to explain the levels of accuracy achieved.

The third hypothesis concerned whether the five instructional groups manifested an accuracy order similar to the acquisition order of naturalistic learners, and whether there were any differences in the accuracy orders of the different groups that might be explained by corresponding differences in the instruction they received. Groups C, D and E received more instruction in particle than the other two rules, while Groups A and B received more instruction in verb-end. Despite these between-group differences, all five groups demonstrated much higher levels of accuracy in the use of particle. Also, although inversion received the least attention in all the classrooms, four out of the five groups manifested higher levels of accuracy in this rule than in verb-end, which received greater instructional emphasis. In other words, despite differences in instructional emphasis among the five groups, the levels of acquisition of the three rules was surprisingly uniform, and accorded with the order of acquisition reported for naturalistic learners.

The one exception was Group D, which failed to display any acquisition of inversion while achieving a fairly high level of verb-end acquisition (0.67). The learners in Group D were relatively poorly motivated. They did not need to continue with German beyond the end of the year. Classroom observation and a diary study kept by one of the learners showed how the group became disillusioned with their studies during the second term. This was reflected in irregular attendance by many of the students and in a poor response to the instruction. However, although these facts can explain the overall lower levels of achievement of this group on particle and inversion, it fails to explain why verb-end was performed more accurately than inversion. The order of instructional emphasis experienced by this group matches the level of acquisition of the three rules. This result is anomalous, therefore. No explanation is available. In particular, it is not clear why the learners in this group produced so few obligatory occasions for inversion (only six in total).

This study was set up to examine whether instruction had an effect on the route of L2 acquisition. The results reported suggest that they do not. The study lends support to claims that the acquisition of syntactical features, such as German word order rules, follows the same sequence in both untutored and tutored learners. The classroom learners followed this sequence even though the order of introduction and emphasis given to the rules in the instruction was different.

One interesting finding of this study is that many of the classroom learners achieved considerable success in acquiring the three word order rules, despite the relatively short period of instruction and despite the psycholinguistic difficulty of the rules themselves. Nearly all the learners acquired particle. Out of the 39 learners, 28 succeeded correctly in producing one or more utterances requiring verb-end (the most difficult of the rules). In contrast, many of the learners studied in the ZISA project failed to acquire inversion or verb-end after several years of living in West Germany, and several did not even acquire particle.

Although comparisons between migrant workers and classroom learners of the kind investigated in this study may not be justified on the grounds of social and educational differences, it is striking that in such a short period of time the majority of the classroom learners achieved some degree of competence in all three word order rules. It does not follow, therefore, that instruction is worthless. Instruction may serve to accelerate acquisition and also may contribute to higher levels of ultimate success (Long, 1988a). One of the central tasks facing classroom SLA researchers is to explain why learners who receive instruction seem to outperform learners who learn naturalistically despite the fact that instruction itself does not affect the route of acquisition.

Conclusion

The contribution of the research reported above to the construction of a theory of L2 acquisition lies in the evidence it provides to show that the acquisition of features such as German word rules is determined principally by internal mechanisms rather than by input.

In order to explain the acquisitional sequence for word order, the ZISA researchers suggest that development proceeds in accordance with the cognitive complexity of the operations involved in the production of the rules. A rule that can be performed using a simple processing operation is acquired before a rule that requires a more complex operation. Thus, acquisition is subject to psycholinguistic restrictions; one processing operation serves as a prerequisite for another, more complex operation. Clahsen (1984) identifies a number of processing strategies that students have to learn to apply:

Canonical word order strategy. This strategy leads learners to produce sentences in accordance with a 'natural' word order that corresponds with the deep structure relations between sentence elements. In applying this strategy, learners avoid any processing that involves an interruption of the canonical order.

Initialisation/finalisation strategy. When learners master this strategy, they are able to apply permutations to the canonical order that entail moving elements to sentence-initial or sentence-final position. Elements in these positions are more salient and easier to memorise than sentence-internal elements.

Subordinate clause strategy. Clahsen suggests that subordinate clauses are processed differently from main clauses. Subordinate clauses are considered marked in relation to main clauses. The learner needs to recognise that the normal processing strategies that apply to main clauses will not apply to subordinate clauses. The subordinate clause strategy allows for the prediction that reorderings of sentence elements will be mastered in main clauses before subordinate clauses. These strategies — which are general in nature — can be applied to German word order rules in order to explain their sequence of acquisition.

Not all researchers explain the existence of a developmental sequence for German word order rules by means of general learning strategies. Researchers such as Du-Plessis *et al.* (1987) and Jordens (1988) argue that L2 learners have continued access to Universal Grammar, on which they draw in systematic ways. These account for the sequence of word order acquisition. Jordens, for instance, claims that the main problem facing learners of L2 German is that of sorting out how two possible word orders — SVO and SOV — are related. Learners learn that the underlying word order is SVO when they discover the distinction between finite and nonfinite verb categories. Subsequently, they learn that this underlying word order needs to be restructured depending on whether the clause is main or subordinate. Jordens illustrates how deep structure representations of initial, intermediate, and final state grammars can account for this.

Irrespective of whether an explanation based on general learning strategies or Universal Grammar is invoked, the research can be used to support the general claim that instruction does not affect the sequence of word order acquisition. It would appear that the process of word order acquisition that learners follow is not influenced by learning context.

In reaching this conclusion, however, it is not intended to suggest that input is unimportant in L2 acquisition. Input is valuable because it acts as a trigger for the acquisition of learnable rules. In this respect, the position adopted by researchers like Pienemann (1986) who seek to explain acquisitional sequences in terms of general learning strategies is not dissimilar to that held by those such as White (1987) who invoke explanations based on Universal Grammar. Both Pienemann and White recognise that input interacts with the learner's current knowledge. Both are concerned with trying to specify what constitutes the most suitable input for learning to take place. Both acknowledge that it is possible to manipulate the input (e.g. by giving instruction in specific features or through the correction of overgeneralisations) in order to facilitate learning. Both draw attention to the internal factors that constrain it.

There is, however, one important difference between a cognitive theory of language learning and one based on Universal Grammar. In a cognitive theory, such as that propounded by Pienemann, instruction needs to be directed at the next stage in the acquisitional sequence for it to be successful. In a theory based on Universal Grammar, such as that advanced by White, instruction serves to trigger the setting of a particular parameter, which can in turn lead to further reorganisation of the learner's grammar. Pienemann sees the relationship between input and acquisition as a direct one; White sees it as both direct and indirect.

Research based on typological universals lends support to the view that instruction can accelerate acquisition as a result of an indirect triggering effect. Zobl (1983) has suggested that learners have a projection capacity that enables them to acquire unmarked rules on the basis of input relating to associated marked rules. A number of studies based on typological universals (e.g. Eckman, Bell & Nelson, 1988; Gass, 1982; Zobl, 1985) lend support to this position. This concept of projection is an extremely powerful one, but it cannot be easily reconciled with the notion of acquisitional sequence as defined by Pienemann. Here is a case of different theories of SLA, drawing on very different background disciplines, offering opposing explanations, both of which find support in empirical research. It testifies to the need for different branches of SLA research to pay attention to each other's work in order to reconcile apparent contradictions.

The practical implications of the effects of instruction on the acquisition of German word order rules are also not entirely clear-cut. On the one hand, the research suggests that Krashen's (1985) claim that grammar instruction has no role in the 'acquisition' of new structures is not tenable. Instruction can result in acquisition (in Krashen's sense), providing certain conditions are met. However, as Long (1985b) has noted, it is more or less impossible for teachers to ensure that these conditions are met in the course of their day to day teaching. Teachers cannot be expected to know when learners are ready to acquire the next word order rule in the sequence. Also, individual learners will achieve readiness at different times, requiring the teacher to individualise instructional schedules to suit each learner. Another proposal might be to limit formal instruction to variational features. These are features that are not subject to processing constraints and that can be acquired at any time. Pienemann's (1984) study showed that formal instruction did have a positive effect on the acquisition of German copula. This proposal is certainly more feasible, but the problem is that not much is currently known about which features are variational and which are developmental. This proposal must remain no more than a future possibility. It would seem, therefore, that even though Krashen is theoretically wrong about what formal instruction can achieve, he may be right to advocate that teachers base their teaching on activities that lead to meaning-focused interaction. In other words, classroom learners should be invited to proceed in the same way as naturalistic learners. This would also safeguard against the possibly damaging effects of premature formal instruction, which Pienemann (1984; 1986) has reported.

There are, however, two major objections to this position. The first is that learners will fail to acquire the more difficult rules (e.g. inversion and verb-end) once they have achieved communicative adequacy. Learners may need form-focused instruction to make them aware of grammatical features that have little communicative importance and yet constitute target language norms. In other words, formal instruction may serve to prevent fossilisation. The second objection is that naturalistic acquisition is often a very slow process; instruction may not alter the way in which learning takes place, but it may help to speed it up. Long's (1983c) review of the effects of formal instruction supports such a contention; classroom learners appear to learn more rapidly than naturalistic learners. The 39 learners investigated in the study reported in this article also seemed to outperform naturalistic learners. These two objections constitute powerful arguments in favour of formal instruction.

The question arises as to how formal instruction is able to prevent fossilisation and accelerate acquisition if it only works when certain conditions have been met. There are a number of possibilities. One is that the advantages recorded for classroom learners may be the result of instruction in variational features. This is likely, but classroom learners also seem to do better in developmental features, so it cannot constitute a complete explanation. A second possibility is that by recycling the teaching of developmental structures, the teacher can ensure that every learner will be 'ready' sooner or later to benefit from the instruction. The principal objection to this is that premature instruction may have a deleterious effect on learning. Another possibility is that instruction has a delayed rather than an immediate effect. In other words, instruction at one point in time primes the learner so that acquisition becomes easier when a state of readiness is finally reached. As Lightbown (1985b: 108) puts it, 'formal instruction may provide "hooks", points of access for the learner'. It should be noted that each of these possibilities does not exclude the others. Formal instruction may work in all three ways.

The study reported in this article has provided evidence to support the hypothesis that the sequence of acquisition of grammatical structures such as German word order rules is the same in naturalistic and instructed L2 acquisition. This, in turn, provides support for the view that instruction directed at a particular structure will not result in acquisition unless the leaner is developmentally ready. It was noted, however, that the learners in this study progressed more rapidly than naturalistic learners reported on in other studies. One explanation for this (although by no means the only one) is that the instruction helped to accelerate acquisition. It has been suggested, therefore, that instruction may have a delayed rather than an immediate effect.

Appendix

Word Order Acquisition

	Time 1									Time 2								
	Particle			*Inversion*			*Verb-end*			*Particle*			*Inversion*			*Verb-end*		
	1	*2*	*3*	*1*	*2*	*3*	*1*	*2*	*3*	*1*	*2*	*3*	*1*	*2*	*3*	*1*	*2*	*3*
A																		
1 Maria	0	0	0	1	3	0	0	0	0	4	4	0	6	11	0	0	1	0
2 Begona	0	1	0	0	1	0	1	3	0	7	8	0	7	11	0	0	3	0
3 Myriam F.	0	0	0	0	1	0	2	4	0	1	2	0	0	4	0	2	2	0
4 Gabriella	0	1	0	2	9	1	1	2	2	5	6	0	17	20	0	6	8	0
5 Myriam L.	1	1	0	5	7	0	5	7	0	2	2	0	6	8	0	10	13	0
6 Miguel	3	3	0	1	1	0	0	0	0	2	2	0	3	4	0	2	4	1
7 Nellie	1	1	0	0	0	0	2	2	0	0	1	0	0	2	0	4	6	0
8 Giles	1	1	0	3	6	0	2	2	0	6	6	0	8	9	0	7	9	0
B																		
9 Helen	0	0	0	2	3	0	0	8	0	3	4	0	2	6	0	1	5	0
10 Caroline	2	3	0	0	3	0	2	3	0	3	3	0	2	3	0	5	8	0
11 Gareth	0	0	0	3	5	1	1	3	1	1	4	0	1	6	0	2	11	0
12 Sandra	1	1	0	0	4	1	3	8	1	3	3	0	2	7	0	11	15	0
13 Debbie	3	3	0	0	2	0	5	5	0	7	7	0	0	2	0	6	7	0
14 Angela	2	3	0	6	6	2	0	4	0	5	5	0	10	13	0	2	13	2
15 Cathy	0	0	0	3	9	0	1	6	0	4	5	0	4	9	0	2	15	0
16 Jane	0	0	0	6	11	2	0	0	0	6	6	0	6	13	0	2	5	1
C																		
17 Dominque	12	18	0	4	7	0	1	7	0	4	4	0	1	4	0	0	11	0
18 John F.	9	10	0	2	6	0	0	2	0	5	8	0	2	3	0	1	1	0
19 Jonathan	10	12	0	0	6	0	1	2	0	4	4	0	0	1	0	3	6	0
20 Sharon	3	4	0	0	1	2	0	2	0	6	8	0	0	0	0	1	2	0
21 M.-Anne	10	11	0	0	2	0	0	3	0	5	5	0	1	2	0	1	2	2
22 Andrew R.	6	8	0	9	12	0	0	3	0	4	4	0	3	5	0	2	4	0
23 Annie F.	7	8	0	2	4	0	0	3	0	7	8	0	6	7	0	2	4	0
24 Louise	10	11	0	2	3	0	1	3	0	5	5	0	2	2	0	5	6	0
25 Lynne	8	9	0	1	5	0	2	7	0	7	7	0	1	3	1	2	10	7
D																		
26 Sally	7	7	0	2	2	0	2	3	0	9	9	0	0	1	0	4	5	0

| | Time 1 | | | | | | | | | Time 2 | | | | | | | | |
| | Particle | | | Inversion | | | Verb-end | | | Particle | | | Inversion | | | Verb-end | | |
	1	*2*	*3*	*1*	*2*	*3*	*1*	*2*	*3*	*1*	*2*	*3*	*1*	*2*	*3*	*1*	*2*	*3*
27 Andrew G.	1	5	0	2	4	0	0	2	0	3	3	0	0	2	0	2	4	0
28 Lisa	6	9	0	1	4	0	2	3	0	7	10	0	0	0	0	3	4	0
29 Paula	3	3	0	0	0	0	0	1	0	0	3	0	0	0	0	0	0	1
30 Kelvin	4	6	0	1	3	0	0	0	0	5	6	0	0	1	0	0	0	0
31 Caroline	9	10	0	0	2	0	0	0	0	4	4	0	0	1	2	0	0	0
32 Elizabeth	2	4	0	0	5	0	0	2	0	4	5	0	0	0	0	0	1	0
33 Caroline	5	8	0	1	4	0	0	2	2	1	2	0	0	1	0	3	4	7
E																		
34 M.-José	2	3	0	1	3	0	1	1	0	8	8	0	2	2	0	0	1	0
35 Andrew C.	3	3	0	4	4	0	2	8	0	4	4	0	2	6	0	2	10	0
36 Mohamed	7	8	0	3	7	1	1	1	0	10	13	0	3	5	0	0	3	0
37 Antonio	5	7	0	0	1	0	0	0	0	5	7	0	0	5	0	0	1	0
38 Bimarck	7	8	0	6	13	0	0	5	0	5	5	0	2	3	0	3	5	0
39 Rosemarie	0	2	0	0	1	0	0	0	0	3	3	0	0	0	0	0	0	0

Note 1 = Score; 2 = Obligatory; 3 = Non-Target Productions.

5. The Role of Practice in Classroom Learning

Introduction

One of the advantages of the growth of empirical studies of classroom language learning is that cherished assumptions about language teaching can be subjected to scrutiny. Elsewhere (Ellis, 1988a), I have argued that this is the appropriate way to set about making use of the findings of second language acquisition (SLA) research. That is, what is needed is not research applied but applied research. The starting point in such an approach should not be the research itself but a pedagogical issue of importance. The research provides a means for examining whether the assumptions that lie implicit in pedagogic prescriptions are justified.

This is the approach that will be followed here. The pedagogical issue which is the focus of attention is 'practice'. This construct is an extremely slippery one, however, meaning many things to many people. We shall begin, therefore, by defining what we mean by 'practice'. Following this, various pedagogic claims for practice will be examined and a number of quantitative studies which have investigated the effect of practice on language learning will be considered. The results provided by these studies are inconsistent and conflicting. We will argue that a more qualitative approach — one that examines how 'practice' works out in actual classroom interaction — is needed to illuminate the nature of the relationship between practice and learning. Finally, a number of hypotheses, compatible with the available research, will be advanced regarding the role that practice plays in classroom language learning.

What Do We Mean by 'Practice'

Most methodologists distinguish two general stages in the teaching of linguistic knowledge; presentation and practice. These stages correspond to Rivers & Temperley's (1978) distinction between 'skill/knowledge getting' and 'skill/knowledge using'.

In order to make sense of the term 'practice', therefore, we need to see it as in opposition to 'presentation'. The purpose of the presentation stage is to help the learner acquire new linguistic knowledge or to restructure knowledge that has been wrongly represented. The teacher's job in this stage of the lesson is described by Byrne (1986:2) in this way:

> At the presentation stage, your main task is to serve as a kind of *informant*. You *know* the language; you *select* the new material to be learned. . . and you *present* this in such a way that the meaning of the new language is as clear and memorable as possible.

In the presentation stage it is the teacher who does the talking — provides input — while the learner listens and understands. Any production on the part of the learner is incidental, designed simply to introduce the new language into the memory store.

The 'practice' stage follows the 'presentation' stage. One of the assumptions of 'practice', therefore, is that the learner already knows the forms that are the target of the practice but needs to gain control over them. The purpose of practice is to activate the new knowledge to the point where it can be used automatically and correctly in normal communication. For this reason the learner is required to engage in *extensive production* of utterances containing the new structure. In contrast to the presentation stage, emphasis is placed on learner participation, and the teacher needs a new role in order to accommodate this:

> You do the minimum of talking yourself. You are a skillful conductor of an orchestra, giving each performer a chance to participate and monitoring the performance to see it is satisfactory. (Byrne, 1986)

Thus, practice is something that learners have to do in order to make the transition from knowing a feature to using it in real-life communication. A clear analogy exists with learning to play the piano; before the learner attempts to play a whole piece, she practises scales and short phrases.

Helping learners to achieve control over their knowledge requires different kinds of practice. A common distinction found in most training manuals is that between *controlled* and *free* practice. Controlled practice takes the form of various drills which require the mechanical production of specific linguistic forms. Free practice involves engaging in simulated communication which has been set up to provide opportunities for the use of those forms that have been presented and practised in a controlled manner. Controlled and free practice are best viewed as the poles of a continuum. The continuum reflects the degree of focus required by the learner. In controlled practice the learner is required to focus more or less exclusively on the correct production of the target features. In free practice the learner is concerned with meaning rather than with form. In between the two poles are other kinds of practice (e.g. guided and meaningful or contextualised practice).

It is possible to produce a fairly tight definition of controlled practice, as follows:

Controlled practice

(1) takes place when the learner has already internalised the specific feature which is the learning target;
(2) involves production on the part of the learner;
(3) involves the isolation of a specific linguistic feature;
(4) requires the learner to focus attention on this linguistic feature;
(5) requires the learner to carry out a mechanical operation that leads to correct production of the target feature;
(6) involves the provision of teacher feedback regarding the accuracy of the learner's production of the target feature;
(7) provides the learner with the opportunity to repeat incorrect productions correctly.

Although the list is an obvious one, it is important to be explicit, as only in this way is it possible to carry out a rigorous empirical investigation. Each defining characteristic of controlled practice represents, in fact, a largely untested assumption about the nature of language learning.

Free practice is not so easy to define. The problem lies in establishing clear criteria for distinguishing 'free practice' from 'communicative use'. One possible criterion is the *purpose* of the performance. It can be argued that when the learner is concerned with *learning* the L2, she engages in free practice, but when the learner is concerned with conveying a real message, she engages in 'communicative use'. A similar distinction might be made in the case of the pianist who plays a concerto in his studio as a preliminary to a full public performance. The distinction is not an easy one where the classroom language learner is concerned, however. For one thing, the learner may be engaged in both learning and communicating at the same time. That is, she may be entirely focused on meaning content but be fully aware that the real reason why she is taking part in the activity is to learn the language.

The whole idea of practice is, in fact, predicated upon a particular view of what language teaching consists of. Traditional methodology (the methodology we have been discussing to date) envisages a three part process (cf. Brumfit, 1979):

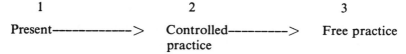

A communicative model of teaching presupposes a different process; 'communicative use' provides the basis for any focused language work:

1   2   3

Communicative ----->   Present------------->   Controlled practice

   It is not clear whether any descriptive differences between learner output in free practice and communicative use will occur. If, in both cases, the performance is concerned with the exchange of meaningful messages, one might expect the same type of discourse to arise. Differences may arise if the learner spontaneously introduces the new features during free practice (i.e. without recourse to any conscious manipulation or editing of output). This, of course, is exactly what is intended by those who advocate the traditional methodology, but the everyday experience of teachers is that new material is frequently not reflected in free practice: '. . . students often seem to master a structure in drilling, but are then incapable of using it in other contexts' (Haycraft, 1978: 36). Studies of the effects of formal instruction on L2 acquisition support Haycraft's view (e.g. Felix, 1981; Ellis, 1984a; Pienemann, 1984). There are definite constraints on what is 'learnable' and, therefore, on what can be freely used.

   It may be that we would do better not to try to draw any distinction between 'free practice' and 'communicative use', but to classify both as 'unfocused performance'. It would follow that the only real distinction is between focused and unfocused performance, as I have proposed elsewhere (Ellis, 1988a). Focused performance would include any kind of practice where the learner is consciously attending to the accurate production of specific target forms — irrespective of whether the language exercise is mechanical or meaningful (i.e. contextualised). Unfocused performance would occur when the learner is oriented towards meaning exchange. Practice, according to this view, would correspond to focused performance and would be largely analogous with controlled practice, as described above.

   All this may seem nothing more than semantic nit-picking, but it is in fact crucially important to come to a clear understanding of what is meant by 'practice'. The term is bandied about in a loose, ill-defined way with the result that precise research becomes very difficult and pedagogic prescriptions opaque.

The Pedagogic Claims for 'Practice'

In considering the pedagogic claims we will restrict the discussion to 'controlled practice'. The term practice from now on will be used to refer exclusively to controlled practice.

In traditional methodology — as outlined above — practice has a clear purpose. Practice helps to make perfect by helping the learner to gain control over new knowledge. This claim is closely associated with the precepts of behaviourist learning theory. Providing that the stimulus is carefully identified with a particular response and care is taken to ensure that the learner produces correct responses, 'habit strength' is built up. It is interesting to note that even in an age when behaviourist theory is largely discredited, the view that language consists of a set of habits which can be developed through concentrated practice does not die, as this quotation from Gower & Walters (1983:83) indicates:

> Repetition practice helps to develop habits. However, in real life we are mostly able to choose which language to use and as we are largely non-mechanical beings this makes for a profoundly complex activity. Habit formation is a small, if essential, part of learning to communicate.

For Gower & Walters the 'small part' which habit formation comprises justifies some 15 pages describing the teaching strategies needed for controlled practice. A quick survey of the current batch of training manuals (e.g. Hubbard et al., 1983; Harmer, 1984) reveals a similar firm commitment to controlled practice.

It is not necessary to invoke behaviourism in support of practice, however. Cognitive learning theory can also provide a rationale. Seliger (1977) suggests that the cognitive effects of practice counter what Ausubel (1971) refers to as 'obliterative subsumption', by which process new material is submsumed within existing networks so that its distinguishing features are lost. Seliger gives the example of the learner who overgeneralises the inverted word order of non-embedded questions in embedded questions: 'I don't know how is he going to do it.' Practice serves to draw the learner's attention to the salient features of a new structure so that the essential attributes are not obliterated through overgeneralisation or transfer. According to this view, therefore, practice has much the same function as 'presentation' — to develop awareness of linguistic form and in this way to overcome the effects of other, powerful cognitive processes. This is rather different from the kind of claim advanced by many methodologists, namely that practice aids control. Presumably a cognitive view places less emphasis on the need for sheer *quantity* of practice.

Most advocates of a communicative methodology are not prepared to abandon practice. Littlewood (1981a) justifies the inclusion of structural practice as 'a point of departure' for more communicative (i.e. meaning-focused) activities. He justifies his position like this:

> . . . we are still too ignorant about the basic processes of language learning to be able to state dogmatically what can and cannot contribute to them. Structural practice may still be a useful tool, especially when the teacher wishes to focus attention sharply and unambiguously on an important feature of the structural system. (Littlewood, 1981a: 9f.)

Littlewood's communicative approach does not really differ from the traditional approach in the sequence of teaching operations it proposes. The difference is only one of emphasis — free practice or communicative use (we have claimed they are synonymous) is allocated more time with a corresponding reduction for controlled practice. Other proponents of a communicate methodology are more radical, advocating a re-ordering of the customary three steps of the teaching process, so that instruction commences with communicative use (cf. Brumfit's model, outlined above). Even here, however, a place is still provided for the controlled practice of those features of which the learner displays a lack in mastery.

There are, however, a number of 'natural' methods which reject any role whatsoever for practice. Prabhu (1987) proposes that grammatical competence can best be acquired if the learners are engaged throughout in meaning-focused activity. Prabhu set up the Communicational Teaching Project in South India to explore to what extent 'task based teaching' was feasible and whether it promoted the successful acquisition of grammar. Prabhu writes about the project:

> Attempts to systematize input to the learner through a linguistically organized syllabus, or to maximize the practice of particular parts of language-structure through activities deliberately planned for that purpose were regarded as being unhelpful to the development of grammatical competence and detrimental to the desired preoccupation with meaning in the classroom. (Prabhu, 1987: 1f)

Thus Prabhu rejected controlled practice because he believed it obstructed the learner's engagement with meaning and so impeded learning. Instead, Prabhu and his aides developed a series of reasoning-gap activities designed to stimulate meaning-focused interaction in the classroom.

To sum up, three different pedagogic positions regarding the role of practice are evident in the current literature:

(1) Practice is *necessary* to ensure that learners develop correct language habits or to enable them to overcome 'obliterative subsumption'.
(2) Practice is not necessary for language learning but is *desirable* either as a precursor to communicative language use or as a means of dealing with problems that arise in communicative language use.
(3) Practice is neither necessary nor desirable for language learning and, in fact, can have a *detrimental* effect.

We can now turn to the available empirical research to see which of these positions it lends most support to.

Empirical studies

We will begin by examining a number of quantitative studies. These provide conflicting results regarding the effectiveness of practice. We consider why this is and then go on to consider qualitative approaches.

Quantitative studies

Quantitative approaches entail the collection of data relating to the practice opportunities afforded to different learners (the independent variable) and data relating to the learning outcomes of the same learners (the dependent variable). Scores on the independent variable are then correlated with scores on the dependent variable in order to establish whether there is any significant relationship between the two.

A number of such studies are summarised in Table 5.1. The results are extremely varied. Some studies (e.g. Seliger, 1977; Naiman *et al.*, 1978; Ellis & Rathbone, 1987) report positive relationships between the amount of practice and learning. One study (Ellis, 1984b) reports a negative relationship; that is, those learners who received the most opportunities for practice displayed the smallest gains in acquisition. Other studies report either no relationship between practice and learning (Day, 1984) or only a very weak relationship (Ely, 1986).

What explanation can be given for these mixed results? One of the problems is that different researchers work with different definitions of 'practice'. For Seliger (1977), for instance, practice consists of any speech act produced by a learner in the classroom. For Ellis (1984b) 'practice' consists of nominated opportunities for learners to produce utterances containing the target feature when presented with picture cues. Other researchers operationalise the construct in different ways. It is not always clear whether 'practice' — in the sense we have defined it above — is the target of study or whether it is participation in general. In the case of the latter, unfocused as well as focused production is included.

Another problem lies in the way that the dependent variable — learning — is measured. Three of the studies (Naiman *et al.*, 1978; Day, 1984; Ely, 1986) employed general measures of proficiency while the other three (Seliger, 1977; Ellis, 1984b; Ellis & Rathbone, 1987) obtained measures of the learners' knowledge of specific grammatical features. One possible explanation for the difference in the results obtained in the Seliger and Day studies (which followed similar designs) is the different way that learning was measured. It is also worth noting that in only two studies (Ellis, 1984b; Ellis & Rathbone, 1987) was any attempt made to relate practice in the production of a specific grammatical structure to the acquisition of that structure.

The main problem, however, lies in the difficulty of interpreting correlational statistics. A coefficient of correlation tells us only whether there is a significant *relationship* between two variables; it does not tell us about the direction of the relationship. All the studies in Table 5.1 were designed on the assumption that practice influences acquisition, either negatively or positively. Such an assumption may not be justified, however. It would be possible to argue that it is how much a learner knows that affects the amount of practice she receives. For example, weak learners might find themselves nominated to practice more frequently than strong learners. It would also be possible to argue that the relationship between practice and learning is interactional in nature; that is, the amount of learning influences the amount of practice which in turn affects the amount of learning. The diversity of results obtained suggests that a theoretical model in which practice is treated as a determinant of learning is far too simplistic. The whole relationship is much more complex, subject to the myriad variables that govern classroom behaviour.

The results of the Ellis & Rathbone (1987) study, in particular, give reason for querying whether the 'practice-causes-learning' model is tenable. They found that the amount of practice in V-end was not significantly related to the acquisition of V-end but was significantly (and positively) related to scores on a discrete-item test of grammatical proficiency. This test did not, in fact, include any items for V-end. In other words, practice in feature x was related more strongly to knowledge of features a,b . . . n than to knowledge of feature x itself. Clearly a 'practice-causes-learning' explanation does not work here. However, a 'learning-causes-practice' explanation is possible. The learners' general knowledge of L2 German in some way governed the quantity of practice they took part in.

TABLE 5.1 *Survey of quantitative studies of the role of practice in language learning*

Study	Subjects	Practice	Measures of learning	Results
Seliger (1977)	6 adults learning English	Amount of verbal interaction in the classroom; any student speech act counted as an interaction; initiations and responses scored separately	Cloze test; structure test; aural comprehension test	Total interaction scores correlated significantly with both structure and aural comprehension scores; percentage of initiations correlated significantly with aural comprehension.
Naiman et al. (1978)	Learners of L2 French in Grades 8, 10 and 12 of anglophone schools in Canada	Various measures of classroom behaviour (e.g. student hand-raising; student complete/partial responses; student correct/incorrect responses)	Comprehension test; imitation test	Positive significant correlations between hand-raising, complete responses, correct responses and students responding above 10 times and both measures of learning found; negative significant

Study	Subjects	Practice	Measures of learning	Results
				relationships existed between incorrect/ partially correct responses and both learning measures.
Day (1984)	26 adult learners of L2 English in Hawaii; divided into high and low input generators	Responses to teacher general solicits; self-initiated turns	Oral proficiency (interviewer assessments of learners' grammatical, pragmatic and sociolinguistic competence); cloze test	No significant correlations between classroom participation and oral proficiency or cloze test scores.
Ellis (1984b)	13 children learning English as a L2 in Britain	Contextual-ised opportunities to produce WH Qs; number of practice exchanges per learner	Gains in the accuracy of production of 'when' Qs in an elicitation game played before and after instruction	Children who had fewest opportunities for practice showed greatest gains.
Ely (1986)	72 first-year adult learners of L2 Spanish at university in	Number of self-initiated utterances in Spanish, i.e. volunteering	Oral fluency in a story reproduction task (= absence of	Self initiations correlated significantly with oral

Study	Subjects	Practice	Measures of learning	Results
	USA; half in first and half in second quarter	a question or a response	self-interrupted elements); oral correctness (based on error counts in stories); written correctness (based on final written examination)	correctness in beginners. No other significant correlations reported.
Ellis & Rathbone (1987)	39 adult learners of L2 German; beginners	Number of occasions each learner attempted to produce a sentence with V-end in controlled practice; number of correct V-end sentences	Accuracy of V-end production in an oral narrative; discrete item test of general grammatical proficiency	Number of correct V-end sentences (but not total V-end practice) correlated significantly with V-end-tion. Both correct and total practice of V-end correlated with general grammar proficiency. Relationship with general proficiency stronger than with V-end acquisition.

The quantitative research into the role of practice which has been undertaken to date provides a salutary warning of the dangers of nomothetic enquiry in such a complex area as classroom language learning. Such research risks making assumptions about the nature of the relationship between instruction and learning which may not be warranted. In formulating researchable hypotheses, simplistic cause–effect models of teaching may be invoked — perhaps because such models are implicit in many pedagogic prescriptions — with consequent confusion in the results obtained. A wiser approach is to conduct careful *qualitative* studies first.

Qualitative studies

Qualitative studies involve the careful analysis of interactional protocols. That is, the researcher examines what is actually *said* and *done* in the name of practice. Alternatively, qualitative studies may ask learners to introspect or retrospect on learning processes. Both kinds of research provide insights into a number of key aspects of practice:

(1) The nature of the learner's contribution to practice sessions.
(2) The nature of the teacher's contribution to practice sessions.
(3) Factors determining the distribution of opportunities for practice.

We will briefly consider each of these.

Controlled practice results in three-phase interactional exchanges, in which the teacher initiates, the learner responds and the teacher supplies feedback. Three-phase exchanges are not restricted to controlled practice however; they predominate in any teacher-dominated interaction where the pedagogic goal is to elicit a pre-determined response from the learner (Sinclair & Coulthard, 1975; Pica, 1987). What differentiates IRF exchanges in controlled practice from similar exchanges in more meaning-focused instruction is their interactional *goal*. In practice sessions the goal is to perform a specific linguistic feature correctly. This affects both the learner's and the teacher's contributions.

Studies of classroom interaction in which a learner is attempting to perform a new target structure reveal the difficulties which are often experienced. Ellis (1984a) provides the following protocol in which a 13-year-Punjabi girl is struggling to perform a drill practising markers of plurality:

1. **T:** Now, what is this?
2.   (holds up pen)   **S:** This is a pen.
3. **T:** What are these?

4.	(holds up two pens)	S: This are a pen.
5.	T: These are ____?	
6.		S: Are pens.
7.	T: What is this?	
8.	(holds up a ruler)	S: This is a ruler.
9.	T: What are these?	
10.	(holds up two rulers)	S: This is . . . are . . . This are a rulers.
11.	T: These are rulers. What are these?	
12.		S: This are a rulers.
13.	T: Not 'a'. These are ____?	
14.		S: Rulers.
15.	T: Rulers.	
16.		S: Rulers.

The task requires the learner to encode a number of plural markers: (1) the plural demonstrative article ('these'), (2) the plural copula ('are'), (3) the zero article, and (4) the plural noun form ('rulers', 'pencils' etc.). As Ellis observes, this learner fails to perform one or more of these markers in each attempt (see Table 5.2).

TABLE 5.2   *Production of plurality markers by one learner in controlled practice*

Utterance	Missing plurality markers
4	(1), (3), (4)
6	(1)
10	(1), (3)
12	(1), (3)
14	(1), (2), (3)
16	(1), (2), (3)

One explanation of this is that the task of producing plural sentences is beyond this learner's competence. Although the learner probably 'knows' what is required of her, she is unable to comply because she has not reached the appropriate stage of development.

It is not certain what abilities a learner requires to perform successfully a drill such as the one above. Clearly, if the learner already controls the linguistic features which are the focus of the practice, correct production should pose no problem. In such a case, however, the practice is not achieving anything, except allowing the learner to display knowledge that has already been thoroughly acquired. What happens when the learner lacks the requisite control, as with the Punjabi girl? Hosenfeld (1976) set out to answer this question by asking learners to report on the strategies they used when performing drills. She concluded that what was being practised were procedures for getting right answers rather than the grammatical items themselves. Correct responses merely indicate that the learner has accessed the appropriate cognitive strategies for reproducing the target structure; they do not show that learning is taking place. Qualitative studies, therefore, lead one to be sceptical whether any grammar-learning takes place in controlled practice.

Other qualitative studies have looked at the nature and consistency of the teacher's feedback — in particular what the teacher does when the learner's response contains an error. McTear (1975), for instance, finds that teachers sometimes give up the task of correction and are often inconsistent, sometimes correcting an error and sometimes not. Allwright (1975) points out that teachers, in fact, may have a duty to be inconsistent as they need to respond to individual differences among the learners. Finally, it has been shown (Long, 1977) that the procedures a teacher uses to correct an error may not always be explicit, so that learners have to interpret the teacher's treatment of error. The effectiveness of the treatment will depend on whether the learner is able to make the right interpretation. We can see many of these factors at work in the feedback provided by the Punjabi girl's teacher.

We now turn to consider the factors that influence the distribution of practice opportunities in a classroom. Ellis & Rathbone (1987) address this issue. They note that practice may be *volunteered* or *nominated* and that this can influence the learner's production. For example, if responses are nominated in a predictable manner (e.g. alphabetically or line-by-line), learners are able to prepare in advance, whereas volunteered responses are likely to be more spontaneous.

One factor that influences who teachers nominate to respond in practice sessions is the learners' existing levels of competence. The protocol below shows what can happen:

1. T: Nun, erm, auf der nächsten
       Seite. Und warum sind sie im
       Schirmgeschäft? Mary.

2.   S1: Erm, sie sind im
                                                 Schirmgeschäft, weil, erm
                                                 (.2.) sie (.) möchten eine
                                                 Schirm kaufen.

3. T: Was meinen die anderen? Ist

das richtig, was Mary sagt?
(.3.) Roger, Sie schütteln den
Kopf. Verstehen Sie? Sie
schütteln den Kopf. Shaking
your head. Wie sagen Sie es?
Warum sind sie im
Schirmgeschäft?

4.
                                      S2: Erm, weil sie einen Schirm
                                           kaufen möchten.

5. T: Weil Frau Meyer einen
       Schirm kaufen möchte. Und
       Mary sagte, weil Frau
       Meyer möchte einen Schirm
       kaufen.

The focus of the practice here is V-end. The teacher begins by nominating
S1, who fails to produce a correct sentence. She then turns to S2, who has
shown signs (i.e. by shaking his head) that he is both able and prepared to
provide a correct answer. This he does. S2 functions as a kind of proxy
teacher; he is called on to supply correct answers when other students make
mistakes. It is not surprising, perhaps, that it is S2 who receives the most
opportunities for practice in his class.

However, teachers probably vary considerably in the implicit principles
they follow in deciding who to nominate for practice. Some may try to be
egalitarian by ensuring that all students receive equal shares. Others may try
to direct practice at those students who are most in need of it. Purely local
factors can play a part. Thus, in the case of Ellis & Rathbone's study, the
teachers tended to favour those learners who had elected to continue with
German beyond the end of the year at the expense of those students who had
decided to give it up. In short, a whole host of factors affect who gets
nominated and how often they get nominated.

What factors govern volunteered responses? One factor is the learner's
language ability. Learners who already 'know' how to perform a structure are
more likely to try their hand. Learners who are uncertain are more likely to
hold back. This leads us back to the argument already advanced, namely that
it is acquisition that determines practice rather than vice versa. There are other
factors, however. The nature of the practice activity can influence whether a
learner is allowed to volunteer. In the Ellis & Rathbone study, volunteered
responses occurred more frequently in freer practice activities (e.g. when
students were allowed to compose their own sentences) than in text book
exercises. Even more important is the personal inclination of the individual

learner. Some learners dislike being asked to perform in front of their peers and, therefore, rarely volunteer. Other learners are keen to try and feel no anxiety about risking themselves in public. Ely (1986), in the study referred to earlier, provides quantitative evidence of this; he found that risk-taking was a significant positive predictor of classroom participation, accounting for nearly 30% of learner variance. Ellis & Rathbone provide evidence from diary studies kept by some of the learners in their study to illustrate the marked difference in attitude to practice that learners hold. One learner dreads teachers' questions:

I was really tense in this class when she was asking us questions . . .

As usual I was quite frightened when asked questions.

I was quite frightened when asked questions again. I don't know why; the teacher does not frighten me but my mind is blocked when I'm asked questions. I fear lest I give the wrong answer . . .

Another learner, however, has no qualms about making mistakes and welcomes the opportunity to take part in productive practice:

Again today, volunteers were asked to read a passage. I find it irritating that no one seems to want to volunteer apart from one or two people. I'd rather volunteer and make an idiot of myself. . . I think this is important because I want to learn really quickly.

Quite apart from their general attitudes towards practice, learners can vary in the extent to which they willingly participate on a day to day basis, as a result of purely personal factors or even the time of the day. A host of potentially interacting factors determine to what extent and when a learner volunteers answers in class.

These qualitative studies lead us to see controlled practice in a very different light from that shed by the quantitative, pseudo- experimental studies. Practice comes to be seen as a *social* event involving *personal* investment on the part of the learner. Practice consists of a particular kind of interaction which is negotiated by the participants in accordance with the social and personal factors that prevail in a given teaching context. Once practice is seen in this way, it becomes difficult to seek a direct, causative link between practice and learning. There are simply too many intervening variables. Thus, even practice that meets clear definitional criteria will be implemented variably and have different outcomes.

Discussion

So far we have considered the pedagogical arguments for controlled practice and reviewed the empirical research which has examined the role that practice plays in language learning. We observed that mainstream pedagogy — in the form of both traditional and communicative language teaching methodology — finds a definite place for controlled practice. The empirical research, however, suggests that the relationship between controlled practice and learning is far more complex than is presupposed in most methodological prescriptions and that there is no clear evidence that controlled practice does in fact promote L2 acquisition. Although it would be difficult to come to any firm conclusion on the basis of the limited research that has been conducted to date, it is clear that controlled practice can mean very different things in different classrooms depending on the social and personal relationships that prevail between the teacher and the learners. In other words, it is a mistake to treat even controlled practice as a monolithic phenomenon.

In this section we will consider a number of other points that bear on the role of controlled practice, drawing more generally on the results of SLA research.

First, the nature of the linguistic feature which is the instructional target may influence whether the practice works or not. Meisel, Clahsen & Pienemann (1981) distinguish *developmental* and *variational* features of SLA. Developmental features are features that are constrained by strategies of language processing. They are acquired sequentially because the development of each feature can take place only when the necessary processing strategies have been activated. Pienemann (1984) has shown that formal instruction is powerless to change the sequence of acquisition of developmental features such as German word order rules. He found that only those learners who were ready to learn INVERSION (i.e. were at the immediately preceding stage), benefited from instruction; learners who were not ready showed no improvement and some even regressed. Variational features are features that are not constrained by language processing strategies and, theoretically therefore, can be acquired at any time. Johnston (1987) argues that because variational features are 'computationally simple' they are teachable. He reports the results of a study designed to teach immigrant German children the copula. This showed that they responded quite positively, with the rate of omission of copula dropping by over 50% in some cases after a week of targeted teaching of various kinds. Practice, therefore, may have differential success depending on the structure that is the focus of the instruction.

The second point concerns how controlled practice is viewed. In the preceding sections we have viewed it as 'focused instruction' in accordance with a pedagogical perspective. However, controlled practice can be viewed simply as 'input'. That is, in the course of engaging in controlled practice the learner is exposed to a variety of L2 features, not just the specific feature which is the instructional target. For example, a lesson planned to practice markers of plurality (as in the protocol considered earlier), also exposed the learners to input in the use of the copula:

> What *is* this?
> This *is* a pen. etc.

It is possible that such input — although not the focus of the lesson — will facilitate the acquisition of developmental features the learner is ready for or variational features such as copula. It is also possible that because drills model specific L2 features with high frequency (e.g. Verb-*ing*) over-learning will take place (cf. Lightbown, 1983). If we view controlled practice as 'input' we have to recognise that what is learnt may not be the same as what is taught; the lesson may have been designed to teach feature x, but the learners do not acquire x, although they do acquire y. Researchers and methodologists may not be comfortable with this possibility, as, once again, it is potentially threatening to the value that is traditionally placed on practice. Also, if we view practice as 'input', we are forced into asking whether the input provided in this way is of equal quality for the purposes of facilitating SLA as input provided through meaning-focused communication.

The third point concerns the temporal relationship between practice and acquisition. The assumption that underlies pedagogic statements about controlled practice is that the relationship is an *immediate* one; that is, as a result of engaging in controlled practice, acquisition (at least in the form of a strengthening or automatising of knowledge) takes place then and there. It is perfectly feasible, however, that practice has a delayed effect. Figure 5.1 suggests how this might arise.

$$\text{INPUT}$$
$$\text{-----}>$$

```
                    ┌──────────────────────────────┐
                    │ EXPLICIT        IMPLICIT      │
PRACTICE--->        │ KNOWLEDGE--->KNOWLEDGE        │  --->OUTPUT
                    └──────────────────────────────┘
```

FIGURE 5.1   *The delayed effect of practice*

Controlled practice contributes directly to explicit (i.e. declarative) knowledge, but not to implicit (i.e. procedural) knowledge. Implicit knowledge is dependent on meaning-focused input which the learner processes in accordance with the current state of her interlanguage. Communicative output draws predominantly on implicit knowledge. However, controlled practice contributes indirectly to implicit knowledge in that the existence of explicit knowledge sensitises the learner to the occurrence of specific features in the input which otherwise would not be attended to. According to this view of classroom L2 acquisition, therefore, controlled practice has a *delayed* effect. The real value of such practice is in enabling learners to formulate declarative knowledge. If this is so, however, we need to ask whether controlled practice is the best way of raising consciousness about the formal properties of a language. Controlled practice is designed to automatise rather than to sensitise and for this reason is time-consuming. There may be more efficient ways (such as problem-solving tasks) of helping learners develop useful explicit knowledge.

The points discussed in this section are all speculative. They should be considered as hypotheses that are grounded in current SLA research and theory. They all lead in the same direction — namely, to question the conventional pedagogic arguments advanced in support of controlled practice.

Summary and Conclusion

One of the functions of applied linguistics is to submit pedagogical assumptions to close scrutiny. In this article we have used both the results of empirical SLA research and SLA theoretical perspectives to examine the pedagogic claims that are frequently made for controlled practice.

The following is a summary of the main points that have been raised:

(1) A model of teaching in which practice is seen as determining learning (the 'practice-causes-acquisition' model) is simplistic and not tenable. Controlled practice is a form of classroom interaction and, as such, is a varied phenomenon subject to a host of social and personal factors. It is for this reason — above any other — that quantitative studies of practice have produced conflicting results.

(2) Frequently, it is acquisition that determines practice, rather than vice versa. That is, how much of the L2 a learner already knows controls how much practice she gets, as qualitative studies of practice have shown. Frequently the way practice is conducted by the teacher reflects her assessment of the proficiency attained by individual learners. In this way, practice may simply serve to reinforce the learners' and the teacher's

preconception about who is succeeding and who is not succeeding. That is, a kind of self-fulfilling prophecy may be acted out through practice.

(3) Controlled practice is designed to automatise items that are already part of the learner's interlanguage; qualitative studies suggest that it does not achieve this. Frequently learners fail to produce correct exemplars of the target structure and the teacher connives at this. Controlled practice may do little more than develop the strategies needed for reproductive competence.

(4) Even if controlled practice is credited with *causing* learning, there are strong theoretical grounds for believing that only some grammatical features (i.e. 'variational' features that are computed simply) can be influenced easily by practice. Controlled practice will only facilitate the acquisition of 'developmental' features if the necessary processing prerequisites have been established.

(5) Controlled practice is a source of 'input'; the learner may select from this input what she is ready and prepared to process, irrespective of what structure is the target of the practice.

(6) The real role of controlled practice may be to raise the learner's consciousness about language form. This consciousness may not be convertable into implicit knowledge immediately but may facilitate it in the long term. There may be better ways of raising the learner's consciousness than controlled practice, however.

We are led to conclude that in the case of controlled practice the old axiom 'practice makes perfect' may not apply to language learning or, at least, not in the way that many teachers and methodologists think it does. Practice may only facilitate acquisition directly if it is communicative, i.e. meaning-focused in nature.

Section 4
Variability and Second Language Acquisition

The two papers in this section consider the nature of variability in L2 performance and its relationship to acquisition. Both papers are theoretical in nature and make no real attempt to apply the general arguments advanced to language pedagogy. However, the theoretical position which these papers present has been motivated to a considerable extent by my interest in pedagogical issues.

Language-learner language displays enormous variability. This is true for both naturalistic and classroom learners. The latter, for instance, may be successful in performing a specific linguistic feature accurately in the context of a controlled practice exercise but fail to do so in more communicative language use. It was this phenomenon that first motivated me to investigate how L2 acquisition takes place and which led me to examine variability. How we explain this phenomenon will have a profound effect on what approach to language pedogogy we decide to adopt.

My own approach to explaining variability has been psycholinguistic rather than sociolinguistic (although I have drawn on a number of constructs used by sociolinguists). It has attracted considerable criticism from sociolinguists who approach the study of variability from a different point of view (e.g. Preston, 1989) and from linguists for whom variability is an uninteresting and trivial phenomenon (e.g. Gregg, 1990). These criticisms are in some cases legitimate, but I do not think they invalidate my overall position, if this is viewed from a psycholinguistic/pedagogic perspective.

It may help the reader if I briefly summarise what the main premises of my current position are.

(1) The acquisition of new linguistic forms may be socially motivated (i.e. by the need to communicate effectively and in contextually appropriate ways) or psychologically motivated (i.e. by the wish to know more of the language).

(2) Newly acquired forms are likely to co-exist with previously acquired forms, at least initially. This can result in *free-variation* (where the two

forms are used randomly in the same types of language use) or in *systematic* variation (where the the use of the two forms is distributed with some degree of regularity in accordance with social factors).

(3) Systematic variation also occurs in accordance with linguistic context. Thus the learner finds it easier to to employ a target language variant in some linguistic environments than in others.

(4) Planning variability arises as a result of processing factors. When learners have time to plan, they are more likely to attend to form and to access target-language rather than interlanguage variants. When there is no time to plan, the learner will tend to fall back on those forms which are easiest to process (i.e. early interlanguage forms).

(5) Synchronic (or horizontal) variability is closely related to L2 development (vertical variability) in a number of ways:

   (a) Leaners seek to maximise the communicative effectiveness of their interlanguage systems by eliminating free variation. This manifests itself in the restructuring of form-function relationships in the learner's interlanguage. Thus, free variation serves as a precursor of systematic variation.

   (b) Leaners extend the range of a new linguistic item as they acquire the ability to use it in an increasing number of social contexts.

   (c) Learners also extend the range of a new linguistic item as they acquire the ability to use it in an increasing number of linguistic contexts.

   (d) As learners overcome processing contraints, they are able to use new linguistic forms in unplanned as well as planned discourse.

The general picture that emerges from this summary is that L2 acquisition is a gradual process which involves a reduction in variability as target language variants spread to an increasing number of social and linguistic contexts and as the ability to access them under different conditions of use develops.

'Sources of variability in interlanguage' (*Applied Linguistics* 6: 118–31) discusses the relationship between free and systematic variation and illustrates how form-function relations get restructured. 'Interlanguage variability in narrative discourse: style shifting in the use of the past tense (*Studies in Second Language Acquisition* 9: 1–20) examines planning variability. The reader interested in the application of variability theory to language pedagogy might like to refer to 'Contextual variability in second language acquisition and the relevancy of language teaching' which can be found in Section 6 of this volume.

6. Sources of Variability in Interlanguage

The Horizontal and Vertical Dimensions of Interlanguage

Following Corder (1977), it is possible to identify both a horizontal and a vertical dimension to interlanguage. The horizontal dimension refers to the interlanguage that a learner has constructed at a specific point in time. The vertical dimension refers to the developmental stages through which the learner passes over time. The main purpose of this paper is to propose an alternative account of how horizontal and vertical variability are related, based on a central role for non-systematic language-learner language. First I consider briefly the key issues of systematicity and variability.

It is now axiomatic that interlanguage is systematic. This is true from both the horizontal and the vertical perspectives. That is, we portray the interlanguage which the learner has constructed at any stage of development as an internally consistent system, while we also view the process of development from one stage to the next as ordered and regular. The theoretical case for the systematicity of interlanguage was made initially in a series of papers in the late 1960s and early 1970s (Corder, 1967; Nemser, 1971; Selinker 1972). Although interlanguage theory has been subsequently developed in a number of ways, the essential claim that interlanguage is systematic has remained intact.

It has become increasingly acknowledged, however, that interlanguage is also variable (see, for instance, Dickerson, 1975; Huebner, 1979). The variability is evident in both the horizontal and the vertical dimensions. Each interlanguage which the learner forms contains alternative rules for performing the same function. On some occasions one rule is used, on another a different rule. Also, despite the striking uniformity in the developmental profile of different learners, there are variations in the overall course of development that learners follow.[1] Interlanguage constitutes an unstable system and as such is permeable to invasion by new linguistic forms. Its dynamic quality is reflected in tremendous variability in language-learner language and also in overlapping stages of development as one set of variable rules is revised in favour of another.

To claim that interlanguage is on the one hand systematic and on the other variable is potentially contradictory. However, theoretical developments in linguistics which have provided the tools for describing the competence that underlies native speaker performance as variable rules (e.g. Labov, 1970; Bailey, 1973) or as overlapping grammars (Bickerton, 1973) indicate that systematicity and variability are reconcilable. It has been hypothesised (e.g. by Tarone, 1983) that interlanguage, like any other natural language, is systematically variable. Furthermore, it has been proposed that systematic variability serves as a mechanism of change — as Widdowson (1975) has put it, 'change is only the temporal consequence of current variation'. According to this view of second language acquisition, then, interlanguage is to be explained in terms of two principal hypotheses:

1. Interlanguage is composed of a series of variable systems.
2. Systematic horizontal variability in interlanguage is the precursor of vertical growth.

It is this position that I wish to examine. In order to do so, I shall first investigate in what ways language-learner language is systematically variable. I shall then argue that there is also substantial non-systematic variability in the horizontal dimension of interlanguage. To illustrate this I shall look at some data from a longitudinal study of a second-language learner and show that current interlanguage theory based on systematic horizontal variability cannot comfortably account for them.

Systematic Variability

The study of how language users systematically vary their use of linguistic forms has been a major area of sociolinguistic enquiry. Two major types of variability have been identified and described: situational variability and contextual variability.

Situational variability consists of the alternation of two or more linguistic forms in accordance with extra-linguistic factors. A number of quite complex models have been proposed to account for the range of situational factors that are involved (e.g. Crystal & Davy, 1969; Brown & Fraser, 1979). Brown & Fraser usefully group these factors into two sets according to *scene*, which includes such factors as setting, type of activity, and subject matter, and *participants*, which covers factors relating the individual characteristics of language users (e.g. sex, age, ethnicity) and interpersonal role relationships.

Whereas the study of variability in native-speaker speech has covered a full range of extra-linguistic factors, the study of systematic interlanguage variability has been more restricted, operating primarily with the model of variability proposed by Labov (1970). Labov showed that there was systematic variability in the speech of New Yorkers. He collected data from a range of speech styles from the 'vernacular' (where language use is at its most natural and systematic) to the 'careful'. His subjects varied in their use of socially prestigious sounds such as /θ/ according to the amount of attention they paid to their speech. In the natural style there were fewer instances of /θ/ than in the careful style. Thus Labov hypothesises that social factors to do with the level of formality of language use are linked to how much attention users pay to their speech. It should be noted that this model of systematic variability considers only participant factors; no account is taken of factors to do with scene.

Labov's model has proved attractive to researchers in (SLA). It has been used to explain why learners are able to perform according to target language competence on one occasion, but not on another. For instance, classroom learners are able to use a target language rule in a language exercise, but fall back on to a more primitive interlanguage in ordinary communication. In the classroom the learner attends closely to the language he produces and so performs according to his careful style, while in ordinary conversation he attends to meaning rather than to form, and so performs in his vernacular style. However, as Labov showed for native speaker use, performance differences from one setting to another will not be absolute, but relative to the *degree* of attention paid to form. The learner operates a stylistic continuum, producing on any single occasion varying proportions of the correct target language and interlanguage forms. A further reason for the attractiveness of Labov's model is the methodology that goes with it. This consists of the cross-sectional collection of data, using a number of elicitation instruments to reflect differing degrees of attention. This methodology has proved readily applicable to second-language users. Examples of studies which have made use of Labov's model and methodology are Dickerson (1975), Dickerson & Dickerson (1977), and Schmidt (1977). Tarone (1983) provides an excellent summary of what is revealed by these and other studies about interlanguage variability:

> . . . the data we have examined . . . indicate that interlanguage does vary systematically with elicitation task and, further, that when a task elicits a relatively more careful style, that style may contain more TL (target language) forms and more prestige NL (native language) variants than the relatively more casual style elicited by other tasks.

Thus the Labov model, developed to describe native speaker use, can be successfully applied to interlanguage performance. It accounts for stylistic variability, that is variability determined by participant factors.

The second type of variability that has been identified in interlanguage is contextual variability. This is evident when the language user varies his use of linguistic forms according to the linguistic environment. A good example of how this has been treated in sociolinguistic theory is again Labov (1970). Labov examined the copula in Black English Vernacular and developed a variable rule to account for when it was deleted. He noted that the presence or absence of the copula was related to its syntactic position. For instance, it was more likely to arise if the preceding noun phrase was a pronoun. Its occurrence was also more likely when the following grammatical structure was 'gonna' than when it was a noun phrase.

Interlanguage is also marked by contextual variability. Dickerson (1975), for instance, found that the phonetic quality of specific phonemes produced by Japanese learners of English varied according to the phonetic environment. When /z/ was followed by a vowel, for instance, the subjects used the correct target language sound 100% of the time right from the beginning of the study, but when it was followed by silence they used /z/ only a proportion of the time, also employing other variants. Grammatical examples of contextual variability can also be found. I have observed Zambian learners of English use the third person singular of the present simple tense correctly in simple sentences or in the initial clause of complex sentences but use the uninflected form in the second clause of complex sentences. For example:

Moses lives in Lusaka.
Moses lives in Lusaka, but he work in Kafue.

As with situational variability, contextual variability constitutes a continuum, with some linguistic contexts associated with the use of one variant and other contexts with another, but with all variants occurring in varying proportions in all contexts at some stage of development.

In summary, then, a full account of the systematic nature of horizontal variability in interlanguage requires that both situational and contextual variability be considered. In the case of situational variability this would involve investigating the effects of factors relating to both scene and participants. In the case of contextual variability it would involve studying how the linguistic environment constrains the operation of interlanguage rules at different stages of development. A full account would also need to consider how situational and contextual variability are connected — how the two sets of factors interact for specific linguistic forms. It might be possible to rank the frequency of the third person singular form from high to low as follows[2]:

1 + careful style; + simple sentence/first clause complex sentence
2 + careful style; + second clause complex sentence
3 + vernacular style; + simple sentence/first clause complex sentence
4 + vernacular style; + second clause complex sentence

However, I know of no model of interlanguage variability that has attempted this. Neither do I recall any study which has investigated the full range of situational factors (i.e. considers scene as well as participants). In general the models of interlanguage which have taken account of systematic variability have been of a restricted nature.

It is, however, not beyond the bounds of researchers to develop more complex models. Before doing so, however, it is worth considering to what extent non-systematic variability is important for understanding interlanguage use and development.

Non-systematic Variability

Native-speaker language use is characterised by non-systematic as well as systematic variability. This non-systematic variability is of two types. The first type is the result of performance lapses, the numerous false starts, deviations from rules, changes of plan in mid-course, etc. of which Chomsky (1965) speaks. This type is not part of the language user's competence. It occurs when the language user is unable to perform his competence. However, not all non-systematic variability is of this type. The second type, which is of greater interest to me, is that variability that is the result of competing rules in the learner's competence. These rules are acted upon quite haphazardly.

It is not difficult to find examples of such non-systematic variability. The examples, however, are likely to be idiosyncratic. I sometimes say /da:tə/ and sometimes /deitə/, sometimes /ɔfn/ and sometimes (ɔftn/, sometimes /skedju:1/ and sometimes /ʃedju:1/. Examples can also be found at the grammatical level. To the best of my knowledge I alternate quite haphazardly between 'who' and 'that' as subject relative pronouns with human referents in non-restrictive relative clauses.[3] I shall argue later that such non-systematic variability is contrary to a general principle of linguistic organisation, but for the moment, I merely wish to draw attention to the existence in the native-speaker's competence of variants that serve no situational or contextual function. In this type of variability, linguistic forms exist in free variation.

Non-systematic variation is, I believe, extremely important for understanding how interlanguage evolves.

Some Data

Before turning to the theoretical development of my position, I want to consider some speech data. It must be emphasised that these data are intended to *illustrate* a phenomenon that I believe to be widespread in L2 acquisition, whether tutored or untutored, namely non-systematic variability. The intention, however, is not to report on an empirical study and the data are not presented with a view to testing any research hypothesis, but to illustrate, using authentic rather than contrived examples. I shall examine these data in the light of a number of current theories of SLA and argue that they fail to provide a satisfactory explanation because they are based on the assumption that interlanguage variability is systematic.

The data I wish to discuss as examples of this problem consist of just two utterances:

1. No look my card.
2. Don't look my card.

They were produced by an 11-year-old Portuguese boy (whom I shall call 'J') who was the subject of a longitudinal study. When J arrived in Britain he was placed almost immediately in a language centre where he received day-long instruction in English. At the start of the study J was an almost complete beginner. His productive English was limited to a few words. The data were collected inside the classroom using a pencil-and-paper record of all the spontaneous speech (i.e. *not* speech elicited in instructional drills of any kind) that J produced. An audio recording of each lesson was used to check the accuracy of the pencil-and-paper record. J was visited once each week for a minimum of one hour throughout the school year.

Before discussing these data, a few comments about J's use of negative utterances are in order. In the first month J produced a total of 18 spontaneous negative utterances.[4] Out of these, 17 used the 'no' negator, as in utterance (1) above, and only one used 'don't'. Thus utterance (2) was the solitary example of a 'don't' negative in the first few weeks of the study. In the next month, however, the proportion of 'don't' negatives increased substantially, although 'no' negatives were still more frequent. It was not until the sixth month that negatives containing 'not' (i.e. either 'don't' or 'aux + not') were in the majority. This pattern of development parallels that reported in other studies (e.g. Cazden *et al.*, 1975; Wode, 1976).

In what way can these data be explained? I propose to examine a number of theoretical positions which have been advanced to explain-interlanguage variability. I am indebted to Tarone's (1983) excellent review of three paradigms for the study of interlanguage, which I shall draw on extensively. I shall add one paradigm to Tarone's list.

1. The homogeneous competence paradigm

This is the first of Tarone's three paradigms. It attributes to the learner a unitary competence, which is considered to underlie speech production. This competence is not always manifest in performance, because of various processing constraints which distract the user. The homogeneous competence paradigm sees variability as a performance characteristic in accordance with Chomsky's theory of language. The data might be explained as follows in such a paradigm:

> J possesses a single rule for negative utterances. This rule constitutes his competence. In actual performance, however, he may manifest variants of this rule. These do not, however, reflect his competence.

But such an explanation is not very helpful or convincing. What is the negative rule which constitutes J's competence? Is it the most frequently occurring rule (i.e. 'no' + V) at this stage of his development? If this is so, then the more target-like form ('don't' + V) would have to be treated as deviant. If, however, the target-like rule is held to represent J's competence, then there is the problem that this was manifest on only one occasion in the first month.

2. The capability paradigm

The second paradigm Tarone considers is the capability of paradigm. This derives from the Labovian theory of systematic stylistic variability which has already been discussed. It rests on the assumption that the learner's competence (or 'capability' as Tarone prefers to call it) is heterogeneous, made up of a continuum of styles, ranging from the careful to the vernacular. Which style the learner calls upon is determined by the degree of attention paid to language form, which in turn is a reflection of social factors to do with participant factors. Tarone favours this paradigm. She emphasises that it enables interlanguage to be portrayed as systematic both because it is describable through a set of variable and categorical rules, and because it has internal-consistency.

This paradigm might afford the following explanation of the data:

> J possesses two rules for negative utterances. The 'no' + V rule (the least target-like) is a feature of his vernacular style. The 'don't' + V rule (the most target-like) is a feature of his more careful style. Thus in utterance (1), J is engaged in casual speech and is not attending to form, while in utterance (2), he is engaged in more formal speech and is attending to form.

But this explanation is again not convincing, as it does not correspond to the facts of the situation. As far as I could tell, J was attending to meaning in both utterances. In both cases his aim was to prevent other pupils looking at his word bingo card. Also the social parameters of the situation were the same for both utterances. It is difficult to account for the variability illustrated by these two utterances in terms of stylistic differences.

3. The dual competence paradigm

This is the third of Tarone's paradigms. It is the pardigm of Krashen's Monitor Model (Krashen, 1981a). Briefly, Krashen distinguishes 'acquisition' and 'learning', arguing that the latter is involved in language performance through the use of the Monitor, a device for editing utterances initiated by means of 'acquired' knowledge.

The data might be explained as follows in a dual competence paradigm:

> J has 'acquired' the 'no' + V negative rule, but he has 'learnt' the 'don't + V rule. Thus utterance (1) reflects 'acquired' knowledge and unmonitored performance, while utterance (2) reflects the application of 'learnt' knowledge through the Monitor.

This explanation fails for the same reason that the capability paradigm foundered. There was no indication that J was Monitoring in utterance (2). Krashen (1981a) lists three conditions for the use of the Monitor. The first is that there is sufficient time. But J produced utterance (2) in the same spontaneous manner as utterance (1). The second is that the learner is focused on form. But J was clearly focused on meaning. The third condition is that the learner 'knows' the rule (i.e. is able to state what it is). I am unable to say whether J had any metalingual awareness of the 'don't' + V rule, but I very much doubt it.

4. The multiple competence paradigm

This is the paradigm I wish to add to Tarone's three. It posits that the learner does not possess a single interlanguage system, but a number of separate and overlapping systems. It has been recently advanced by Selinker & Douglas (1985). They suggest that the process of second language acquisition involves the building of a number of interlanguage systems, which may share some rules, but which also contain some unique rules. The construction of these interlanguages is linked to the creation of 'discourse domains'. They define a discourse domain as 'a personally and internally created area of one's life that has importance'. As an example they refer to a Polish applied linguist, whose English they have observed to vary according to whether he is operating in the domain of 'being an international professor who lectures in English' or in the domain of 'telling stories about Poland in English after drinking several vodkas'. They argue that he has formed separate interlanguages, consisting of at least some unique rules and corresponding to the two domains.[5]

An explanation according to this paradigm may look like this:

J has two different domains. Relating to one of these domains, J has constructed an interlanguage with the negative rule, 'no' + V. Relating to the other domains J has constructed another interlanguage where the negative rule is 'don't' + V.

It is difficult to determine exactly what J's domain (or domains) was. Selinker & Douglas do not provide clear behavioural criteria for determining whether one or another 'internally created area' is being drawn on. However, given that both utterances were produced in the same situation, were addressed to the same kind of listener, and performed the same illocutionary meaning, the variation they represent cannot convincingly be attributed to J's having internalised separate domains. The domain — which might be described as that of 'playing games with one's peers in a classroom' — is constant.

What criteria can be used to determine whether language-learner variability is systematic or non-systematic? One possibility might be to use a statistical criterion, to say, for instance, that systematic variability can be held to exist only if each of the two or more forms in question is used above a specified frequency. It might, therefore, be rather arbitrarily argued that at this stage of J's development 'no' and 'don't negatives are in free variation because only one instance of a 'don't' negative out of a total of 18 negative utterances occurred. Implicit in the arguments I have advanced in discussing the four paradigms above are other criteria, which I would now like to make more explicit. I suggest that non-systematic variability can be held to exist when (1) the two forms occur in the same situational context, (2) the two forms help perform the same illocutionary meaning, (3) the two forms occur in the same linguistic context, (4) they occur in the same discourse context, and (5) there is, in the manner of their production, no evidence of any difference in the amount of attention paid to the form of the utterances. Using these criteria, J's use of 'no' and 'don't' negatives as manifest in the data that have been discussed can be said to be in free variation in his interlanguage.

Varibility and Acquisition

Strong claims have been made about the relationship between systematic horizontal variability and vertical development. I shall begin by reviewing these claims. I shall then argue that in order fully to understand the relationship between variability and acquisition, it is necessary also to consider non-systematic variability, as this provides an explanation of how the learner's vernacular style evolves in its own right.

According to the capability paradigm outlined by Tarone (1983), second language acquisition proceeds in one of two ways. New interlanguage forms are internalised spontaneously when the learner participates in natural communication. These forms enter interlanguage directly in the vernacular style. In addition, forms which initially enter the more permeable careful style as a result of conscious study spread across to the vernacular style. It is in this latter way, then, that variability is linked to acquisition. As Littlewood (1981b: 156) puts it, the careful style acts as a norm which 'will pull the learner's whole repertoire in the direction of a range of variation similar to that found in the native speaker's use of the language'. Or, as Widdowson (1975) puts it, the learner discovers how to act on his knowledge. What the learner can first do in situations that permit close attention to linguistic form, he will later be able to do in natural communication.

In this view of the relationship between variability and acquisition, second language learning is encompassed within a sociolinguistic theory that emphasises the regularity and predictability of language variation. It is significant, however, what this view does not explain. It does not explicate the process by which new forms are internalised spontaneously into interlanguage. It does not account for how the vernacular style develops in its own right. However, Tarone and Widdowson both recognise that acquisition cannot be explained in its entirety by the flow of knowledge from the careful to vernacular styles or from code to context rules.[6] How can we use variability theory to explain the self-contained growth of context rules? I want to argue that this can be done if due attention is paid to non-systematic variability in interlanguage.

At any single stage in the development of a second language, the learner's interlanguage is composed of competing rules. In some instances these rules will be related to situational or contextual factors. But in other instances the use of the competing rules will be arbitrary — they will be manifest in the same linguistic environment and they will be used to perform the same communicative function with the same social signification. In these instances the learner's grammar is independent of both situation and context. The data produced by J which were discussed in the previous section are an example of such non-systematic variability.

The claim that performance variability is not always systematic is not a new one. Bickerton (1975) has also disputed the 'contextual' theory of linguistic variation. He writes:

> While with the help of a little hindsight, a plausible contextual explanation can be given for many stylistic shifts, there are many more that operate in quite unpredictable ways. (Bickerton, 1975: 183)

Bickerton argues that the situation is only one factor among many. Linguistic variability is and never will be entirely predictable. Indeed, it cannot be, for if it were to be so, linguistic change would no longer be possible.

New linguistic forms emerge in all natural languages. They can arise quite spontaneously and do not need to be socially motivated. Bickerton, for instance, points out that the Martha's Vineyarders in Labov's (1963) famous study were not led to introduce new phonological features as a result of the influx of outsiders, but rather intensified and exploited a feature that was already available in their repertoires, in order to maintain their own identity. Natural language is unstable and so is subject to invasion by new forms. Interlanguage is a special type of natural language in that it is characterised by a very high level of instability. It is subject to constant bombardment by new linguistic forms, many of which are 'taken in', when, to begin with, they exist side by side with existing forms. It is possible that the guiding force in this process is not social but psycholinguistic, for example the operating principles proposed by Slobin (1973). It is likely that the nature of the linguistic forms to which the learner is exposed is also an important factor, as suggested by Wode (1980). The important point, however, is that initially these new forms are not absorbed into the system. Rather they float around as alternatives to forms which are already part of the system. Thus, when J acquired the 'don't' + V negative rule to add to the 'no' + V rule that was already part of his repertoire, he did so not because he needed an alternative negative rule, but because he was 'open' to input. Initially the new rule was in free variation with the older rule.

It is not efficient, however, to operate a system in which two forms have total identity of function. Who would build a computer with redundant input commands? The presence of two forms in free variation, therefore, is in conflict with the economy principle of linguistic organisation. This states that in ideal form a linguistic system will contain enough and no more distinctive features than are required to perform whatever functions the user wishes to communicate. Although the economy principle does not determine what gets into interlanguage, it does determine what takes place once it is in. The economy principle sees to it that the new forms are either integrated into the system by ensuring that they contribute to distinguishing meanings, or are eliminated. In Piagetian terms, the economy principle does not explain how a new feature is assimilated, but does explain how it is accommodated.

What evidence is thre for this view of interlanguage? Strong evidence can be found in research that examines form-function correlations in interlanguage. If, as has been claimed, acquisition begins with the incidental internalisation of new features; it can be expected that in the first place new forms will serve existing functions rather than the exact function(s) they serve in the target language. The learner will draw haphazardly on forms in free variation to perform whatever functions he needs to communicate. This is precisely what has been observed to take place. Wagner-Gough (1975), for instance, found that her subject, Homer, acquired the progressive morpheme early (like other learners), but she observed that it was used to refer to present, past, and future time. Wagner-Gough (1975: 158) comments:

> The progressive did not occur in semantic contrast with any other tense in his speech, and furthermore, it did not seem to emerge as a form whose adult function was clear to him.

Also when Wagner-Gough examined Homer's use of simple verb forms, she found that they were used for a range of functions more or less identical to the progressive. Homer used both forms in semantic free variation. Einstein *et al.* (1982) also examined the use of the progressive and simple verb forms, this time in a cross-sectional study of adult ESL learners. The results they obtained could be explained by hypothesising that the simple and progressive forms were first stored as one form/function and only later differentiated. They write:

> . . . ultimately what is being learned is how to use the appropriate form of the simple present or present progressive with an appropriate meaning. (Eisenstein *et al.*, 1982: 389)

Further evidence comes from Huebner (1981). He investigated the use of two formulas in the speech of a Thai learner of English. He found that the acquisition of the forms of the formulas preceded the acquisition of their functions. He suggests that the acquisition of function may be an evolutionary process involving the gradual narrowing of functional range. In general, second language acquisition research has focused on morphosyntactic development, so that there are few studies which have investigated the relationship between form and function either at a single point in time or over time. In those studies that have done so, however, there is clear evidence that, to begin with, the learner acquires forms which he uses to realise existing functions and only later does he sort out specific functions for them to perform.[7]

To summarise, second language acquisition can be seen to involve (1) the assimilation of new forms, and (2) the sorting out of form-function correlations. To explain the process of development we need explanations for both (1) and (2). Assimilation results from the learner being 'open' to forms occurring in the input and operating on these by means of one or more interlanguage strategies. This leads to the formation of an initial 'hypothesis' regarding the target language rule. Initial hypotheses may or may not correspond to standard target language rules. Iresspective of whether correspondence does or does not exist, new forms will continue to be assimilated until the learner is no longer 'open' to input. New intake is likely to result in two or more forms being used in free variation. This is where the economy principle comes in. Unless alternative forms can be justified by allocating them to different functions, redundant forms will be eliminated from the interlanguage. The learner will endeavour to maximise his linguistic resources by creating a system in which different forms serve different functions. The first stage consists of forms used in free variation, but subsequent stages involve the progressive sorting of forms into functional pigeon holes. It is likely that the first sorting will not establish form-function correlations that correspond to those of the target language. This may take several sortings and may never be entirely achieved. The learner will try to avoid the elimination of forms that have entered his interlanguage — he can scarce afford to lose valuable linguistic material — so he will be driven to resolve the profligacy of forms by creating his own system of relationships. This will be continually subject to revision as long as new forms are assimilated. Each new form creates further profligacy which can be resolved only by continued functional reorganisation or the elimination of redundant forms.[8]

It is easy, now, to see why two types of variability arise in interlanguage. Non-systematic variation occurs when new forms are assimilated but have not yet been integrated into the learner's form-function system. Systematic variation occurs when the new forms have been accommodated by a restructuring of the existing form-function system to give the new forms their own meanings to perform. Situational variability is one aspect of this process.

This complex process can be adequately represented only by what Huebner (1979) has called the 'dynamic paradigm'. But such a paradigm poses problems for the description of interlanguage. One solution is to adapt Gatbonton's (1978) diffusion model. This is based on Bickerton's (1973) proposal for a polylectal grammar in creole studies. Gatbonton developed the model of account for phonological development in interlanguage. The model consists of two phases: (1) an acquisition phase, in which a new form systematically spreads across the phonetic environment of an original form, and (2) a replacement phase, in which the original form is systematically eliminated from each phonetic environment until finally the new form has completely taken over. The adaptation I have in mind to make it fit form-function relations is in the replacement phase; instead of the new form taking over the function(s) of the original form (which can and does take place), the forms are systematically restricted to specific functions.

The diffusion model can reveal the vertical systematicity which occurs in the development of a sub-system such as negatives. Below is an example of its application to J's development of the two negative rules illustrated in the data discussed earlier. J began with a single negative rule ('no' + V) and used this to perform both commands and statements. Later he internalised a second negative rule ('don't' + V). First he used this with the earlier rule in commands, while continuing to use only 'no' + V in statements. Next he used both rules to perform both meanings. This completed the acquisition phase. The reorganis-ation phase begins when the use of forms in free variation gives way to their systematic variable use. It can be seen to commence when forms are distinguished in terms of situational, contextual, and discourse use. The clearest manifestation is when there is evidence of a learner preference for one form over another in the performance of a particular illocutionary meaning. Thus for J the reorganisation phase begins when he first eliminates the use of 'no' + V for commands while continuing to use both forms for statements. It continues when later 'don't' + V is restricted to commands and 'no' + V to statements. The process of acquiring negatives is, of course, not yet complete. Also the picture provided in Table 6.1 is idealised: before Time 5 was reached, other forms (e.g. aux + 'not') had begun to appear. But the table is an accurate reflection of a small section of the development of negation which J went through. It demonstrates the nature of the dynamic process in which form-function correlations are worked out.

TABLE 6.1 *The diffusion model applied to form-function relationships (based on Gatbonton, 1978)*

	Meaning	
	Commands	*Statements*
Acquisition phase		
Time 1	(1)	(1)
Time 2	(1), (2)	(1)
Time 3	(1), (2)	(1), (2)
Reorganisational phase		
Time 4	(2)	(1), (2)
Time 5	(2)	(1)

(1) = 'no' + V rule
(2) = 'don't' + V rule.

It should also be pointed out that in addition to the gradual sorting out of form-function relationships, the learner needs to extend steadily the linguistic environments in which new forms can be used. This process, which gives rise to the contextual variability discussed earlier, runs concurrently with functional development. It contributes to the remarkable horizontal variability that is so characteristic of interlanguage.

Summary and Conclusion

In this paper I have sought to explore in what way interlanguage can be described as a series of variable systems. I have argued that this is an accurate characterisation if due recognition is given to functional as well as formal development. I have also argued that variability is not just a concomitant of development, but one of the mechanisms by which it takes place.

Horizontal variability is of two basic types: systematic and non-systematic. Systematic variability can be described by relating the occurrence of specific formal features to either situational or contextual factors. However, it is the non-systematic variation that is the key to understanding the vertical dimension of interlanguage. Interlanguage involves at least three essential processes:

(1) the internalisation of new linguistic forms
(2) the progressive organisation of form-function relationships
(3) the elimination of redundant forms.

(1) is responsible for non-systematic variability, (2) and (3) for resolving the

problems which this creates. The existence of non-systematic variability therefore is a necessary condition for continual development. Whereas a theory of second language acquisition based on systematic learner variability (e.g. Tarone's capability model) talks of the 'spread' of forms from one style to another, a theory of second-language acquisition based on non-systematic variation helps to explain how the acquisition of the vernacular style takes place directly. This explanation is, of course, non specific to interlanguage: it also accounts for the creole continuum. The resolution of non-systematic variability underlies all language change.

Notes

1. The extent and the causes of variation in the sequence of development in second language acquisition are a matter of debate. Dulay, Burt & Krashen (1982) argue that there is a clearly defined 'natural' order. However, other researchers (e.g. Wode, 1980) have argued that variability in the order of development can take place as a result of first language transfer when there is a 'crucial similarity measure' operating between the interlanguage rule and the first language rule.
2. This ranking is offered as an illustration of the way in which situational and contextual factors may interact. It is an obvious simplification. For example, stylistic variability is treated as a dichotomy rather than a continuum, while it is highly likely that use of the third person singular -s will be influenced by a number of linguistic environments, not just the one considered here.
3. It is, of course, not easy to be sure that these forms are in free variation. I may have missed the true symstematicity that is there. However, I am conscious that other variants (e.g. long /ɑː/ and short /æ/ in words like 'path') do serve stylistic functions. If my intuition is to be trusted, therefore, these variants are in free variation.
4. The longitudinal study was carried out in the classroom. All the utterances occurred in classroom interaction. For the purpose of this analysis only the learner's spontaneous speech was considered. However, there were no negative utterances in the context of classroom exercises during the first month. Negatives were not taught until much later.
5. The example of the vodka-drinking professor was given in an earlier version of the paper by Selinker & Douglas that was published in *Applied Linguistics* 6, 2.
6. Code rules characterise what the learner *knows*; they correspond to what the learner recognises as the correct norm. Context rules characterise what the learner *does*; they are called upon when the learner needs to use his knowledge for some communicative effect.
7. Sampson (1982) offers a rather different account of what she calls 'a dialectal model of form and function'. She argues that when a learner internalises a form, he acquires it together with the function which it performed in the situation in which it occurred. Thus

   The learner may be expected to use a given form in a given function because the meaning of the form is associated with the particular function (Sampson, 1982: 16).

Sampson continues to argue that the learner is not likely to generalise the form to a new function. Thus for Sampson, acquisition is the process of learning which other functions a form that is acquired initially as a specific form-function correlation is connected with. This is rather different position from the one I am advocating. I am claiming that the learner rapidly extends a new form to cover a range of functions and that acquisition is the process of discovering which of these functions can and cannot be served by it. Sampson does not cite any studies which support her position. The few studies which have investigated form-function relationships seem to be more compatible with the position I have advanced.

8. The elimination of redundant forms must take place if the learner is eventually to achieve native speaker competence. This is so because at least some of the forms that are acquired are not just used in a different functional distribution from the target language, but are formally different from the target language (e.g. past tense forms like 'costed'). Presumably the learner eliminates such forms (rather than trying to exploit them functionally) because subsequent input demonstrates that they are not present in the target language.

7. Interlanguage Variability in Narrative Discourse: Style Shifting in the Use of the Past Tense

There is now evidence to show that second language (L2) learners perform variably on different tasks. Dickerson (1975) showed that Japanese learners of English varied in their use of /z/ according to whether they were performing in free speech, dialogue reading, or word list reading. That is, the learners were more likely to produce /z/ or /z/-like variants on some tasks than on others. Similar results in the phonological production of L2 learners have been provided by other studies (e.g. Dickerson & Dickerson, 1977; Schmidt, 1977). These studies have been reviewed by Tarone (1983).

There have, however, been few studies of morphological or syntactic variability in L2 performance.[1] Godfrey (1980) examined the use of tense markers by Spanish and Japanese learners of English of different proficiency levels on a story-telling task. Godfrey found that the learners varied in their use of tense markers according to their L1 background, the linguistic context (i.e. whether the linguistic context was an 'easy' or a 'difficult' one), the specific verb tokens used, the discourse context (e.g. whether the discourse context constituted an episode boundary), and the learners' level of proficiency. This study shows that even within a single discourse type there is considerable variability in L2 performance. However, the study did not consider style shifting across tasks. Tarone (1985) examined style-shifting in the use of three grammatical morphemes (third person singular present tense verb -s, the article, and the noun plural -s) and one grammatical structure (direct object pronouns). She used three tasks — a written grammar test, an oral interview, and oral narrative[2] — hypothesising that these would require different degrees of attention to form and that accuracy levels in obligatory contexts for the forms under consideration would reflect attention levels in a consistent way. She found that there was variability according to task and that, with the exception of noun plural -s, this variability was evidenced in more than two styles (i.e. there was a different accuracy level on each task).

Taken together, Godfrey's and Tarone's studies suggest that variability is manifest in both L2 morphology and L2 syntax. There is a need, however, for further studies in these areas.

Tarone's study also addressed the question of whether style shifting in morphology and syntax operates in a consistent direction for all linguistic forms, as seems to be the case in L2 phonology.[3] She found that the third person singular decreased in accuracy from the grammar test to the oral narrative, but that the article and direct object pronoun increased in accuracy. In other words, she provides evidence for suggesting that style shifting is not constant where grammatical features are concerned. Tarone attempted to explain this finding by suggesting that the narrative task (hypothesised to require the least attention to form) in fact led the learners to attend to discourse cohesiveness to a greater extent than the other two taks, and that the article and object pronouns (but not the third person singular) act as important markers of discourse cohesion.

The studies of style shifting referred to above have been conducted using the theoretical and methodological framework of Labov (1970). Labov argues that because variability in language use is systematic, it should be treated in terms of competence rather than performance. Language users have the capacity to utilise variable means in accordance with their perception of appropriate language behaviour in different situational contexts. He claims that in addition to categorial rules the grammar of a native speaker contains variable rules that describe which of one or more linguistic forms is used in a given context. Tarone (1983) draws on Labov's work to propose that L2 learners possess a capability continuum comprised of a range of styles from the careful to the vernacular. Like Labov, she argues that the regularities of the learner's variable use of interlanguage rules represent an abstract linguistic system rather than just slips of the tongue or other performance phenomena. Thus, both the native speaker and the L2 learner possess a variable *competence*, the difference being that the L2 learner's system is characterised by the presence of more variable rules than the native speaker's system because interlanguage is more permeable to invasion by new forms. Which variant the learner or the native speaker uses is a product of the degree to which attention is focused on form. Linguistic features that manifest themselves in the learner's careful style (associated with close attention to form) will not necessarily be evident or not evident with the same frequency in the vernacular style (associated with attention to meaning rather than form).[4]

A rather similar theoretical framework to Tarone's is that proposed by Ochs (1979). She makes a distinction between unplanned and planned discourse. The former is discourse that lacks forethought and organisational preparation. The latter is discourse that has been thought out and organised prior to expression. The concept of discourse planning applies to both the overall structure of discourse (i.e. the sequence of speech acts) and to the lexico-grammatical resources used to express individual acts. Because there are varying levels of planning, planned and unplanned discourse are seen as poles on a continuum. Ochs argues that for unplanned discourse, speakers rely more on morphosyntactic structures acquired early on, whereas for planned discourse, they make greater use of structures that emerge later. Thus, formal differences can be expected depending on the kind of discourse that is produced. The planned/unplanned distinction is clearly much the same as the careful/vernacular distinction discussed by Labov and Tarone. In both cases the language user/learner is credited with a variable system which he or she draws on differently according to the degree of attention to form (but see note 4).

This view of interlanguage as a variable system raises an important question about L2 acquisition research. This concerns the claims that acquisition follows a natural order of development (Dulay & Burt, 1974b; Krashen, 1981a). The natural order has been investigated with the implicit understanding that the learner possesses a homogeneous rather than a variable competence. That is, the learner is credited with a knowledge of L2 rules which is taken to underlie all language use. Crediting the learner with a variable interlanguage system leads to two possibilities regarding the natural order hypothesis: (1) the same natural order will be reflected in all styles and (2) different styles will manifest different natural orders. (1) is possible if the same interlanguage rules occur in all styles and if the accuracy order of these rules remains the same in all styles. In such cases, the accuracy levels of linguistic features may vary from one style to another, but the rank order of these features remains constant across styles (see Table 7.1).

TABLE 7.1 *Accuracy levels of linguistic features across styles*

Linguistic features	Style A		Style B	
	Accuracy level	*Rank order*	*Accuracy level*	*Rank order*
a	20%	1	40%	1
b	30%	2	60%	2
c	35%	3	70%	3

(2) is possible if it is found that different rules occur in different styles (i.e. there are categorical differences) or if it is found that different styles produce different accuracy orders. The available evidence suggests that there are categorical differences across styles (see Tarone, 1985) and also that there are

different accuracy orders. Krashen (1981a), for instance, allows for different accuracy orders according to whether the learner is monitoring using learned knowledge. However, Krashen's theory predicts that there will be only two accuracy orders, one resulting from the use of acquired knowledge and the other from the use of learned knowledge. According to variability theory, there are potentially as many accuracy orders as there are styles. There is clearly a need to reconsider the claims regarding a natural order in the light of variability theory. This will involve establishing whether accuracy orders do change according to style, and if this proves to be the case, considering which of the orders obtained is to be considered primary where L2 acquisition is concerned or whether the notion of natural order is vacuous.

There is a further issue raised by the methodology that has been used to investigate style shifting. Research based on the Labov/Tarone framework has made use of tasks designed to elicit differing levels of attention to form. These have involved very distinct types of language use (e.g. dialogue versus narrative versus grammar tests). But as Tarone's stdy shows, this raises problems of comparability of performance on at least some structures, as the type of discourse can influence which forms are focused on (see comments above about the use of articles and direct object pronouns in oral narrative). Ochs' framework suggests that there is no need to resort to tasks leading to such different types of language use, as a single discourse type can reflect varying degrees of planning. Thus, style shifting will be apparent in a single discourse type. Ideally, if we wish to investigate the L2 learner's variable competence, we need to establish what variability is the product of engaging in different types of language use (which could be referred to as *text type variability*) and what variability is the product of fluctuations in attention to form (which might be called *planning variability*).[5]

The research reported in this article is concerned with planning variability in one type of language use: narrative discourse. It has been designed to address the various issues discussed above. The following hypotheses are tested:

(1) L2 learners manifest different levels of accuracy in interlanguage morphology in narrative discourse according to the amount of time available for discourse planning.

(2) When the time available for planning narrative discourse varies, L2 learners display both categorical and variable regularities in interlanguage morphology. That is, some learners will manifest zero use of specific morphological forms in one style and variable use in a second style, whereas other learners will manifest variable use in both styles but with different accuracy levels.

(3) Learners will display consistently higher accuracy levels in interlanguage morphology in planned narrative discourse than in unplanned narrative discourse. That is, the direction of style shifting corresponds to the amount of planning time available.
(4) Accuracy orders for interlanguage morphology in L2 learners' narrative discourse will differ according to the amount of planning time available. More than two accuracy orders will be observed.

The Study

Subjects

A total of 17 subjects participated in this study: 4 male and 13 female. They were all enrolled in a part-time EFL class at Ealing College of Higher Education, where they received six hours of instruction per week. All students enrolling for part-time classes are interviewed individually by members of the EFL department and assigned to an appropriate class according to their proficiency level. Altogether there are six levels, with Level 1 corresponding to complete beginners and Level 6 to Cambridge Proficiency. The subjects in this study were all in Level 2, which can be characterised as post-beginner or early intermediate. They had been studying English (at Ealing and elsewhere) for different lengths of time, the shortest being two weeks and the longest five years. At the time of data collection they had been at Ealing for two weeks.

The subjects differed on a number of dimensions. They were of mixed language backgrounds: German, French, Spanish, Portuguese, Polish, Farsi, Japanese, and Korean. They also differed in their abilities to write English; some were fluent and fairly accurate writers, whereas others had substantial problems with spelling and punctuation. It should be noted that all the subjects had experienced some contact with English outside the classroom, many staying with English families.

Structures

The structures chosen for this study all belonged to a single subsystem of English grammar: past tense verbs. The decision to select structures from a single subsystem was made to avoid the problems of comparing performance across totally unrelated structures in a cross-sectional study (see Hatch (1983) for a discussion of these problems).[6] The structures were:

(1) *Regular past tense form.* The regular past tense form consists of the addition of *-ed*, *-d*, or *-t* to the simple form of the verb in writing. In speech it consists of the addition of /id/, or /t/ to the simple form.
(2) *Irregular past tense form.* The irregular past tense form involves some change in the simple form of the verb other than the addition of regular past tense markers. Included in this category are also the past tense forms of auxiliary verbs (e.g. 'did', 'had', 'would').
(3) *Copula past tense form.* The copula past tense form consists of 'was' or 'were'. It occurs both as a main verb and as an auxiliary verb in the construction of the past progressive tense.

Tasks

The 17 subjects performed three tasks all involving story telling. These were:
(1) *Written narrative.* In order to elicit written narratives, we asked the subjects to write a story based on a picture composition from Heaton (1975). This consisted of six pictured about a theft. Two robbers (a man and a boy) stole a basket from an Indian man at an airport. They escaped in a car. When they later opened the basket they found it contained a snake.
(2) *Oral narrative 1.* After writing the written narrative the subjects recorded an oral version of the same story in a language laboratory.
(3) *Oral narrative 2.* The subjects were given another picture composition also from Heaton and were asked to record an oral version of the story in the language laboratory. This story was about a boy who got off a bus late one evening and dropped one of the packages he was carrying. A stranger picked up the package and pursued the boy across a park. The boy was frightened and tried to run away. Eventually the man caught up with him and gave him the package.

Procedure

The subjects were first asked to complete a short questionnaire giving information about the L1, how long they had been studying English, and how long they had been in England. They were then provided with paper and asked to write a story based on the first picture composition. To encourage the use of past tense forms, we asked them to begin with 'One day . . .'. Some assistance was given with spelling, punctuation, and vocabulary. However, any verbs written on the blackboard were always in the simple form (i.e. no past tense form was provided). Their written stories were collected after one hour.

For the second task, the subjects were taken to a language laboratory and asked to record an oral version of the story. They were allowed to record the story twice, but only the second attempt was transcribed. For this task, the subjects kept their copies of the picture composition. They were asked to begin their stories with 'One day . . .'.

The third task was also recorded in the language laboratory. The subjects were given the second picture composition and were allowed to look at it for two minutes. They were then asked to record an oral version of the story without further preparation. They recorded the story only once, once again beginning with 'One day . . .'.

The rationale behind the tasks and the procedure followed was that there would be different opportunities for planning narrative discourse. It was hypothesised that Task 1 would provide the greatest opportunity for planning, given that the subjects had ample time to both determine the content of the story and to search through their lexico-grammatical repertoires. Task 2 would provide less opportunity for planning, as the requirements of oral performance restrict the time available for locating correct and appropriate lexico-grammatical means. Task 3 would be more difficult than Task 2 because the subjects needed to determine the content of the story and had little or no opportunity to practice the linguistic means of expression.

Thus, it was anticipated that the subjects would be able to attend to the form of past tense verbs most carefully in the written task, less carefully in Task 2 (the first of the oral tasks), and least carefully in Task 3 (the second of the oral tasks). However, it is not claimed that these tasks tap performance at the poles of the stylistic continuum. The written task was not intended to elicit the careful style and the second oral task was not intended to elicit the vernacular style. It was anticipated that the tasks would elicit performance representative of different points on the continuum.

Tense Continuity in Narrative Discourse

As Frawley & Lantolf (1985) observe, it is well known that events in narrative discourse are related in the historical present by native speakers. That is, past tense usage is not obligatory in this type of discourse. It is also recognised that when beginning L2 learners engage in narrative discourse they do not typically make use of tense distinctions, preferring other devices (e.g. adverbials in conjunction with general discourse principles) to realise temporal relationships between events (see Perdue, 1984: 197–200).

These observations are potentially problematic for a study seeking to investigate the use of past tense forms in narrative discourse. However, as Godfrey (1980) points out, once a particular tense continuity is established, it must be maintained. That is, if a speaker elects to use past tense to narrate events at the beginning of a story, there is an obligation to continue in this tense sequence unless the sequence of events is interrupted in some way (e.g. by providing background information). It was for this reason that the subjects of this study were asked to begin each narrative with 'One day . . .', which, it was hoped, would trigger the initial use of past tense forms. As the analysis was to be passed on the notion of *obligatory occasions* (see below), it was essential to establish whether the subjects did indeed elect to use past tense continuity. An inspection of the opening utterances in each subject's stories revealed that the past tense continuity was chosen by 16 out of 17 subjects (the exception being Subject 4 — see Appendix).[7] Therefore, an analysis based on obligatory occasions would seem in order.

Analysis

The length of the written stories varied from a half to one and a half sides of A4 paper. Approximately one hour of oral data for each story was collected. These oral data were transcribed by the researcher in normal orthography (except for highly deviant pronunciations, which were transcribed phonetically). Any verb which could not be clearly transcribed was excluded from the analysis. Obligatory contexts for the three past tense forms were then established using the procedure described by Brown (1973). Each verb was scored as correct or deviant in contexts requiring the use of the past tense. Repetitions of any verb (common in the oral tasks, particularly in Task 3) were not counted. However, in cases where the first attempt was deviant and the second attempt correct, both attempts were included in the scoring, that is, both unmonitored and monitored forms were scored. No allowance was made for a verb marked for past tense but marked incorrectly (e.g. 'losed').

Results

Table 7.2 shows the percentage of correct forms for past regular, past irregular, and past copula on each of the three tasks. It provides an overview of the results obtained. It can be seen that where regular past tense verbs are concerned, there is a decrease in accuracy from Task to Task 3. For the irregular past tense, accuracy levels remained more or less constant across the three tasks. For the past copula, the accuracy levels on Tasks 1 and 2 were almost identical, but on Task 3 they were markedly lower. A detailed discussion of the results follows, using χ^2 (incorporating Yates correction) to measure the significance of the difference in proportions of correct and deviant past tense forms in the three tasks.

TABLE 7.2   *Overview of results (% correct)*

	Regular past	Irregular past	Past copula	Total
Task 1	77	60	76	70
Task 2	57	57	75	62
Task 3	43	55	60	54

The raw scores for each subject on each of the three past tense forms investigated in the three tasks are given in the Appendix. Table 7.3 gives the overall frequencies of correct and deviant past tense forms on the three past tense forms taken together. It provides a general indication of performance in the use of the past tense in the three tasks. The difference in frequencies of correct and deviant forms between Task 1 and Task 2 is significant at the 0.05 level ($\chi^2 = 4.5$). The difference between Task 2 and Task 3 is also significant at the 0.05 level ($\chi^2 = 4.0$), whereas the difference in frequencies between Task 1 and Task 3 is significant at the 0.001 level ($\chi^2 = 16.6$). Accuracy in the use of past tense forms decreased from Task 1 to Task 3, with Task 2 intermediate.

TABLE 7.3   *Overall frequencies of correct and deviant past tense forms*

	Task 1	Task 2	Task 3
Correct	204	188	163
Deviant	88	117	141

Table 7.4 gives the results for regular verbs. A significant difference in the observed frequencies of Task 1 and Task 2 occurs ($\chi^2 = 10.0; p > 0.01$) and also between Task 1 and Task 3 ($\chi^2 = 21.6; p > 0.001$). However, the difference in frequencies between Task 2 and Task 3 failed to reach significance ($\chi^2 > 3.29; p > 0.10$). Accuracy in the use of regular verbs decreased from Task 1 to Task 3, with Task 2 again intermediate.

TABLE 7.4   *Correct and deviant forms in regular past*

	Correct			Deviant		
	Total	Mean	SD	Total	Mean	SD
Task 1	82	4.82	2.01	24	1.44	0.80
Task 2	58	3.41	1.28	44	2.59	0.85
Task 3	29	1.71	0.78	39	2.29	0.81

Whereas regular past tense forms decreased in accuracy from Task 1 to Task 3, irregular verbs maintained a more or less constant level of accuracy across tasks (see Table 7.5). There were no significant differences in accuracy levels from one task to another.

TABLE 7.5   *Correct and deviant forms in irregular past*

		Correct			Deviant	
	Total	Mean	SD	Total	Mean	SD
Task 1	68	4.00	1.52	46	2.71	1.74
Task 2	69	4.06	0.95	53	3.21	2.20
Task 3	83	4.88	1.56	68	4.00	1.25

Accuracy scores for the past copula were almost identical for Tasks 1 and 2, but there was a significant difference between Tasks 2 and 3 ($\chi^2 = 4.36$; $p > 0.05$) and also between Task 1 and Task 3 ($\chi^2 = 4.51$; $p > 0.05$). The frequencies are given in Table 7.6.

TABLE 7.6   *Correct and deviant forms in past copula*

		Correct			Deviant	
	Total	Mean	SD	Total	Mean	SD
Task 1	54	3.18	1.23	17	1.00	0.41
Task 2	61	3.59	1.22	20	1.18	0.50
Task 3	51	3.00	1.22	34	2.00	1.33

The accuracy orders for the three past tense forms varied according to task (see Table 7.7). The principal cause of the differences lay in the marked decrease in accuracy scores for regular verbs across tasks.[8] Thus, whereas regular verbs had the highest accuracy score in Task 1, in Task 2 they scored lower than the copula and about the same as irregular verbs, and in Task 3 they scored lowest of all three past tense forms by a wide margin.

TABLE 7.7   *Accuracy orders for three past tense forms in the three tasks*

Rank	Task 1	Task 2	Task 3
1	Regular Pa	Cop Pa	⎧ Cop Pa
2	Cop Pa	⎰ Regular Pa	⎨ Irregular Pa
3	Irregular Pa	⎱ Irregular Pa	Regular Pa

Bracketed structures indicate that the difference in overall scores for these structures was less than 1% for the group as a whole.

Discussion

This study set out to examine four hypotheses about interlanguage variability. Each of these hypotheses is now discussed in the light of the results reported above.

Hypothesis 1

The results of this experiment are consistent with the hypothesis that past tense forms occur as a product of the difference in opportunities to plan narrative discourse. However, when the three past tense morphemes are examined separately, it is clear that style shifting is not present to the same extent. It is most clearly evident in regular past tense forms, less so in the past copula, and hardly at all in irregular past tense forms.

What explanation can be given for these findings? One possible explanation of the extensive style shifting in regular past forms is a linguistic one. Recall that the subjects in this study used the regular past tense most accurately when they had time to plan (i.e. in Task 1). Because this structure is constructed according to a regular and relatively simple rule, learners are able to call on the rule when they are attending to form. Krashen (1982: 97) has argued that conscious monitoring can only take place with rules that are easily learned; these are 'rules that are easiest to describe and remember'. Rules that require only the addition of a bound morpheme, such as the regular past, are considered easy to learn. It can be hypothesised that the first verb structure learners acquire is the simple form, which is unmarked in comparision to the regular past form. When learners have little opportunity to plan their discourse, they are likely to resort to the unmarked form; when they have more planning time, they can apply the rule for regular past. Most of the errors in obligatory contexts requiring the regular past in Tasks 2 and 3 did indeed consist of the substitution of the simple form.

As an illustration of how the subjects substituted simple forms for past tense forms, consider the following examples from Subject 6 (see Appendix), example 1 from Task 1 (planned) and example 2 from Task 2 (less planned):

(1) A policeman who was there whistled. But it was too late. The thief and his young collaborator had taken a car and had disappeared on the traffic. They stopped on a forest but they had haven a big surprise when they opened the case. It contained a big snake and they knew nothing.
(2) The policeman was in this corner whistle but it was too late. The two thieves escape with the big suitcase, took their car and (pause) went in the

traffic. They passed near a zoo and stop in a forest. There they had a big surprise. The basket contain a snake.

Interestingly, three of the simple forms in (2) (i.e. 'whistle', 'stop', and 'contain') occur in the past tense in (1). These instances of simple forms in Task 2 occur in the second half of the narrative. No instances of simple forms occur in the first half. It is as if this subject was unable to sustain the effort of controlling the regular past rule throughout.

In contrast, the irregular past tense cannot be considered an easy rule. It is possible that past tense forms have to be learned as separate tokens, each past tense form constituting a distinct lexical item in the learner's interlanguage. It should be noted that many past tense forms occur with high frequency in the input and are also used frequently (e.g. 'said', 'went', 'stood', 'saw', 'took'). Such forms are therefore highly practiced. As a result, these forms may not be very sensitive to planning level and therefore do not style shift very much. Although errors consisting of the overgeneralisation of the regular past (e.g. 'losed') and of the substitution of the simple form did arise, they were rare and tended to occur only with less common verbs. It might be hypothesised that style shifting in the irregular past will occur to a greater extent (a) with learners who are just beginning to acquire these forms (the learners in this study were at the intermediate level rather than at the beginning level), and (b) with less common irregular verbs. In such cases, overgeneralisation of the regular form and substitution of the simple form are likely variants.

There is style shifting with the past copula, but this is most evident between Tasks 2 and 3. It will be recalled that Task 3 required the subjects to perform without opportunity to plan either the content or the means of expression, whereas Task 2 did not require the content to be planned. Little style shifting occurred between Tasks 1 and 2, where the difference lay in the time available to search lexico-grammatical resources. The important factor in the use of past copula, then, may be the extent to which the learner is familiar with the content of his or her message. Evidence for this interpretation can be found in the type of errors that occurred. In the majority of cases these involved copula deletion. For example, subject 12 produced these utterances in Task 3[9]:

Little boy coming out in the XXX.[10]
The child very upset and he stop.
The child crying.

When L2 learners are confronted with processing problems of the kind experienced in Task 3, it may be that they resort to semantic simplification (Ellis, 1984a). That is, they reduce the number of propositional elements they encode in utterances. Omission of the copula may take place because the copula is not a major meaning–bearing element. In contrast, main verb deletion hardly ever occurred.

It is interesting to compare the results of this study with those of Hulstijn & Hulstijn (1984). The latter investigated the effects of two variables — pressure of time and focus of attention on grammar (as opposed to content) — on the accuracy levels obtained by 32 adult learners of L2 Dutch in the performance of two word-order rules. They found that the presence or absence of time pressure had no significant effect on accuracy levels, but that focusing on grammar did. On the face of it, these results appear to contradict the results obtained in this study, which has examined planning variability by comparing performance on tasks that vary in the amount of time available to the subjects. However, Hulstijn & Hulstijn do report that the greatest difference in their study was between performance that was focused on content and was subject to time pressure on the one hand and performance that was focused on grammar and was not subject to time pressure on the other. The difference between these two conditions may amount to the same as the difference between this study's Task 3 condition (time pressure plus probable focus on content) and Task 1 condition (no time pressure plus probable focus on form). Interpreted in this way, the results of this study can be seen as corroborative of those of Hulstijn & Hulstijn (1984).

To summarise, there is evidence to support hypothesis 1; style shifting occurs on past tense forms. However, the degree of style shifting appears to vary as a product of the nature of the linguistic form (with regular and easily learned forms style shifting more than irregular forms that are difficult to learn) and as a product of the kind of processing demands placed on the learner (with style shifting in the past copula dependent on whether the learner has the opportunity to plan the content of his or her message). Thus, not all linguistic forms style shift, and those that do style shift do so under different conditions of use.

Hypothesis 2

When the accuracy scores for individual learners on the three past forms are examined, there is clear evidence of both variable and categorical regularities. For example, as Subject 6 moved from Task 3 to Task 2, he produced the regular past more variably; and as he moved from Task 2 to Task 3, absence of the regular past became categorical. On Task 1, performance was categorically correct; on Task 2 it was variable; and on Task 3, it was categorically incorrect (use of the simple form being the variant) (see

Table 7.8). This subject's use of the regular past is an almost perfect example of style shifting. One other learner showed an almost identical pattern of style shifting on the past regular (Subject 11), whereas many others showed a shift from categorical accuracy on Task 1 to variable accuracy on the other two tasks. As might be expected, however, such regular style shifting was less evident on the past irregular. Performance on the copula reveals cases of variable regularity giving way to the categorical use of variant forms (in particular zero copula), but more commonly of increased variability as the learner moves from Task 2 to Task 3.

TABLE 7.8 *Variable and categorical regularities across three tasks in one learner's performance*

	Task 1	Task 2	Task 3
Past regular	100%	50%	0%

Hypothesis 3

The results of the study are consistent with the claim that the amount of planning time available to the learner has a systematic effect on accuracy levels. The direction of style shifting for all three past tense forms remained consistent with the highest accuracy levels apparent on Task 1, where the learners had ample time to plan both the content of their narratives and to locate lexico-grammatical resources, and the lowest accuracy levels apparent on Task 3, where learners were acquired to plan both content and expression more spontaneously. Intermediate accuracy levels were found on Task 2, where the narrative content was familiar but constraints were placed on the time available for expression. Thus, style shifting correlates with the opportunity for discourse planning.

The consistency of the direction of style shifting found in this study is in contrast to Tarone's (1985) findings. However, as has already been pointed out, Tarone's tasks involved a variety of discourse styles, and the inconsistency in the observed style shifting of different structures may have been the result of learners attending to discourse cohesiveness on some structures and not on others. In this study, style shifting was examined in a single discourse style (oral narrative), so the discourse factor was controlled for. The results suggest that *planning variability* may be consistent across structures; Tarone's results suggest that *text type variability* can be reflected in style shifting that follows opposite directions according to the discourse functions of different structures.

Hypothesis 4

The final hypothesis predicted that different styles would produce different accuracy orders for the same linguistic features. The results support this hypothesis (see Table 7.7). The kind of task used to collect data determines the accuracy order obtained. As three different orders arose, corresponding to the three tasks, the results do not appear to support the predictions of Krashen's Monitor Model, which states that only two orders will emerge according to whether acquired or learned knowledge has been used. Instead, the results confirm the predictions of a variable competence theory (Ellis, 1984a): accuracy orders vary according to style, and as many orders as styles are possible.

It is unfortunately not possible to directly compare the orders obtained for the three past tense forms in this study with the orders for the same forms reported by different morpheme studies, as none of these studies investigated past copula. It can be noted, however, that there is little agreement in the order of past regular and past irregular in the morpheme studies. Dulay & Burt (1974b), using spoken data elicited by the *Bilingual Syntax Measure*, place past regular before past irregular, as does Larsen-Freeman (1976), using both spoken and written data.[11] However, Hakuta (1974) gives the opposite order, whereas Rosansky (1976) brackets them as acquired at the same time. The present study found similar differences, but according to task. Thus, in the planned writing task, the regular past is more accurate than the irregular past (Dulay & Burt's and Larsen-Freeman's order); in the planned oral task, the accuracy scores were almost identical (Rosansky's order); and in the unplanned oral task, the irregular form was more accurate than the regular (Hakuta's order).

What does this suggest about the so-called natural order so widely discussed in L2 acquisition literature? This study casts doubt on whether there is any such thing as a natural order for all styles, at least where past verb forms are concerned. If learners are credited with a variable rule system which produces different accuracy levels according to which variant is employed, there seems to be no basis for investigating a natural order. One way out might be to argue, that the natural order is apparent only in the vernacular style. This style can be considered primary in that it reflects informal language use and is the most systematic. But the crucial point is that we can no longer go on talking about a natural order as a universal and stable phenomenon. Orders are a reflection of styles. If we want to maintain the notion of an acquisitional order, we would do well to stop basing this on accuracy orders (which simply reflect the learner's variable competence) or on some notional criterion level (which will not produce a consistent order, because whether learners attain the chosen level will again depend on the style). Instead, we should do as Bickerton (1981) recommends and treat the first occasion a structure appears as the point of acquisition. This, of course, would mean that cross-sectional studies could no longer be used to address the question of acquisition order.

Summary and Conclusion

This paper has considered L2 planning variability by investigating style shifting in a set of morphological structures in a single discourse type (narrative discourse). Planning variability can be distinguished from text type variability, which arises when L2 learners are asked to produce different types of discourse. The results of this study show that planning variability can be systematic and consistent where past tense forms are concerned. That is, for the L2 learners investigated, the influence of the target language seems to be most apparent in planned discourse where there is the opportunity to attend to form.

Planning variability is seen as a feature of the learner's competence, not just of his or her performance. At any one stage of development, the learner possesses two or more rules for at least some structures and calls on these differently according to whether the discourse is planned or unplanned. The influence of the target language variant is most apparent in planned discourse and least apparent in unplanned discourse. However, not all structures in the learner's interlanguage manifest style shifting or manifest it to the same degree. Some structures will have been thoroughly acquired in the sense that they are categorical in all styles. Other structures will display style shifting; in the case of regular and easily learned forms this may be substantial, but in the case of irregular forms, which are difficult to learn, it may be negligible. Because the learner's competence is variable in at least some rules, different accuracy orders will occur in different styles. For this reason it makes little sense to equate accuracy orders with acquisition orders, and little sense to talk of a single natural order.

This study has examined style shifting in a small population of low-intermediate L2 learners. The results obtained cannot be generalised to other populations of L2 learners. We need further studies carefully designed to isolate the planning variable — the focus of this study — from other potentially confounding variables such as topic, familiarity with topic, first language background, and level of proficiency. We also need to establish the extent to which planning variability arises in other types of discourse (e.g. conversation). Finally, future studies should obtain baseline information concerning style shifting by native speakers.

This study has, however, indicated the importance of planning time in accounting for variability in L2 performance. It has suggested a number of important questions which require investigation:

(1) *In what ways is style shifting affected by linguistic factors having to do with the nature of different grammatical rules?*
     One way in which this question might be tackled is to examine how patterns of style shifting change on marked and unmarked linguistic forms.[12] It might be hypothesised that style shifting is more pronounced on marked linguistic forms.

(2) *Are style shifting patterns maintained at different developmental stages? That is, are they consistent from one developmental stage to the next, reflecting, for example, the increased influence of the target language?*
     Most of the available research into style shifting has been cross-sectional. Therefore, we do not know very much about the developmental effects. Kellerman (1985) has noted that some structures are subject to a U-shaped pattern of development: an initial high accuracy level is superseded by a low level before the accuracy level once again rises. It would be interesting to explore U-shaped behaviour in terms of style shifting at different developmental stages.

(3) *What is the relationship between planning variability and text type variability?*
     One way to examine this might be to investigate performance on the same structure both within a single discourse type, where planning opportunities are varied, and across discourse types, where factors such as discourse cohesiveness do and do not operate.

(4) *How does style shifting operate in interlanguage lexis?*
     Just as some phonological and grammatical forms are more prevalent in one style than in another, so too may lexical forms be. In this study, the effects of planning time on the use of past tense forms led to marked differences in the frequencies with which the three forms were used in different tasks. For instance, in Task 1 irregular verbs constituted 17.2% of total past verbs; in Task 3, 37.2%. One explanation is that the irregular verbs used constituted a lexical core, which is drawn on more extensively when planning pressures arise. But we need to explore much more thoroughly what lexical style shifting consists of to complement what we are beginning to find out about phonological and grammatical variability.

(5) *What differences arise in the patterns of style shifting manifested in native speaker and non-native speaker discourse?*
     Ochs (1979) noted that native speakers may resort to structures acquired early on in unplanned discourse. Thus, it should not be taken for granted that native speakers perform at a 100% criterion level in all

structures in all types of discourse. We need to investigate to what extent non-native English speakers achieve similar patterns of performance as native speakers when faced with the same planning constraints.

The few studies of interlanguage variability which have taken place to date indicate that it is a highly complex phenomenon, particularly where grammatical structures are concerned. We need to develop our understanding of this complexity. The study of interlanguage variability is of central importance for describing and explaining the process of L2 acquisition.

Notes

1. Studies of L2 variability have focused on phonology rather than on syntax or morphology (see, for instance, Beebe, 1980b; Sato, 1984). In addition to the studies of morphological and syntactic variability mentioned above, the reader might also consult Eisenstein *et al.* (1982); Hulstijn & Hulstijn (1984); Hyltenstam (1984).
   Although there have been few studies of grammatical variability in interlanguage, studies of L2 acquisition (in particular longitudinal studies) have frequently drawn attention to variability phenomena. For example, Cancino *et al.* (1978: 209) write:
   > We did, however, think that perhaps traditional grammatical descriptions in the form of rules could be made of such linguistic subsystems as negative, interrogative or auxiliary. Our attempts to write rules for the negative proved fruitless. The constant development and concomitant variation in our subjects' speech at any one point made the task impossible.
2. Tarone set out to examine six structures, but dropped two of these (subject pronouns and feminine gender) from the analysis because the data for these structures proved inadequate. She also intended to use four tasks, but dropped one (an oral description task) because it proved too difficult for the subjects.
3. Sato (1985) found that style shifting was not consistent in all phonological segments of the speech of one Vietnamese learner. It is possible, therefore, that the direction of style shifting is also not consistent in phonology.
4. Sato (1985) rightly points out that there is no objective way of determining how much attention a subject is paying to form in different tasks. Therefore, the claim that different tasks produce different levels of attention can only be an assumption. One way of overcoming this methodological problem may be to make use of Ochs' (1979) framework. Objective means for determining whether discourse is planned or unplanned can be found if the *degree* of planning is equated with the *time* made available for planning.
5. Each text type (continuous narrative, dyadic conversation, grammar tests, etc.) is likely to reflect planning variability according to the planning opportunities available. Thus, for instance, performance on a grammar test can be expected to vary as a product of how much time the learner is given to do the test. It makes good sense to investigate style shifting as a result of attention to form within text types so as to control for registerial variability inherent in different text types.
6. The main objection that Hatch (1983) raises is that in order to establish whether a morpheme has been acquired, it is necessary to look at how this morpheme appears *in contrast to others in its class.* Contrasting dissimilar morphemes (past

regular and articles, for example) does not enable the researcher to carry out the kind of contrast required, and therefore sheds little light on their acquisition.

7. This subject chose to adopt a present tense continuity. It is interesting to note that this subject succeeded in maintaining her chosen tense continuity in Task 1 but was less successful in Task 2 and least successful in Task 3. On the surface, then, this subject's scores work in the opposite direction from those predicted to occur (i.e. her past tense scores increase rather than decrease from Task 1 to Task 2). But if her performance is scored from the point of view of her chosen tense continuity, it can also be seen to become more variable across tasks. However, for the purpose of the analysis, no allowance was made for this; her present tense forms were scored as deviant and her past tense forms as correct.

8. In a discussion of Larsen-Freeman's (1976) morpheme study, Krashen (1982) also notes that the regular past decreased in accuracy from a task eliciting monitored performance to a task eliciting unmonitored performance.

9. It is also possible that omission of copula occurs as the result of the influence of the learner's first language. A further analysis is needed to establish this. However, even if the L1 is a cause, it does not rule out the explanation offered here. Copula deletion may be the result of multiple, interacting causes.

10. XXX denotes utterance elements that could not be deciphered.

11. In light of the results of this study, a difference in the orders of past regular and past irregular between performance on Larsen-Freeman's writing and oral tasks might have been expected. This did not, in fact, occur. Although irregular past did increase in accuracy on the writing task, this increase was insufficient to produce a different order for the two morphemes. It is possible that Larsen-Freeman's writing task did not tap planned performance to the same degree as the writing task in this study. It should be noted, however, that it is not writing *per se* that leads to increased accuracy on the past regular, but *planned* writing. Free writing can be expected to display accuracy levels similar to those in free speech.

12. Linguistic markedness has been investigated in terms of Chomsky's theory of universal grammar and also in terms of typological universals. Simply put, linguistic features that are universal are considered to be less marked than linguistic features that are peripheral or relatively rare in the world's languages.

Appendix: Raw Scores on the Three Tasks

Subject	L1	Task Pa reg C	Pa reg D	Pa irreg C	Pa irreg D	Pa cop C	Pa cop D	Task 2 Pa reg C	Pa reg D	Pa irreg C	Pa irreg D	Pa cop C	Pa cop D	Task 3 Pa reg C	Pa reg D	Pa irreg C	Pa irreg D	Pa cop C	Pa cop D
1	Japanese	3	5	3	1	0	5	2	6	2	1	2	2	1	6	2	6	1	6
2	Farsi	2	2	3	10	5	1	1	1	1	9	4	3	2	3	7	8	0	3
3	Farsi	2	1	4	6	0	3	1	5	6	10	0	6	1	5	0	8	1	6
4	Spanish	0	4	0	5	0	2	0	4	2	4	0	2	0	2	1	4	2	2
5	German	8	0	8	3	4	0	5	1	5	3	5	0	7	2	7	3	4	0
6	French	9	0	5	1	4	0	4	4	7	0	5	0	0	3	5	3	6	0
7	German	3	2	1	7	2	0	2	3	4	5	4	0	0	0	4	4	1	2
8	German	6	4	1	1	4	2	5	4	4	2	3	1	1	2	8	0	6	0
9	Portuguese	5	1	3	1	5	0	4	0	1	2	7	0	4	1	7	2	1	3
10	German	4	1	3	3	6	0	4	0	3	0	6	1	2	0	4	7	6	0
11	Spanish	6	0	9	0	7	0	2	5	7	1	8	1	0	2	4	3	7	0
12	Farsi	0	2	2	4	0	2	0	3	2	9	0	1	0	2	1	6	1	6
13	Polish	7	0	6	1	2	0	6	1	5	2	3	0	3	0	8	4	3	0
14	Japanese	10	0	5	0	3	0	7	2	7	0	3	0	3	0	7	1	1	0
15	Japanese	7	1	5	1	6	0	7	3	4	0	4	1	2	2	7	3	5	5
16	French	2	0	7	1	4	0	2	0	5	3	3	0	1	5	7	2	4	0
17	Farsi	8	2	5	1	2	2	6	2	4	2	4	2	2	4	4	4	2	1

C = correct; D = deviant

Section 5
Learning Styles and Second Language Acquisition

My interest in learning styles is a fairly recent one. The bulk of my empirical work has focused on identifying and describing how L2 *learning* takes place rather than on investigating how individual *learners* set about their task. In other words, I have been primarily concerned with the universal properties of acquisition rather than individual differences in learners. This was in part a reflection of the general trend in SLA studies and in part a response to my feeling that the learner factors discussed in the literature were so multifarious and often so ill-defined as to defy effective enquiry. The change in my attitude was brought about in part by the general reawakening of interest in how individual learners learn an L2 and in part by the 'global' nature of the idea of learning-style, which I found attractive because it offered the possibility of conducting research which might have general applicability.

Of course, the study of learning style, like that of other learner factors, is not without its problems. There is, for instance, no general agreement about what it consists of and, as a result, no agreement about how to measure it. A number of researchers have made use of constructs and instruments borrowed from general psychology (e.g. field dependency/independency, as measured by the *Group Embedded Figures Test*). Other researchers have developed definitions of learning style based on direct observations of how L2 learners vary in the ways they learn. Of these two approaches, it is the latter which seems the most promising.

Inevitably, given the looseness of the construct and the uncertainty about how best to measure it, the two articles in this section are exploratory in nature. Their value, perhaps, lies less in the results which they provide than in the formation of the questions that need to be answered. These are:

(1) Does learning style affect the subconscious strategies that learners use to process L2 input as acquisition or does it affect only the conscious tactics they employ to obtain and analyse input?
(2) What is the relationship (if any) between learning style and other factors that contribute to individual differences (e.g. aptitude, motivation, personality)?

161

(3) Is it possible to identify one learning style that works best for learning? Or are there many ways to be a successful language learner?

(4) Is classroom L2 learning facilitated when there is a match between the instructional style and the learners' learning style? Conversely, is it impeded when there is no such match?

(5) Which methods for investigating learning style are likely to be most profitable for SLA?

All of these questions are touched upon in one or both articles but the answers provided are best seen as partial and speculative.

Both articles address learning style in classroom learners. The subjects are the same learners as those used for the study of the acquisition of German word order rules (see Section Two), i.e. experienced foreign language learners. 'Individual learning styles in classroom second language development' (published in de Jong & Stephenson, 1990: 83–96) attempts to relate differences in the extent to which learners opt for linguistic accuracy or spoken fluency with the general distinction between a norm-oriented and a communicative-oriented learning style. This distinction looks promising, but clearly much more work has to be done. 'Classroom learning styles and their effect on second language acquisition' (*System* 17: 249–62) is a case study of two learners, which uses multiple sources of information to try to build up a picture of their approach to learning a foreign language and how this interacts with the instruction they experienced.

8. Individual Learning Styles in Classroom Second Language Development

Research into the relationship between learning style and second language acquisition has been mainly concerned with *cognitive style*. This term refers to the way in which learners process information. The construct is premised on the assumption that different learners have characteristic modes of operation which function across a variety of learning tasks, including language learning.

The principal measure of cognitive style used in SLA research has been the *Group Embedded Figures Test* of field dependency/independency developed by Witkin *et al.* (1971). This requires subjects to identify a simple geometric figure within a more complex design. Learners who are able to carry out this task easily and rapidly are said to be 'field independent', while those who cannot do so are 'field dependent'. It has been hypothesised that field independents will do better in classroom learning because they will be better able to analyse formal grammar rules. However, SLA research which has used the *Group Embedded Figures Test* has been far from conclusive (cf. Ellis (1985) and McDonough (1987) for reviews of the literature). Field independency appears — at best — to be only weakly correlated with second language (L2) proficiency.

However, the hypothesis that L2 acquisition is influenced by the way in which learners orientate to the learning task remains an appealing one. The relative failure to find any consistent relationship between cognitive style and language learning may be the result of the test measure which has been used. The crucial distinction with regard to learning style may be between learners who are *norm-oriented* as opposed to those who are *communicative-oriented* (Clahsen, 1985; Johnston, undated). Norm-oriented learners are those who are concerned with developing knowledge of the linguistic rules of the second language, while communicative-oriented learners are those who seek to develop their capacity to communicate effectively in the L2 irrespective of formal accuracy.

According to this proposal, learners vary in the way in which they view the language learning task. This task can be viewed as a modular one in accordance with the theory of L2 acquisition proposed by Bialystok & Sharwood Smith (1985). The general construct 'language' is subdivided into different modules according to which aspect (e.g. linguistic versus pragmatic) is involved. Each module is further subdivided to reflect the general distinction between 'competence' and 'performance'. Thus, in the case of the linguistic module, acquisition entails both the development of *knowledge* of the actual rules that constitute the language and *control* of the knowledge which has been acquired. We can speculate that norm-oriented learners choose to focus on acquiring linguistic knowledge, while communicative-oriented learners endeavour to develop channel control mechanisms.

There are a number of interesting pieces of research that reflect the basic distinction between norm-oriented and communicative-oriented learners. Hatch (1974), on the basis of an extensive review drawing on 15 observational studies of 40 L2 learners, distinguished 'rule formers' (i.e. learners who progress steadily by building up their knowledge of L2 rules) from 'data gatherers' (i.e. learners who gain rapidly in fluency but who do not appear to sort out any rules). Seliger (1980) found that some learners were 'planners' who endeavoured to organise their productions prior to performance, while others were 'correctors' who preferred to go first for fluency and then to edit subsequent performance as necessary. Dechert (1984) describes two different learners' approaches to the retelling of an oral narrative; one was 'analytic', characterised by long pauses at chunk boundaries, an absence of filled pauses and corrections, very few additions to or omissions from the original story and serial, propositional processing. The other was 'synthetic', characterised by shorter pauses at chunk boundaries, many filled pauses and corrections, considerable changes to the original story and *ad hoc* episodic processing.

Schmidt (1983) reports on a particularly illuminative case study of a Japanese painter called Wes. The study covered a three year period. Schmidt found little development in this learner's grammatical competence over this period, but considerable development in sociolinguistic, discourse, and strategic competence. Schmidt suggests that the type of progress Wes demonstrated was a product of his learning style and that the acquisition of grammatical competence is in part, at least, independent of the acquisition of the general ability to communicate effectively.

We can also speculate — as does Schmidt — that learners with different learning-task orientations will also vary systematically on individual learner factors such as motivation and aptitude. For example, a norm-oriented learner might be expected to score highly in tests of grammatical analysis such as the 'Words in Sentences' section of the *Modern Language Aptitude Test*

(Carroll & Sapon, 1959). Communicative-oriented learners, on the other hand, might be expected to do better on tests of word memory, on the grounds that vocabulary is particularly important for communication.

The purpose of the study reported in this paper is to explore these speculations with reference to the acquisition of German as a second language in a classroom context by a group of 39 adult learners. The study has these aims:

(1) To test whether field dependency/independency is related to the acquisition of linguistic knowledge and channel control.
(2) To investigate the extent to which the acquisition of linguistic knowledge and channel control proceed independently of each other.
(3) To explore which individual learner factors relate respectively to norm-oriented and communicative-oriented learners.

Each of these aims will be considered separately.

Subjects and Instructional Context

The subjects were 39 adult students taking beginning courses in German at two institutions of higher education in London. They were aged between 18 and 41 years with different first language backgrounds: English, Spanish, French, Mauritian Creole, and Arabic. All the learners were experienced classroom learners, having reached A Level or equivalent in at least one second language other than German. Although the course was designed for complete beginners, 14 of the students already had some limited knowledge of German.

The courses the learners were taking were part of a degree programme leading to a BA in Applied Language Studies. They lasted a full academic year, although the period of this study covered only two terms (approximately 22 weeks). The students were taught in separate groups, receiving between 7 and 12 hours of language instruction per week. Two course books were used with different groups. One book provided a traditional structural course and the other a notional-functional course. In fact, however, the methods of instruction varied little between groups. In general, the overall approach was a traditional one, involving extensive explanation of formal grammar points together with various kinds of practice and translation exercises. None of the groups received much opportunity to use German in natural communication. In other words, the instruction was *accuracy* rather than *fluency* focused (Brumfit, 1984).

Field Dependency/Independency

The *Group Embedded Figures Test* (Witkin *et al.*, 1971) was administered to the 39 learners at the end of the study. The test provided measures of the degree of field independency of each subject. A number of different measures of learning were obtained as follows.

Word order acquisition score

The learners performed an information gap activity in pairs at the ends of term 1 and term 2. This required them to describe to each other pictures making up a story in order to reconstruct the narrative and then to tell the complete story. The intention was to obtain a corpus of relatively spontaneous speech. Transcriptions were prepared and obligatory occasions for three German word order rules obtained. The three rules were particle, inversion and verb-end. Research into the naturalistic acquisition of German (Meisel, 1984) has shown that these rules are developmental in the sense that learners acquire them in a fixed sequence.

The percentage of correct suppliance of each word order rule was computed. In order to obtain the maximum score a learner must have produced a minimum of three obligatory occasions and performed correctly in all of them. Learners who produced fewer than three obligatory occasions were penalised by reducing the maximum score possible by 33% if they produced only two obligatory occasions, and by 66% if they produced only one. Learners who produced no obligatory occasions scored zero. Learners who produced three or more obligatory occasions were awarded a score out of 100% according to the percentage they performed correctly.

The word order acquisition score was designed to provide a measure of the learners' level of acquisition of linguistic knowledge at the end of term 1 (Time 1) and term 2 (Time 2).

Word order acquisition gain score

This was calculated by subtracting the word order acquisition score at Time 1 from that at Time 2. It was intended to provide a measure of the rate of acquisition of linguistic knowledge.

Speech rate score

This was computed using the same speech data as for the first two learning variables. The score consisted of the numbers of syllables produced in one minute of speech after disfluencies (i.e. repetitions, corrections, fillers, and parts of words) had been discounted. The speech rate score was designed to provide a general measure of the learners' channel control at Times 1 and 2.

Speech rate gain score

This was calculated by subtracting the speech rate score at Time 1 from that at Time 2. It was intended to provide a measure of the rate of acquisition of channel control.

Vocabulary proficiency score

This was obtained by means of a test used by the Department of German as a Foreign Language at the University of Münich. The test consisted of 31 items requiring learners to complete a sequence of four words with the appropriate item. For example, 'Tag: hell — Nacht: . . .' The items became progressively more difficult. The students were given ten minutes to complete the test, which was administered once only at Time 2.

Grammar proficiency score

A discrete item grammar test (also from the University of Münich) was administered at Time 2. The test consisted of 30 items arranged in order of difficulty. A sliding marking scale was used giving weight to the more difficult items. The students were given 20 minutes to complete the test.

A cloze score

The passage for the cloze test was a written version of one of the picture compositions used in the information gap activity, prepared by a native speaker of German. The first 50 words of the text were given in full. Thereafter, every tenth word was deleted. The score was out of 25. The students were allowed 15 minutes to complete the test.

Pearson product-moment correlation coefficients between the field independency scores and the scores for the various measures of learning were obtained. These are displayed in Table 8.1. The coefficients are all negative. However, no relationship reaches statistical significance. For this sample of learners, therefore, cognitive style as measured by the *Group Embedded Figures Test* is unrelated to measures of the acquisition of linguistic knowledge or of channel control.

TABLE 8.1   *Correlations between field independency and learning variables*

Learning variables	Correlation with field independency
1) Word order acquisition	
Time 1	–0.05
Time 2	–0.27
2) Word order acquisition gain	–0.22
3) Speech rate	
Time 1	–0.09
Time 2	–0.11
4) Speech rate gain	–0.01
5) Vocabulary proficiency	–0.00
6) Grammar proficiency	–0.19
7) Cloze	–0.15

N = 39   All correlations nonsignificant: $p > 0.05$

Acquisition of Linguistic Knowledge and Channel Control

The second aim of the study was to investigate to what extent the measures of linguistic knowledge were independent of the measures of channel control. If the scores obtained could be shown to be unrelated, this would provide support for the modular theory of language acquisition proposed by Bialystok & Sharwood-Smith (1985), and would also suggest that learners differ according to whether they are norm, or communicative oriented.

The same measures of learning as described in the previous section were used. Two kinds of statistical analysis were carried out. First, Pearson product-moment correlation coefficients were computed between the measures of linguistic knowledge and the measures of channel control. Second, a principal components factor analysis was run to gain further insight into the relations between the two sets of variables.

The Pearson product-moment correlations between the measures of linguistic knowledge and speech rate obtained at Times 1 and 2 are shown in Table 8.2. The coefficients are all small, well below the 5% level. These results suggest that for this group of learners acquisition of linguistic knowledge and channel control develop separately.

TABLE 8.2   *Correlations between linguistic knowledge and channel control*

| Linguistic knowledge | Speech rate | |
	Time 1	Time 2
Word order acquisition		
Time 1	–0.16	
Time 2		0.04
Vocabulary proficiency		0.04
Grammar proficiency		0.07
Cloze		0.14

N = 39   All correlations non-significant: p > 0.05

However, a significant negative correlation between *gains* in word order acquisition and in speech rate from Time 1 to Time 2 was found (r = –0.44; p < 0.01). Thus, those learners who showed the greatest gain in acquisition of the three word order rules manifested the smallest gain in general oral fluency and, conversely, those learners who developed the ability to process speech the most rapidly displayed the smallest gain in knowledge of the word order rules.

A principal components factor analysis was carried out using the scores obtained on all the learning variables at Times 1 and 2. Two factors were extracted in accordance with the hypothesis that linguistic knowledge and channel control constitute independent aspects of acquisition. The results (see Table 8.3) show that the knowledge variables all load positively on Factor 1, while the speech rate scores produce loadings around zero. The pattern is reversed for Factor 2. The 'Control' variables load strongly and the

TABLE 8.3   *Results of factor analysis (two factor solution)*

Variable	Factor 1	Factor 2	Eigenvalue	% of variance
Speech rate (Time 1)	–0.03	0.88	3.06	43.7
Speech rate (Time 2)	0.09	0.82	1.48	21.1
Word order acquisition (T1)	0.64	–0.05	0.86	12.4
Word order acquisition (T2)	0.66	0.16	0.75	10.7
Vocabulary proficiency	0.78	–0.03	0.44	6.2
Grammar proficiency	0.91	0.00	0.29	4.2
Cloze	0.86	0.10	0.11	1.6

knowledge variables only weakly. There is, therefore, reason to assume that the factors represent 'Knowledge' and 'Control' respectively, and, that these two aspects of acquisition are independent.

Taken together, these results indicate that for this group of learners a clear distinction can be made between the acquisition of linguistic knowledge on the one hand and of channel control on the other. It should be noted that the two modules were found to be independent irrespective of whether the measurements of each module were obtained from the same or different data sets. Thus, speech rate was weakly correlated with *both* word order acquisition and general proficiency. Furthermore, development in one module is linked to a lack of development in the other. Learners may choose which aspect of acquisition to place emphasis on and progress differently according to the choice they make. Some learners opt to develop the rule system of the target language, while others prefer to develop fluency.

Individual Learner Factors and Knowledge/Control

The results reported above give credence to the claim that learners differ in the general way they orientate to the learning task. They suggest that there are norm-oriented and communicative-oriented learners. Here we explore whether individual learner factors such as motivation and aptitude can be used to distinguish such learners.

There is a rich literature dealing with the relationship between learner factors and language learning. Gardner (1980) summarised years of research in Canada by concluding that a general index of attitude and motivation and standard measures of aptitude together account for around 27% of the variance in learning (measured by means of grade scores) obtained by instructed foreign language learners. Gardner and other researchers, however, have been solely concerned with the relationship between learner factors and linguistic knowledge. There has been no research — to the best of our knowledge — that has investigated the relationship between learner factors and channel control.

In this study a number of measures of different learner factors were obtained at the beginning of the study. The measures were:

(1) *Integrative motivation* The measure of integrative motivation was derived from the subjects' responses to a number of statements of the kind:
This language will enrich my background and broaden my cultural horizons.
They were included in a questionnaire administered at the beginning of the

study. The subjects rated each statement on a scale from 1 (unimportant) to 3 (very important). The ratings were then aggregated.

(2) *Instrumental motivation* This measure was obtained in a similar way to that for integrative motivation. The students responded to statements such as:
This language seems easier than others I could have taken.

(3) *Expectancy of achieving native speaker fluency* The learners were asked to rate how probable they thought it was that they would one day achieve native speaker fluency in German. The scale was from 0 (completely improbable) to 5 (completely probable). This measure was designed to provide an indication of how the subjects saw themselves as learners of German in the long term.

(4) *Aptitude (words in sentences)* This was assessed by means of Part IV of the *Modern Language Aptitude Test* (Carroll & Sapon, 1959). The test requires the subjects to identify the function of words within a sentence. There were 45 items. A time limit of 13 minutes was set.

(5) *Aptitude (memory)* This was measured by means of a test (Skehan, 1982) that assesses the subjects' abilities to memorise words in an unknown foreign language (Finnish). The subjects were given five minutes to memorise the words and two minutes to write down all the words they could remember.

(6) *Aptitude (sound discrimination)* This was measured by means of Part 5 of Pimsleur's (1966) *Language Aptitude Battery*. The test requires the subjects to learn phonetic distinctions and to recognise them in different contexts. There were 30 items.

(7) *Aptitude (sound-symbol association)* This was measured using Part 6 of Pimsleur's (1966) *Language Aptitude Battery*. The subjects were required to listen to words and select the closest written version in a multiple-choice format. There were 30 items.

Table 8.4 presents the Pearson product-moment correlations between the various measures of acquisition described previously and the measures of individual learner factors. In general, the results are disappointing. None of the learner factors are related to speech rate; the correlations are uniformly low. This is, perhaps, not so surprising as the measures used to assess individual learner differences were developed to determine which factors affected the learning of linguistic knowledge rather than channel control.

The correlations between learner factors and measures of linguistic knowledge are generally stronger, with expectancy of achieving native speaker fluency the best overall predictor of learning outcomes. This factor relates at the 1% level of significance to all three proficiency measures and also to word order acquisition (T1). However, many of the correlations that might have

TABLE 8.4   *Intercorrelations between learning measures and learner factors*

	Individual Learner Factors						
	(1)	*(2)*	*(3)*	*(4)*	*(5)*	*(6)*	*(7)*
Learning measures							
Speech rate (Time 1)	0.15	−0.05	0.06	−0.06	−0.19	−0.17	0.03
Speech rate (Time 2)	−0.03	−0.09	0.18	−0.06	−0.11	0.11	0.14
Word order acquisition (T1)	−0.03	0.12	0.41**	0.14	0.07	0.29	−0.07
Word order acquisition (T2)	−0.02	−0.04	0.18	0.16	−0.07	−0.20	−0.25
Vocabulary proficiency	0.07	0.04	0.45**	0.29	0.33*	0.05	0.04
Grammar proficiency	0.06	0.29	0.42**	0.21	0.09	−0.12	0.03
Cloze	0.03	0.37*	0.40**	0.16	0.29	−0.05	0.26

Key to Learner Factors:
  (1) Integrative Motivation
  (2) Instrumental Motivation
  (3) Expectancy of Achieving Native Speaker Fluency
  (4) Aptitude (words in sentences)
  (5) Aptitude (vocabulary memory)
  (6) Aptitude (sound discrimination)
  (7) Aptitude (sound-symbol association)

$N = 39$ Significance levels: *$p < 0.05$; **$p < 0.01$

been expected to reach statistical significance fail to do so. In particular, integrative motivation and aptitude (words in sentences) — two factors which previous research has shown to be significant in predicting learning outcomes — produce only low correlations, especially where word order acquisition is concerned.

There are a number of explanations for these results, which need not concern us here. It is sufficient to note that for this sample of learners the individual learner factors that were investigated shed little light on the aim of the study which was to explore which factors characterise norm-oriented as opposed to communicative-oriented learners. As might have been expected, given the knowledge-focused direction of previous research into individual differences, none of the affective and aptitudinal measures obtained provide any insights into the personal characteristics of those learners who orientate towards the acquisition of channel control. This is clearly an area where more research is needed.

Summary and Conclusion

The main findings of the study can be summarised as follows:

(1) Cognitive style (measured as field independency) was not significantly related to any of the measures of linguistic knowledge or channel control.
(2) Measures of linguistic knowledge and channel control were unrelated, suggesting that these two aspects of L2 acquisition are independent of each other. However, acquisition of one aspect of L2 was inversely related to acquisition of the other aspect.
(3) Quantitative measures of motivation and aptitude failed to distinguish clearly those learners who were knowledge-oriented from those learners who were control-oriented.

The research reported in this chapter has attempted to explore an issue of considerable current interest in SLA studies. It has been concerned with identifying differences in learning style. The results suggest that the distinction between norm-oriented learners who seek to develop their knowledge of linguistic rules and communicative-oriented learners who are more concerned with acquiring the channel capacity to perform with greater fluency in the target language is a valid one. This distinction may serve as a more profitable focus of research than that between field dependency/independency, with which previous research into learning styles in SLA has been largely concerned.

Substantial future research is needed to determine whether the independence of knowledge and control in L2 acquisition applies to other learner samples. Such research should ideally obtain measures of linguistic knowledge that reflect mainstream SLA enquiry into developmental sequences — as was attempted in this study by means of the word order acquisition score — as well as more traditional measures of proficiency. Such research should also develop adequate measures of channel capacity, drawing perhaps on the work in second language productions by the Kassel team (cf. Dechert, Möhle & Raupach, 1984).

We need to know much more about the kind of competence which communicative-oriented learners develop. We can speculate that in addition to channel control (explored in this study) they will manifest greater acquisition of discourse, sociolinguistic and strategic competence (cf. Canale, 1983) than norm-oriented learners, as Schmidt's study of Wes has shown.

Ideally, also, we need information about the long-term outcomes of learners with different learning styles. Which style leads to greater success in language learning? Do norm-oriented learners eventually catch up with communicative-oriented learners in other aspects of communicative competence? Do communicative-oriented learners eventually acquire adequate linguistic competence? Schmidt's study suggests that they might not do so. What of balanced learners, that is, learners who display an equal tendency for accuracy and fluency? Do they achieve the best of both worlds, acquiring both formal knowledge and satisfactory channel control? Are learning styles fixed or do they change as acquisition proceeds? These are all questions about which we know very little.

Finally, we need research that can help us to identify the personal characteristics of learners with markedly different learning styles. Here a more qualitative approach involving the use of such research techniques as learner diaries may prove more insightful in the first instance than the kind of quantitative approach reported above. Diary studies kept by six of the 39 learners in this study suggest that learning style is revealed with considerable clarity in the way learners respond to such factors as grammar explanations, type of instructional activity, tests and teacher correction.

9. Classroom Learning Styles and Their Effect on Second Language Acquisition: A Study of Two Learners

Introduction

Although second language acquisition (SLA) research has produced evidence to show that the acquisition of a second language (L2) is characterised by regularities, reflected in both the types of errors produced and the sequence by which grammatical properties are internalised (Meisel *et al.*, 1981; Ellis, 1985: Ch. 3), it has also produced results which show that individual learners approach the task of learning a L2 very differently (Wenden & Rubin, 1987). One way of accounting for the differences is in terms of *learning style*. This is defined by Keefe (1979) as '. . . characteristic cognitive, affective and physiological behaviours that serve as relatively stable indicators of how learners perceive, interact with, and respond to the learning environment . . . Learning style is a consistent way of functioning, that reflects underlying causes of behaviour.'

A learner's preferred learning style manifests itself in how she organises learning and copes with L2 input. Seliger (1984) refers to the procedures the learner uses as *tactics*. They vary from learner to learner. However, learning style does not affect the subconscious *strategies* which the learner uses to convert input into intake and which are responsible for the regularities of SLA.[1]

Studies of learning style in SLA have proceeded in two ways. A number of researchers have used constructs borrowed from general psychology and sought to discover to what extent these affect SLA. The construct which has received most attention is that of field dependence/independence. Field-dependent learners are adjudged to be strongly influenced by context; they prefer an integrative approach. Field-independent learners are able to operate in a more analytical fashion. A number of studies (e.g. Hansen & Stansfield, 1981; Day, 1984; Chapelle & Roberts, 1986; Abraham & Vann, 1987) have been carried out to test the hypothesis that field-independent learners are advantaged in formal language learning and do better in language tests that encourage a focus on form while field-dependent learners are advantaged in informal language learning and do better in tests of oral communication. The results of this research are mixed, but in general field-independents appear to outperform field-dependents in both formal and communicative tests.

The other approach to the study of learning style has involved quantitative and/or qualitative techniques for investigating L2 learners in order to discover the characteristics of different learners in using or learning a new language (Dechert, 1984; Wenden, 1986; Willing, 1988). These studies suggest that learners differ on two broad dimensions:

(1) Active versus passive, i.e. the extent to which the learner is prepared to take responsibility for her own learning and to be persistent.
(2) Studial versus experimential, i.e. the extent to which the learner prefers to engage in formal language learning aimed at achieving accuracy as opposed to learning which is aimed at and takes place through communication.

These dimensions constitute continua; learners can fall at any point on them. Some learners, for example, can display a marked preference for studial or experiential learning, while others prefer to learn in a more balanced way.

It is reasonable to assume that a learner's learning style reflects both nature and nurture. The learner's personality and cognitive style result in a general preference to learn in particular ways rather than others. But the learner's previous learning experiences can also affect her learning style, causing her to expect and even require similar experiences in new learning situations. For example, an L2 learner used to a traditional, form-focused method of language teaching or to a transmission mode of education in general, may respond negatively if confronted with a more 'communicative' method. A learner internalises an 'idea' of what classroom learning involves and then acts out this idea in the tactics she adopts. This mental set is not immutable, however. A learner may revise her 'idea' as a result of different learning experiences or after receiving 'training' in new approaches and techniques.

Not much is known about the relationship between learning style and successful L2 acquisition. Two positions are evident in the literature. One is based on the belief that there are many ways to be successful in language learning and that learners will generally do better if they are able to follow their own preferred styles. The other position is more absolute; it claims that some learning styles are more effective than others. Studies of the 'good language learner' (Rubin, 1975; Naiman *et al.*, 1978; Reiss, 1981; 1985) have tried to identify those learning tactics that result in rapid learning and higher levels of achievement.

Classroom language learners may find themselves in a situation where the instructional style matches their own learning style or in one where there is no such match. There is some research to suggest that learners do better when their learning style matches the instruction (Wesche, 1981; Hartnett, 1985), but the research is sparse and limited, making it difficult to draw firm conclusions.[2] In general, Aptitude Treatment Interaction (ATI) research has produced mixed results (cf. Willing, 1988). It may be that learners will do best if trained to adopt the learning style of good language learners (Birckbichler & Ommagio, 1978).

The research reported in this article was set up to explore a number of these issues. Specifically, it addresses the following questions:

(1) In what ways do classroom language learners' learning styles vary?
(2) Do some learning styles result in more effective learning than others?
(3) Do learners do better when their learning style matches the instructional style?

The research is intended to be 'interpretative-exploratory' in nature and is designed to illuminate these issues rathr than to test specific hypotheses. Such an approach seems more appropriate given the absence of a strong theory to explain the role of learning style in classroom L2 acquisition.

Procedure

Subjects

The subjects were two adult learners of L2 German.[3] They were enrolled in an *ab initio* course in an institution of higher education in London. Monique was from Mauritius. Her mother tongue was Creole, but she spoke French and English fluently and accurately. She was an experienced classroom language learner, but, coming from a multilingual society, had also experienced the naturalistic use of her second languages. Simon was British. His mother tongue was Welsh but he spoke and wrote English like a native speaker. He had studied foreign languages at school but had had very limited experience of using these languages for everyday communication. Both subjects were 19 years old. Neither had any previous knowledge of German.

Instruction

The two learners were studying for a BA in Applied Language Studies at a college in London. Both had elected to study German. Both were required to successfully complete the *ab initio* course in order to continue with their degree. Also both intended to continue with German during the remaining three years of the degree programme.

Although Monique and Simon were in different classes they followed a very similar course of instruction for 12 hours per week. Systematic observation of their classrooms[4] revealed that the main characteristics of the instruction were as follows:

(1) The teaching–learning activities were almost entirely form-focused, i.e. there was hardly any opportunity for meaningful communication.
(2) The form-focused instruction was fairly evenly divided between practise and consciousness-raising activities (such as teacher explanation of grammatical points).
(3) The teachers used English (the base language) and German (the target language) for approximately equal amounts of time.
(4) Most of the teaching took the form of teacher–class (i.e. lockstep) interaction. There was very little small-group work. The classes were very small, however (i.e. under ten).

The teaching, therefore, was traditional and grammar-centred. The stated aim of the course was to develop a high level of linguistic accuracy in the use of L2 German.

Data collection

A variety of data collection instruments were used to gather information relating to the individual characteristics of the two learners and their levels of achievement. These instruments are described briefly below.

(1) *A questionnaire.* Both learners completed a questionnaire designed to provide information about the quantity and quality of their previous exposure to different types of foreign language learning, their attitudes to different teaching methods, their self-confidence as language learners, their expectancies regarding the level they would reach by the end of the *ab initio* course and the nature and degree of their motivation to learn German. The questionnaire contained a mixture of objective and open questions. It was completed in the first week of the course.
(2) *Cognitive style test.* The *Group Embedded Figures Test* (Witkin *et al.*, 1971)

was administered to the two learners. This test requires the subjects to identify the location of a simple geometric figure within a larger, more complex design. It is designed to establish how *field-independent* a learner is.

(3) *Language aptitude test.* A total of four aptitude tests was administered. Part IV of the *Modern Language Aptitude Test* (Carroll & Sapon, 1959) tested the subjects' ability to identify the function of words within a sentence. A *Finnish Memory Test* (Skehan, 1982) tested the subjects' ability to memorise words in an unknown foreign language. Part 5 of Pimsleur's *Language Aptitude Battery* (Pimsleur, 1966) tested their ability to learn phonetic distinctions. Part 6 of the same test measured the subjects' ability to associate symbols with sounds.

(4) *Attendance.* Records were kept of the subjects' class attendance during the first 22 weeks of the course.

(5) *Participation.* The subjects' participation in classroom practice was measured by counting the number of times each learner practised a particular German word order rule (verb-end) in sample lessons audio recorded during the first 22 weeks of the course.

(6) *Word order acquisition.* The subjects were paired off with other learners in their instructional groups in order to perform an information gap task. Each learner was given two pictures which, together with the two pictures held by his/her partner made up a story. The learners first described their pictures in order to put together the story. They then told the whole story. Transcriptions were prepared of everything said. Obligatory occasions for the use of three German word order rules (particle, inversion and verb-end) were identified and a composite score was calculated. This procedure was carried out after 10 and 22 weeks of the study. The word order acquisition scores give a general indication of how rapidly and how far the two subjects' acquisition of German progressed.

(7) *Speech rate.* A measure of the subjects' speech rate was derived from the oral narratives performed as part of the information gap task (see (6) above). The number of syllables (discounting repetitions, corrections, fillers and parts of words) in one minute of speech was calculated.

(8) *Proficiency tests.* The subjects completed three proficiency tests after 23 weeks.

    (a) Vocabulary

        The test consisted of 31 items requiring the learners to complete a sequence of four words with the appropriate item, e.g. 'Tag: hell Nacht: . . .'

    (b) Grammar

        The test was part of a battery used by the German as a Foreign Language Department at Münich University. It consisted of 30 discrete items arranged in order of difficulty. Word order rules were not tested. The test was marked according to a sliding scale of difficulty.

(c) Cloze

The passage for the cloze test was a written version of the picture composition (see (6) above), prepared by a native speaker of German. The first 50 words of the text were given in full. Thereafter, every tenth word was deleted, giving a total of 25 blanks.

(9) *Diary studies.* Each subject was asked to keep a journal of their reactions to the course, their teachers, their fellow-students and any other factors which they considered were having an effect on their language learning. They were issued with a set of guidelines about how to keep their diaries and what to look out for. The diaries were collected in at regular intervals, photocopied and then returned immediately to the diarists. The subjects were assured that the material in their diaries would be treated in full confidentiality.

These instruments were designed to provide a comprehensive quantitative and qualitative account of the two learners' development and their responses to the learning task.[5]

Differences in Learning Style

The results of the aptitude and cognitive style tests reveal a number of differences between Monique and Simon (see Table 9.1). Whereas Simon achieves a high score on the Group Embedded Figures Test, Monique's is low. It would appear, therefore, that Simon is strongly field-independent, while Monique is equally strong field-dependent. Differences also emerge with regard to aptitude. Simon provides evidence of a greater capacity for grammatical analysis, for memorisation of vocabulary and for sound–symbol associations. However, the two learners are very similar where sound discrimination is concerned.

A number of differences in orientation and attitude to language learning and, more specifically to learning German, emerge from the questionnaires. Monique rates her ability to speak other foreign languages (French and English) as 'good', whereas Simon rates his ability in this skill in the foreign languages he has studied (French and Italian) as 'very limited'. Monique is doubtful about her writing abilities, whereas Simon is more confident in this area. Monique states that she chose to study German because she was 'fascinated' with the language. Simon, however, chose it because it was different from the Romance languages he had studied previously and because

TABLE 9.1   *Scores on cognitive style and aptitude tests*

Variable	Monique	Simon
Cognitive style	4	16
Aptitude:		
Grammatical analysis	8	16
Memory	8	11
Sound discrimination	19	19
Sound–symbol association	19	23

it was a 'challenge'. Both learners rate their talent for language learning as 'average' but Simon has higher hopes and expectations of achieving a reasonable level of proficiency in German by the end of the academic year. However, Monique rates herself as less likely to feel uneasy or afraid to make mistakes when speaking a foreign language than does Simon.

The diaries provide evidence of differences in the two learners' cognitive orientations and of some similarities in their affective attitudes.

Monique's cognitive orientation is almost entirely studial. Her journal shows that she is obsessively concerned with linguistic accuracy. She places great store on studying vocabularly and she prefers teaching activities that enable her to perform correctly and to self-correct if necessary. She welcomes teacher-correction:

> We did some oral translation and I personally like it because the class is more lively then as we make mistakes and are immediately corrected and she is critical of herself if she makes too many mistakes.
> Coming to my essay, it was full of mistakes which were due largely to the fact that I adventured myself in unknown vocabulary and clauses.

Despite rating herself as confident and adventurous in the questionnaire, the diary shows that she fears making mistakes and measures her progress in terms of how many she produces:

> As usual the sentences I had to say aloud were full of mistakes. I am getting quite anxious now because I seem to be making a whole lots of mistakes . . .

The corollary of her concern with errors, is the attention she pays to formal grammatical description. Her diary is full of references to explanations of various grammatical points and the importance she attaches to them. She acknowledges that this concern for the formal properties of German affects her ability to express herself freely in the L2.

In contrast, Simon's diary reveals a more balanced cognitive orientation; that is, he appears to favour both a studial approach directed at accuracy and an experiential approach involving the meaningful use of German. Grammar is clearly important to him. Learning grammar involves both a clear understanding of the rules involved and practice. There are plenty of references to both these aspects. If he comes across a new grammatical form he seeks out the rule to explain it and he makes considerable efforts to ensure that he understands it:

> I had to leave early and so missed the most important part of the lesson. This was when the class looked at the dative case. I am very worried about this as although I have taken a look at it tonight I have not understood the use of this case at all.

However, although he values the use of grammatical explanation he does not always find it very interesting. He appreciates the opportunity to practise specific grammatical items, but dislikes mechanical repetition and is also critical of exercises which are too taxing. Opportunities for unfocused language use are also welcomed by Simon. He displays little concern for making errors and the diary contains no references to the need for teacher-correction. He always responds favourably when there are opportunities to communicate freely in German and regrets that more such occasions were not made available. He expresses a preference for grammatical explanations in German, suggesting that listening posed few problems for him.

Where affective orientation is concerned, the two learners are quite similar; both display a lack of confidence and considerable personal anxiety. Monique frequently compares herself with other learners. These comparisons are often triggered off by her sense of failure in some classroom task:

> We had to make sentences with these and replace them by pronouns and I was really at a loss and really felt like crying as the others seemed to have grasped it all.

Simon is very conscious of the advantage which learners with some prior knowledge of German held over him. He tends to rate himself (wrongly) as one of the worst in his group and he easily becomes dissatisfied with his progress:

> I seem to be losing confidence as the amount of grammar increases . . . I have to admit that I'm pretty bad at German at the moment.

However the unease and self-criticism that both learners manifest is 'facilitating' rather than 'debilitating' (Scovel, 1978). It is clear that they are very conscientious and hard-working and maintain their language learning efforts throughout the period of study. There are frequent references to self-study in both diaries.

To conclude, both Monique and Simon are highly motivated learners of German. They have positive attitudes to the language. They are not confident learners but they are tenacious. But they differ markedly in their abilities and cognitive orientations. Monique is field-dependent and displays higher levels of aptitude in sound discrimination. She also rates her oral abilities in her other foreign languages highly. This suggests that she is best equipped to learn experientially through the spoken medium. However, the diary shows that she tries to learn studially, concentrating on linguistic accuracy and avoiding free expression. In Monique's case, therefore, there may be a conflict between the learning style to which she is suited and that which she actually adopts. One reason for this might be her previous classroom language learning experiences. Simon is field-independent and is good at grammatical analysis and vocabulary-memorisation. He possesses the necessary abilities, therefore, to pursue a studial approach to learning and the diary provides plenty of evidence of this learning style. However, he is a flexible learner. He enjoys participating in class and likes to engage in real communication in the L2.

Learning Style and Achievement

Table 9.2 gives the results obtained on the various measures of achievement. Monique does poorly on word order acquisition and speech rate, but she gains a high score on the grammatical proficiency test. In other words, she appears unable to perform either fluently or accurately in an oral communicative task but is successful in a written, form-focused task. Simon demonstrates a much higher level of word order acquisition and is able to

TABLE 9.2 *Achievement scores*

Variable	Monique	Simon	Total possible
Word order (22 weeks)	0.22	0.50	1.00
Word order gain (from 10 weeks to 22 weeks)	–0.11	0.11	—
Speech rate (22 weeks)	31	58	—
Proficiency:			
Vocabulary	6	7	31
Grammar	58	50	75
Cloze	11	11	25

speak more fluently. He also does well in the grammar proficiency test, although not quite so well as Monique.

These results correlate with the cognitive orientations evident in the two learners' diaries. Monique concentrated almost entirely on the formal properties of German and this is evident in her high score in the grammar proficiency test. She paid little attention to trying to communicate or to develop fluency in German. This, too, is reflected in her low scores for word order acquisition and speech rate. Simon showed himself to be a more balanced learner, operating both studially and experientially, when opportunities arose. His learning style is reflected in more even results — relatively high scores both in those measures derived from the oral communication task and in the grammatical proficiency test. In the case of these two learners, therefore, there appears to be a match between *how* they set about the learning task and *what* they actually achieve.

From studies of good language learners it is possible to identify four key aspects of successful language learning. These are:

(1) a concern of language form;
(2) a concern for communication;
(3) an active task approach (e.g. learners who take charge of their own learning rather than relying on the teacher and who are persistent in pursuing goals);
(4) awareness of the learning process (e.g. thoughtful learners who make conscious decisions about what study habits and tactics to employ).

The diaries provide ample evidence for assessing the extent to which the two learners manifest these four characteristics. Table 9.3 summarises the results. It suggests that Simon will be a more successful learner than Monique because he provides evidence of all four characteristics of the good language learner. Monique fails to demonstrate any real concern for communication and this also affects her awareness of the learning process because it leads her to emphasise those tactics that are appropriate for studial learning (e.g. memorisation, self-monitoring and planned production). The achievement results lend support to this conclusion. Simon achieves a more all-round

TABLE 9.3   *Characteristics of the two learners*

Characteristic	Monique	Simon
A concern for language form	+	+
A concern for communication	–	+
An active task approach	+	+
Awareness of the learning process	+	+

performance, whereas the proficiency Monique has developed is restricted to the grammar test.

The Relationship Between Learning Style and Instruction

The type of instruction which both learners received has already been described. In general, it was form-focused and teacher-centred. To what extent does each learner's learning style match the instruction provided?

Evidence has already been provided to suggest that Monique is by nature an experiential rather than a studial learner. If this hypothesis is correct, there is a mismatch between her preferred learning style and the instruction. According to this interpretation, Monique adopted a studial approach because her previous educational experiences led her to expect that this was what was required and because it was soon clear to her that this was the approach needed to succeed in the *ab initio* German course. Monique knew that she would be assessed at the end of the academic year in terms of how *accurately* she could write German. In order to obtain the 60% pass mark in the examination, which she needed to continue her degree studies, she adapted her style to the requirements of the course.

Such adaptation is likely to be accompanied by stress and tension, as the learner is obliged to adopt tactics to which she is ill-suited. Monique's diary provides some interesting evidence that this was indeed so in her case. The instructional method was based on the assumption that learners would be given plenty of opportunity to practice new grammatical features. Monique finds this requirement onerous. She dislikes public performance and fears making errors:

I was really tense in this class when she was asking us questions . . .
As usual I was quite frightened when asked questions.
I was quite frightened when asked questions again. I don't know why; the teacher does not frighten me but my mind is blocked when I'm asked questions. I fear lest I give the wrong answer and will then discourage the teacher as well as be the laughing stock of the class maybe. Anyway, I felt really stupid and helpless in that class.

These and other entries testify to the difficulties which Monique faced in coping with the instructional demands and the effects they had on her. Although she did, in fact, participate in considerably fewer practice exchanges than Simon (see Table 9.4), she would probably have benefited from the opportunity to learn silently in the early stages — in accordance with the approach adopted by many naturalistic learners. Monique might well have voted with her feet and given up the course but for the fact that she needed to pass the German examination in order to continue with her degree. Her attendance (96%) was, in fact, very regular.

TABLE 9.4   *Amount of practice and attendance by the two learners*

Variable	Monique	Simon
Number of practice opportunities (verb-end)	10	16
Attendance	96%	86%

Simon appears to find no difficulties with the instructional approach. He approves strongly of the text book used on the course (Schapers *et al.*, 1980):

> *Grundkurs Deutsch* is interesting and diverse. There are several interesting themes and the book is not repetitive and the exercises are not childish as in many other language textbooks.

Individual lessons are classified as 'boring', 'interesting', 'easy', 'difficult' or 'useful'. He dislikes purely mechanical practice, but appreciates contextualised drills, providing they do not overtax his production abilities. He does experience some anxiety in the early stages when asked to perform in class:

> . . . several of us were afraid to say anything for the rest of the lesson for fear of being made fun of again.

But in general he appreciates the opportunity to practise:

> We seem to be concentrating more on speaking German . . . I think this is very good as we have confidence to speak.
> I answered a lot of questions in class and felt much more confident and eager to try new constructions.

On another occasion he complains that 'you are rarely asked questions' in classes where two groups of learners are combined. Simon practises far more than Monique in class. He is clearly more in tune with the style of teaching and is able to accommodate to the types of instructional tasks without difficulty. His attendance is good (86%), although not as good as Monique's, mainly because of poor health.

In Monique's case, therefore, learning style and instruction may not be well matched. In contrast, Simon seems quite well-suited to the type of instruction. Monique does not appear unduly disadvantaged, as she performs well in the grammar proficiency test — i.e. she succeeds in developing the grammatical accuracy needed to succeed in the course. However, she pays a price. The course proves a painful experience and she is unable to perform effectively in a communicative task. This may be the result of the mismatch. Simon does not find everything easy but he copes comfortably with the course demands. His main regret is that his vocabulary is poor (an opinion supported by the results of the vocabulary test — see Table 9.2), but vocabulary was not the main goal of the course.

To sum up, this study suggests that learners do benefit if the instruction suits their learning style, but, if it does not, they may be able to adapt, at some cost to their own ease of mind and the type of proficiency they develop.

Summary and Conclusion

The study reported above has tried to explore how two learners' learning styles affected the way they responded to the instruction they received and the rate and level of their L2 achievement.

The concept of learning style is, at best, a loose one — it is difficult to define with precision and therefore, difficult to operationalise. In order to systematise the study of the learning styles of the two L2 learners of German, two major dimensions of learning style were identified; a cognitive and affective one. The cognitive dimension concerns the extent to which a learner is oriented towards studial or experiential learning. The affective dimension concerns the extent to which the learner is positively or negatively oriented towards the task of learning the L2. Information about these two dimensions was obtained using a variety of instruments — tests, classroom observation, task performance and introspection. By adopting an eclectic research style in this way it was possible to draw up a picture of how the two learners set about learning the L2. Despite the vagueness of the construct, therefore, the investigation of learning style proved possible.

The results of the study showed that the two learners did manifest identifiable styles of learning. One learner, Monique, was almost exclusively studial in her approach. The other, Simon, was more balanced, giving evidence of an ability to operate both studially and experientially. Both learners showed a positive affective orientation, which was reflected in a highly active approach to language learning.

The results also indicated that Monique's chosen learning style may not have been the style she was naturally suited to. In other words, for various reasons — such as previous educational experience or a preparedness to accept the instructional style on offer — learners may go against their own inclinations. A potentially experiential learner like Monique may feel that she is required to operate studially in a classroom context, if this is what she thinks is needed.

Also important in studies of learning style — but generally missing in previous research — is evidence regarding which learning style results in successful learning. This study showed that what the learners achieved reflected what they set out to learn. Thus, Monique learnt how to obtain high scores in tests of grammatical proficiency while Simon learnt how to perform communicative tasks as well as how to do well in grammar tests. If successful learning is defined as the ability to perform both accurately and fluently (Brumfit, 1984), then, arguably, Simon is the more effective learner. In other words, a balanced cognitive orientation might result in greater success than one is skewed towards either accuracy or fluency. Studies of the good language learner support such a conclusion. However, it is necessary to be wary in reaching such a conclusion. The present study lasted only 22 weeks. Learners may change their learning style as learning progresses. Only fully longitudinal studies will show which learning style is ultimately the most efficient.[6]

This study has provided a number of insights regarding the relationship between learning style and instruction. Bialystok (1985) has argued that there needs to be 'minimal congruity' between the learner's cognitive orientation and the type of instruction provided. She comments:

> . . . great disparities between the strategies used by teachers and the present abilities and strategies employed by learners will effectively reduce the potential benefit of instruction.

Congruity can be assured if either the learner or the teacher adapts or if the learner is flexible enough to cope with whatever type of instruction is on offer. In the case of Monique, it was the learner who adapted. Simon was equipped with the abilities needed to cope with the instruction. Learner-adaptation may not always take place, however. Monique adapted because of her positive affective orientation, the result, perhaps of her strong instrumental need to succeed. Other learners may be more negatively inclined and lack instrumental motivation. Also, forcing learners to adapt may create anxiety and discomfort in the classroom, as was indeed evident in Monique. Such responses may inhibit learning.

Matching instructional and learning style can be achieved by deliberate planning (e.g. Wesche, 1981), but given the range of learning styles likely to be present in any group of classroom learners and the absence of reliable and valid instruments for determining learners' learning style such an approach will not usually be possible. Matching is best achieved by the teacher catering for individual needs during the moment-by-moment process of teaching (i.e. by emphasising group dynamics and offering a range of activity types). Matching can also be enhanced if learners are made aware of their own learning style and are encouraged to adopt flexible learning tactics. These should become the goals of teacher and learner training.

Notes

1. The claim that learning style only affects *tactics* and not *strategies* is a controversial one. Many researchers would not agree with Seliger. It is, nevertheless, a reasonable position to adopt. It is incumbent on those who wish to argue that learner factors have a qualitative (as opposed to quantitative) effect on intake to demonstrate this and to explain the regularity of L2 acquisition.
2. One of the problems with the available research which has investigated the effects of matching instructional and learning styles is that of defining 'instructional style'. It is now widely recognised that definitions in terms of global methods (such as audiolingualism or communicative language teaching) are unreliable. Ideally, then studies need to be conducted based on classroom observation designed to identify *actual* rather than *predicted* differences in instruction.
3. The two subjects were part of a larger sample — 39 in all. The research project had a number of aims:
   1. to examine the effects of formal instruction on the sequence of acquisition of L2 German grammar;
   2. to investigate the role played by a number of learner characteristics (e.g. age, motivation, cognitive style);
   3. to examine the effects of classroom participation on the level of proficiency achieved;
   4. to examine the nature of the proficiency achieved by the learners.
4. Observations were carried out every two weeks using an observation coding scheme designed, in particular, to identify the extent to which classroom activities were form or meaning focused.
5. One lacuna in the data collection was introspective accounts of actual task performance. It would have been useful to have obtained verbal accounts from the learners of how they performed typical classroom tasks (e.g. translation).
6. It is possible that equal success can be achieved by learners with very different learning styles — in the long run. The crucial factor may be the extent to which the learner is able to evaluate her own progress and to adjust her learning behaviour accordingly. Thus, a learner who goes initially for communicative fluency but who recognises at some point during her learning career that it is necessary to focus on grammatical accuracy may arrive at the same point as the learner who goes initially for accuracy and concentrates on fluency later or as the learner who displays a balanced orientation from the beginning.

Section 6
From Research to Pedagogy

Whereas the focus of the previous sections has been various aspects of SLA research and pedagogic issues have been secondary, the reverse is true of the three papers in this section. In each case the primary concern is language pedagogy. SLA research serves as a point of departure for a detailed discussion of a number of pedagogic issues.

There are dangers in trying to apply the results of SLA research (see the 'Introduction' to this volume) and it is wise to be cautious. Therefore, the proposals advanced in the three articles need to be treated not so much as 'prescriptions warranted by SLA research' as 'ideas for solving pedagogic problems suggested by SLA research'.

The following questions are considered:

(1) Should teachers seek to intervene directly in the process of their students' L2 development (e.g. by teaching specific grammatical items) or should they intervene only indirectly (e.g. by providing opportunities for natural communication) and so allow learners to build their interlanguages in their own way?
(2) If both direct and indirect intervention are required, how should these be organised? Is it possible, for instance, to design a curriculum that integrates both approaches or should the curriculum be a modular one with separate components for direct and indirect intervention?
(3) In what ways should direct intervention (e.g. grammar teaching) be carried out?
(4) What types of classroom interaction are likely to prove optimal for L2 acquisition?
(5) How can teachers best take account of differences in learners' learning style?

These are questions of central importance to language pedagogy and, not surprisingly, they have provoked considerable controversy.

Although the articles were written at different times (spanning a period of some six years), there is considerable consistency in the views about pedagogy which they present. The position I adopt is a balanced one — one that argues the need for both direct and indirect intervention and, therefore, one that sees merit in both formal and informal instruction. It contrasts with that advanced by Krashen (1982; 1985), who has argued strongly in favour of an approach based more or less exclusively on indirect intervention. While I accept that interlanguage development is far too complex to be influenced directly by instruction and that learners must be allowed to take charge of their own interlanguage development, I argue that the available evidence from SLA studies suggests that formal instruction can *facilitate* natural development. However, for a number of reasons formal instruction is more likely to have a delayed than an immediate effect on acquisition. The learning that results from formal instruction, therefore, may be available only in careful language use in the first place and only after time, when opportunities for communicating in the L2 are provided, will it manifest itself in more casual styles.

A number of proposals can be derived from this basic position. The first is that opportunities for meaning-focused language use are essential to allow for the development of full capacity in an L2. The second is that formal instruction is useful because it can accelerate this process and prevent early grammatical fossilisation. The third is that direct and indirect intervention are best kept apart and provided for by separate components in the overall curriculum. The fourth is that direct intervention should be carried out in such a way that gives due recognition to the likelihood that the learning that takes place will not be available for immediate use in ordinary conversation. This suggests the need for 'consciousness-raising' designed to give learners an understanding of the formal properties of language and how they contribute to meaning rather than for 'practice' directed at total control.

Finally, there are proposals concerning how differences in learning style can be accommodated. Three possibilities are examined — instruction/learner matching, negotiating learning tasks with students and responding to individual needs dynamically through the way a teacher interacts with different learners. All three have their merit, but in most classroom situations it is the last of these which will provide the main way of accommodating learner differences.

Perhaps, the overriding idea that emerges from these articles is the importance of communication in the classroom. It is mainly through communication that learners build their interlanguages and it is also through communication that the teacher responds to learner differences. Above all, the teacher needs to be a good communicator. But in emphasising this, the intention is not to suggest that the teacher does not also require the instructional techniques needed for skilful direct intervention and some specific suggestions for grammar teaching are put forward.

'Second language learning and second language learners: growth and diversity' was first presented in 1989 at the British Columbia TEAL Conference and subsequently published in *TESL Canada* 7: 74–94. 'Contextual variability in second language acquisition and the relevancy of language teaching' was first presented in 1985 at the Ealing College of Higher Education Conference on Variability in Second Language Acquisition and subsequently published in Ellis (1987). 'Grammar teaching — practice or consciousness-raising?' was presented at the 1990 JALT Conference, Tokyo.

10. Second Language Learning and Second Language Learners: Growth and Diversity

The field of second language acquisition (SLA) studies is characterised by two different traditions. One tradition is linguistic and focuses on the process by which learners build up their linguistic knowledge of the second language (L2). Here the focus is on *learning*. Human beings are credited with an innate capacity to learn language which explains why the process of learning manifests distinct structural regularities. Human beings also possess a common set of wants and needs, which they express through language; this, in turn, accounts for commonalities in the way the L2 is used. The other tradition is psychological; it focuses on the different ways in which learners cope with the task of learning and using an L2. Here the focus is on the *learner*. Human beings are individuals; they differ with regard to gender, age, motivation, personality, learning style, self-esteem etc. Each person has her own way of going about things with the result that there is immense diversity in both the way learners learn and in what they achieve. The teacher needs to take account of both of these traditions — she needs to consider how learners learn and she needs to consider how they differ.

The two traditions may appear, at first sight, to be in conflict. How can we talk about the universal properties of L2 acquisition while at the same time admitting that learners are inherently different? There is no conflict, however. Seliger (1984) distinguishes strategies and tactics. The former involve subconscious mechanisms which govern how input becomes intake. They are not open to direct inspection. Instead, we have to infer what they consist of by studying the learner's output. Learning strategies can be seen as part of the cognitive process in which learners form, test and revise hypotheses (Faerch & Kasper, 1980). Alternatively they can be explained with reference to the setting of parameters available to the learner as part of Universal Grammar (Flynn, 1987). Irrespective of which kind of explanation is offered, the assumption is that all learners work on the input data available to them in the same way. Tactics, according to Seliger, are the devices a learner uses to obtain input and to help them make sense of it. They are conscious — or potentially conscious — and they are open to inspection, therefore. Learners use tactics to plan their learning, to monitor their progress, to tackle specific learning tasks and to compensate for communication problems. Tactics are highly variable. No two learners adopt precisely the same set of tactics. Tactics account for why learners vary in the speed with which they acquire an L2.

The two traditions have helped to support different approaches to language instruction. Prabhu (1985) distinguishes *learner-centred* and *learning-centred* approaches. The former is expressed in the language for specific purposes movement; it involves the attempt to identify the needs of individual learners (or groups of learners) and the design of tailor-made courses to meet these needs. It is also evident in the attempt to adapt the teaching method to the learner's learning style, as in Wesche's (1981) study of deductive and inductive learners, who were exposed to instruction that emphasised respectively conscious rule-formation and audiolingual practice. Learning-centred methodologies are based on theories of the learning process. Humanistic approaches are grounded on a general view of how learning — of any kind — takes place. They seek to create the conditions, particularly the affective conditions, needed to ensure successful learning. Other learning-centred approaches emphasise the uniqueness of language. They treat language learning as a distinct kind of learning. The pedagogical proposals advanced by Stephen Krashen are a good example of an approach based on a theory of language learning.

In this paper I want to try to explore both traditions in order to argue that a 'whole' approach to language teaching must give consideration to both the structural nature of learning and the learner qua individual.

Learning

The last twenty years have seen a burgeoning of interest in how learners learn an L2. This interest has been generated in part by the importance of foreign language learning (particularly English) in the modern world and in part by the paradigm clashes first between behaviourist and nativist views of language learning and more recently between cognitive and linguistic explanations. There have been an increasing number of empirical studies designed to investigate how learners acquire a knowledge of the L2. There have also been a plethora of theories to explain how it takes place. It would be impossible to provide an adequate 'state-of-the-art' summary in this chapter, so instead I will outline and illustrate two general models of L2 acquisition, which characterise much of the current research.

The two models involve very different views of what it means to 'develop' an L2 (Ellis, 1989a). According to one view, learners acquire a knowledge of the L2 incrementally, systematically adding new rules to their grammar. I will refer to this as 'development-as-sequence'. According to the other view, L2 learning is not so much a process of adding new rules to existing ones as of gradually complexifying a mental grammar of the L2. Specific structures or sets of features within a linguistic sub-system complexify through the accummulation of new features. The process involves the constant reformation of existing knowledge as new knowledge enters the system. I will refer to this model of SLA as 'development-as-growth'.

Development-as-sequence

The development-as-sequence model is evident in the morpheme studies which were popular in the 1970s. These studies collected cross-sectional data from groups of learners, identified obligatory contexts for the use of specific morphemes such as aux-*be*, plural –*s* and past regular –*ed* and then worked out how accurately each morpheme was produced. Accuracy orders were then drawn up by ranking the morphemes. Some researchers (e.g. Dulay & Burt, 1973) went on to claim that the accuracy order represented the order of acquisition, on the grounds that morphemes that were acquired first would be performed more correctly than morphemes that were acquired later. A number of different groups of subjects were investigated in this way. The accuracy order obtained was remarkably stable — it was obtained irrespective of the learners' L1s or whether they were children or adults. Researchers such as Krashen (1977) used the results of the morpheme studies to claim that there was a 'natural' route of acquisition for an L2.

The morpheme studies are now out of favour. They have been attacked on a number of grounds. In particular, equating accuracy and acquisition orders has been challenged. It has been shown that the acquisition of specific features is characterised by a U-shaped pattern of development, such that learners initially perform a feature with a high level of accuracy, which then falls away until a fairly late stage when it emerges once again correctly in their speech. It has also been shown that the acquisition of a specific form does not necessarily mean that learners have acquired the ability to use the form in a target-like way. For example, a learner may correctly use the progressive –*ing* form in sentences like:

I am colouring my picture.
She is reading.

but also over-use the same form in sentences like:

Sharpening my pencil. (= sharpen my pencil.)
I playing football every day. (= I play football every day.)

Wagner-Gough (1975), in a study of a six-year-old Persian boy learning English in the USA, found that the progressive-*ing* was used for a wide variety of functions in the early stage of acquisition — to express immediate intention, distant futurity, pastness, process-state activity and commands. These are significant criticisms and we would do well not to put too much faith in the morpheme studies.

It does not follow, however, that we have to completely abandon the development-as-sequence model. There is, in fact ample evidence to suggest that certain formal properties of a L2 are acquired sequentially in some kind of natural sequence. The best evidence comes from studies of the acquisition of German word order rules by both naturalistic and classroom learners (Meisel, 1983; Pienemann, 1984; Ellis, 1989b). The developmental sequence is described later.

Learners with different L1s show an amazing consistency in the sequence of acquisition of these word order rules. Each rule, it is suggested, involves certain processing operations which are hierarchical in terms of their psycholinguistic complexity. The acquisition of one set of operations serves as a prerequisite for the acquisition of the subsequent set. A number of studies have been conducted to investigate whether instruction in advanced word order rules can enable a learner to jump stages or to learn the rules in a different order (e.g. Pienemann, 1984; Ellis, 1989b). The results indicate that this is not possible.

The restrictions imposed by processing limitations and the way in which learners slowly overcome them is apparent in all longitudinal case studies of L2 learners. In my own research I investigated the acquisition of English by three classroom learners in a London language centre. I found clear evidence to support the idea of a sequence of development. For example, the learner's ability to produce imperatives of the kind:

Sir, don't tell Mariana the answer please.
(Vocative) + (neg) + V + (NP) + (NP) + (please)

was characterised by clearly-defined stages:

Stage (1):   One element only is encoded, usually the vocative or the object of the required action.
e.g. Sir, sir, sir.

Stage (2):   Two elements only are encoded, usually the vocative or the object of the required action. Imperatives are typically verbless at this stage.
e.g. Sir, sir, pencil.

Stage (3):   Imperatives with verbs appear — the verb taking the imperative or progressive-*ing* form. By this stage the learners are also able to produce three-element strings.
e.g. Sharpening please.
Playing football with sir today.

Stage (4):   A negative particle is used with a verb to form a negative command.
e.g. No looking my card.

The general pattern of development is reminiscent of child L1 acquisition. Learners gradually increase their processing capacity and, in so doing, are able to produce more and more complex structures.

The idea of a 'natural' route of acquisition is not one that all L2 researchers would wish to adhere to. Lightbown (1984) has pointed out that for every study that gives evidence of a standard sequence, there is another that provides counter-factual evidence. There is, however, sufficient evidence to suggest both that there is a general pattern of development and, for some structures at least an order of acquisition. It does not follow, however, that all grammatical properties are acquired sequentially — indeed it would seem likely that there are many features that are not subject to the kinds of processing constraints discussed above.

Development-as-growth

The development-as-sequence model focuses on the formal properties of language, but, if we are to understand fully how learners acquire the competence to use the L2 we need to consider not just forms but also the functions to which they are put. It is when we look at the interrelationship between form and function in a learner's interlanguage, that we see that development involves an organic process of growth. The task facing the learner is to sort out the form-function correlations that accord with target language use. But this takes time. The interim grammars that learners build are functional grammars; they consist of networks of functions linked loosely to networks of linguistic forms. As the learner gradually builds her interlanguage, she reorganises the existing network. One way of characterising the successful language learner is as someone who is able to correlate a range of forms with a range of functions (Nicholas, 1986).

It is possible to identify three major processes in development-as-growth:

(1) Innovation (i.e. the introduction of new forms into the interlanguage system).
(2) Elaboration (i.e. the extension of the communicative base of the new form).
(3) Revision (i.e. the adjustments to the entire interlanguage system resulting from innovation and elaboration).

These processes are not stages; they are overlapping and continuous. Thus while one form is entering the learner's interlanguage, other forms are in the process of becoming elaborated and revision of the system also starts to take place.

The underlying principle of the development-as-growth model is that learners need to perform certain communicative functions and will use whatever resources are at their disposal to do so. Learners have the capacity to create meaning out of whatever linguistic means they possess — in much the same way as any user of language has (Widdowson, 1978). Gradually, these means will become more target-like. One of the primary motivations for acquiring new resources is to extend the range of pragmatic meanings that can be expressed. The acquisition of new linguistic means results, in turn, in a readjustment of existing resources in order to achieve maximal communicative effectiveness. The need for communicative choice, is, therefore the driving force of development-as-growth. If learners lose this desire — because subconsciously or consciously they feel they have achieved sufficient resources to meet their communicative needs, then fossilisation takes place. The learner closes herself off from target language norms and her interlanguage stops growing.

As an example of how this kind of growth takes place let us consider how the three children referred to earlier set about performing the network of meanings relating to the expression of negation. Bloom (1970) identified three broad categories of negation:

(1) *Non-existence*
This can be further sub-divided according to whether the speaker asserts the non-existence of an action-process, e.g.

Mariana no coming today.

or the non-existence of a state-process, e.g.

Miss, no pens. (= Miss, I don't have a pen).
I no understand.

(2) *Rejection*
This can be broken down into instrumental (i.e. the speaker asserts a negative wish), e.g.

Me no out of here.

and regulation (i.e. the speaker tries to control the actions of another person), e.g.

Don't touch.

(3) *Denial* (i.e. where the speaker refutes or corrects what someone else has said), e.g.

No, eleven. (= My team hasn't got ten points. It's got eleven.)

To start with, the three learners did not realise the full range of these meanings. Their earliest negatives expressed instrumental needs and the non-existence of state-process events. Regulatory negatives appeared a little later. Reference to the non-existence of action-processes emerged last. This pattern of development was consistent across the three children. It can be explained largely by the communicative needs of the children in the classroom context. Initially, classroom survival calls for the learner to be able to express non-possession ('No have . . .'), non-knowledge ('I don't know') and negative wishes ('No want . . .'). As the learner grows into her environment, she needs to be able to exert her control over other people ('No do . . .'). Being able to comment on non-events ('X no happen . . .') is of less immediate interpersonal value to the learner and therefore does not occur until later.

If we turn to the linguistic resources the learners used to realise these meanings, we find evidence of an interesting relationship between form and function. The ubiquitous 'no' negator is used in utterances that perform all the functions listed above. The learners also picked up formulas for performing a number of key functions, e.g.

I don't know.
I don't like.
I don't want.

Other negators like 'don't' and 'not' were initially used in free variation with 'no', e.g.

No look my card.
Don't look my card.

but in a restricted manner. They were used principally in regulatory utterances. Not until much later did 'not' begin to be used according to target language norms. The learners, then, created their own system — a system that can be understood only if function as well as form is considered. The main characteristic of this system is that it sought to make use of whatever resources the learners had available in order to distinguish different kinds of meaning, though the manner in which this was done did not at first correspond to target-language use.

To understand how development-as-growth takes place, therefore, we have to see the language learner as a communicator. Initially the learner has few resources so she relies on her ability to exploit the meaning situated in the context of utterance. To facilitate communication she also acquires a set of useful formulas. As resources are built up she seeks to put them to maximum use by building form-function networks. These networks are constantly evolving as the learner acquires new resources and seeks to express increasingly complex ideas. Normally, we can expect the classroom L2 learner to give primacy to interpersonal meanings to start with. The ideational and textual functions of language follow later. The whole process of syntactisation is inextricably linked with the process of learning how to communicate (Givon, 1979).

Summary

To summarise, the development-as-sequence model claims that learners follow some kind of 'natural' route as a result of the processing complexity of different structures. It emphasises the significance of linguistic factors as determinants of acquisition. The development-as-growth model sees language development as part of the process of learning how to communicate. It attaches importance, therefore, to the changing patterns of interrelationship of form and function. Both models are valid; they both capture important structural facts about the process of L2 acquisition.

The Learner

Let us now turn away from the structural facts and consider in what ways learners vary in the way they go about learning an L2. I want to consider two questions:

(1) In what ways do learners differ in their approach?
(2) Are some approaches better than others?

Learning style

One way we can try to answer the first question is by considering learning style. This refers to the idea that learners have characteristic ways of tackling problems which reflect their whole selves — it is the product of their cognitive, social and physiological preferences. A learner's learning style is evident in whatever she is doing — whether it is learning how to swim or how to learn a language. It is partly the product of innate disposition and partly of experience. A learner's previous education, for instance, may have led her to form certain expectations about what it means to learn in a formal setting. There is a rich psychological literature dealing with learning style (cf. Witkin *et al.*, 1971; Kolb, 1976; Gregorc, 1979) which is of considerable potential interest to L2 researchers and teachers, but, for reasons of space, I will concentrate here on ideas derived directly from the study of L2 learners.

Learning style can be usefully discussed in terms of the learner's cognitive and affective orientations to the task of learning an L2.

Cognitive orientation

It is possible to draw a basic distinction between *experiential* and *studial* learners.

Experiential learners are concerned primarily with learning how to communicate in the L2. They believe that the best way to learn is through using the language. However, *using* does not necessarily mean speaking or writing; an experiential learner can also elect to learn through active listening and reading. Experiential learners are likely to be people-oriented and to dislike routinised learning. They are data-gatherers, acquiring useful formulas and vocabulary rather than rules. They are not bothered about making errors and tend to be monitor under-users. Experiential learners are primarily concerned with meaning and fluency rather than form and accuracy.

Studial learners believe that it is important to approach the task of learning the L2 in a systematic way. They seek direction and consciously plan how they will learn. They try to identify specific problems and to deal with them. Thus, they are likely to make use of reference books (grammars and dictionaries) and to keep notes of useful words and phrases. They are usually object-oriented. They are rule-formers, making efforts to consciously understand grammatical structures, often by comparing the way the L2 works with their mother tongue. They dislike making errors and try to avoid them. They tend to be monitor over-users and they like other people to correct them. Studial learners are primarily concerned with form and accuracy rather than meaning and fluency.

This basic distinction between experiential and studial learners is reflected in a wide range of SLA studies. It has been observed in longitudinal case studies of individual learners (Hatch, 1974), in studies of L2 productions (Dechert, 1984) and in studies based on interviews with learners (Wenden, 1986). It is not intended to suggest, however, that learners fall into one of two camps — experiential or studial. Many learners are 'balanced' learners in the sense that they operate both experientially and studially, in accordance with the particular task or situation in which they find themselves. It may also be the case that learners vary in their cognitive orientation at different stages of their learning, starting off, for instance, as studial learners and then becoming more experiential later. We know little about this, however.

Affective orientation

Willing (1988), using Likert-scale type questionnaires, investigated 517 adult ESL learners in Australia and found that some of them could be distinguished according to the experiential-studial distinction. In the case of many of the learners, however, another dimension was also involved. The learners also differed according to how active they were in their approach to learning. The active-passive dimension, then, is also an important aspect of diversity. This dimension reflects the learner's overall affective orientation to the learning task.

Active learners are independent, are able to tolerate the inherent ambiguity in language, persist in problem solving and enjoy taking decisions. They are self-directed and able to manage their own learning. It should be noted, however, that *active* does not just mean active in production; a learner can also be an active listener or an active reader. Passive learners, on the other hand, tend to be reliant on others, are intolerant of ambiguity, like the teacher to explain everything and do not enjoy discovery learning. Again, it should be noted that passivity does not necessarily mean that learners are not prepared to speak or write in the L2, only that they prefer someone else to take charge of what they have to do.

The extent to which a learner is active or passive is probably, in part at least, a product of their personality. But it is also a reflection of their attitude to the language, to native speakers of the language and to the style of instruction they are receiving. Learners approach the task of learning a new language with certain attitudes, which may be positive or negative. These constitute their initial affective disposition. As a result of their experiences while trying to learn the language, their initial attitudes may be reinforced or they may be modified. Whereas a learner's cognitive orientation is relatively stable, her affective orientation is unstable. Learners fluctuate enormously on both a day-to-day basis and over a longer period of time. It is not possible, therefore, to talk about learners who are permanently active or permanently passive. We should rather see individual learners as variable on this dimension.

As an example of how learners vary in their affective orientation let us consider Mary, a learner of German as an L2 in higher education in London. Mary kept a diary of her learning experiences for six months. She started off with what is clearly a very positive attitude:

> I've really been enjoying learning a new language again. It almost feels as if I'm reliving part of my childhood.

Her diary shows how this attitude is reflected in a highly active approach to learning. The early entries make regular references to self-study. Also the competition and pressure which the instructional style encourages have a positive effect on her. She writes:

> I find the competitiveness is helping me to feel obliged to work all the harder.

However, as time passes, her attitudes begin to change. She becomes resentful of the disruptive behaviour of a number of male students in her group and objects to time being wasted because the teacher had to explain points they had missed through poor attendance. Her diary shows a growing sense of frustration. Also she has personal problems with her boyfriend and this has a damaging effect on her ability to concentrate:

> I've been really nervous today. I've got terrible butterflies and I can't stop shaking. I was in no mood for a German lesson . . .

At this stage the diary shows that her mood fluctuates markedly on a daily basis.

By the end of six months, however, her affective response has become consistently negative. The main reason appears to be her resentment of the pressure imposed upon her, linked to the fact that, for her, German is an optional subject which she intends to give up at the end of the academic year. Slowly, then, she turns from being an active, conscientious learner to a much more passive, *laissez-faire* one. This is what she says at the end of her diary:

> . . . seeing as I don't want to study it seriously, I can't see the point of working so hard for it anymore. I haven't done any German homework for weeks. It is my own loss I know, but I can't see the point in doing it anymore. We've been pushed too hard and at last I've broken down. I've lost all my good attitudes and intentions about German lessons that I had before.

This diary shows us just how important affective factors are in determining whether a learner is active or passive in her approach. It shows also that the degree of activity/passivity is determined to a large extent by local factors in the personal life of the learner and in the learning environment. In a way this is encouraging, because it suggests that, with sensitive handling, positive attitudes can be fostered.

Learners, then vary according to what extent they are experiential or studial on the one hand and active or passive on the other. These dimensions are to be seen as intersecting continua. Individual learners can be plotted with relation to where they come on the two continua (see Figure 10.1). Thus, at the extremes we will find active experiential learners, passive experiential learners, active studial learners and passive studial learners. The vast majority of learners, of course, will not fall at the extremes but somewhere in between. Also, learners will change during the course of their learning.

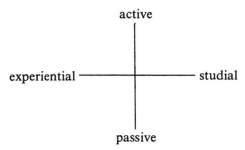

FIGURE 10.1   *Types of learning style in SLA*

The 'good language learner'

So far we have been content to describe how learners' learning styles vary. But we also need to know whether some approaches to the learning task work better than others. The last 15 years have seen a number of studies of the 'good language learner' (e.g. Rubin, 1975; Stern, 1975; Naiman *et al.*, 1978; Reiss, 1985; Abraham & Vann, 1987). These provide a remarkably consistent picture of the tactics used by successful language learners.

In general, the studies point to four key aspects:

(1) A concern for language form

The good language learner pays attention to form. Indeed, according to Reiss' (1985) study, learning tactics reflecting this approach came out on top in a group of 98 college students studying a foreign language at an elementary or intermediate level. The two strategies the learners reported using most frequently were monitoring and attending to form. Other researchers have also found form-focusing tactics a regular feature of the successful language learner. Naiman *et al.* (1978), for instance, mention that learners who treat language as a system engage in effective cross-lingual comparisons, analyse the target-language and make frequent use of reference books. These learners also tried to learn from their errors by asking native speakers to correct them.

(2) A concern for communication

Good learners also attend to meaning. Attention to form and to meaning are not mutually exclusive. Learners seem to benefit from alternting between the two. Gerardo, the more successful of the two learners investigated by Abraham & Vann (1987), is a good example. He took a broad view of language, paying attention sometimes to form and sometimes to meaning. In contrast, Pedro, the less successful, was more or less exclusively concerned with meaning and getting by in conversations. All the good language studies have found that successful learners search for meaning and try to engage in real communication by seeking out opportunities for natural use. They make efforts to get their meanings across using a variety of communication strategies.

(3) An active task approach

Good learners are active in their approach. This can manifest itself in different ways. Active learners take charge of their own learning, rather than relying exclusively on the teacher. They are persistent in pursuing goals. In conversation, the active learner introduces new topics and tries to control the direction the discourse follows. But being an active learner does not mean participating in terms of language production. Reiss (1985) emphasises that her successful learners were typically 'silent speakers'. They listened closely in class and mentally answered questions whether called upon to do so or not. They listened to other students and mentally corrected their errors. They tried to apply new material while silently speaking to themselves.

(4) Awareness of the learning process

Finally, good language learners demonstrate considerable awareness of the learning process and of themselves in relation to this process. They are thoughtful learners who make conscious decisions about what to study and what tactics to employ. They are likely to have a well-developed metacognitive language for talking about their learning and this helps them to monitor how they are progressing. Reiss found that her good language learners were able to give very specific descriptions of how they would approach different learning tasks, while the less successful were often vague and imprecise. Metacognitive knowledge is important because it enables learners to assess their needs, evaluate their progress and give overall direction to their learning.

Summary

To sum up, learners vary according to whether they lean towards learning experientially or learning studially. They also vary according to how active they are in their approach. There are many ways of learning an L2 and doubtlessly a learner's approach will reflect what she wants to achieve. A learner who wants to be fluent and is not bothered too much with accuracy will elect to learn experientially if she can. A learner who wants to pass exams and to achieve a high level of proficiency will probably be more studial. There are obvious dangers in suggesting that one learning style is better than another. However, the evidence of the good language learner research suggests that to be successful (in the sense of achieving both accuracy and fluency) learners need to pay attention to both form and meaning, to be active (particularly in attending to input) and to take charge of their own learning. The successful learner — in some absolute sense — therefore will try to strike a balance between experiencing and studying the language and will be active, both in the sense of being highly responsive to input and in being self-directed. There may, however, be many ways of achieving a balance and learners may grow to be active as learning proceeds.

Instruction

What lessons does the particular view of learning and the learner which I have now presented hold for language pedagogy? First, let me make it clear that I do not see SLA studies of the kind discussed earlier providing definite answers to pedagogical questions. SLA research is only one of many inputs into the process of decision making — teachers ought to and certainly will consider other inputs (e.g. general educational principles and their own practical experience about what works in the classroom). I prefer to treat SLA research as a source of illumination rather than of solutions and to acknowledge that illumination can come from many sources.

I would like to address two questions:

(1) How can we help learners to 'grow' — in the sense of helping them to build their interlanguage systems successfully?
(2) How can we cater for diversity — in the sense of taking account of differences in learners' learning style?

In discussing these questions, I will seek only to outline general positions and not to propose methods or specific techniques.

Helping learners 'grow'

One of the clearest messages of the existing research is that the process of L2 acquisition is controlled by the learner; it is internally rather than externally driven. This is the message of both the development-as-sequence and the development-as-growth models. If learners do progress along a 'natural' route in the process of acquiring an L2 and if this route cannot be rearranged for the learner through instruction, then clearly it is the teacher who has to accommodate to the learner rather than vice versa. It is also impossible for the teacher to regulate in a direct way the process by which learners build, complexify and rearrange form-function networks. The process of interlanguage development is far too intricate and personal for a teacher to intrude into.

The development-as-sequence model does hold out some possibility of direct pedagogic intervention into language learning, however. Perhaps it is possible to organise the instruction so that it corresponds to the natural sequence. For instance, we could try to teach word order rules in the order in which they are acquired, providing learners with chances to practise each structure at just that moment she becomes ready to learn it. There have been a number of proposals along these lines, the most clearly articulated of which is that of Pienemann's (1985). Pienemann suggests that although there should be no attempt to control structures in the input learners are exposed to, they should be asked only to produce structures which are within their processing capabilities. Structures can be taught when they are learnable. But this proposal, while tenable at the level of theory, is unworkable in practice. We cannot expect teachers to know when each learner in their class is ready to acquire the next rule. Also, the research to date is limited to a relatively small set of grammatical features. What should the teacher do about those structures for which no clear developmental evidence is available? Not surprisingly, perhaps, Pienemann's proposal has not received much support.

Does this mean, therefore, that teachers should abandon all attempts to teach grammar? The answer is *no*. What the teacher needs to do is to distinguish two approaches to grammar teaching according to whether the instruction is aimed at direct or indirect intervention. Direct grammar teaching is the traditional approach — the one associated in particular with audiolingualism, the legacy of which is still very much with us today. Direct grammar teaching is predicated on the belief that learners can learn a new structure if they produce if often enough, but, as we have seen, this is a belief which is not supported by the research. Indirect grammar teaching aims to raise the learner's consciousness about the experience of certain forms in the input which are not yet part of her interlanguage. The assumption is that the learner will probably not acquire the forms immediately but will be sensitised to their presence in the input, thereby facilitating subsequent learning, when the learner becomes ready to assimilate them into her interlanguage. Grammar teaching as indirect intervention — aimed at delayed rather than immediate acquisition and concerned with raising awareness rather than achieving productive competence — is viable and may even be necessary to prevent early fossilisation.

The development-as-growth model suggests the importance of learners having the opportunity to engage in real communication. The process by which form-function networks are constructed and modified is fired by the need to use language to express interpersonal and ideational meanings in the construction of discourse of various kinds. The provision of instructional activities which can serve as the crucible for this process is the main challenge facing the teacher. The thrust of communicative language teaching methodology in the 1980s has been to provide the teacher with the means for creating meaning-focused communication in the classroom. In particular, learners need to have the chance to perform a range of language functions and not to be restricted to 'responding to questions', as happens in so many classrooms (Long & Sato, 1983). Interlanguage growth results from the need to realise different kinds of meaning. If there is no need, there is neither motivation nor opportunity to learn.

How then can the teacher generate in the learners a felt need to communicate in the L2? I would like to suggest the following guidelines:

(1) Never force learners to produce. Let each learner decide for herself when she wants to speak.
(2) Never force learners to produce in some pre-determined way. Let them choose how to express themselves.
(3) Do your best to understand what the learner is trying to say.
(4) Help learners to express what they want to say. You can do this by means of requests for confirmation and paraphrasing.
(5) Give learners the chance to initiate their own topics.

(6) Help learners to extend a topic. You can do this by means of expansions, extensions, prompts and prods. But take care not to push a learner too far.
(7) Be prepared to correct learners, but never allow the process of correction to take over from the process of trying to communicate with them.

With the exception of the last point, this list is similar to a list produced by Wells (1986) in his summative guidance to parents who want to help their children learn to talk. Wells argues that children have to work out the way language is organised for themselves, but they need help in doing so. The L2 learner is the same. Of course, the task facing the language teacher is very different from that facing the mother. The teacher only sees the learner a few hours every week. She also has to work in a one-to-many, not a one-to-one situation. But the general principles of how to go about facilitating language learning remain the same.

It is worth noting that if we view teaching as a way of providing the learner with an optimal learning environment, we will be rejecting a means-end view of the curriculum in favour of the kind of process orientation that is currently in favour (Breen, 1987; Nunan, 1988). The content of a language programme (as defined in a syllabus or a set of materials) is of considerably less importance than the classroom interactions which occur in the process of teaching. We should also note that these interactions grow out of the management of business and social relationships in the classroom as much as out of the tasks officially designated for learning.

Catering for diversity

We can cater for diversity in learning style in two different ways. We can seek a match between the instructional style and the learner's learning style — try to ensure, for example, that experiential and studial learners receive appropriate programmes. Alternatively, we can try to train learners to cope efficiently with their own learning and/or, perhaps, to adopt a learning style that we consider most likely to result in successful language learning. The first approach seeks to accommodate diversity, the other tries to help the learner become more effective.

There is no time to explore both of these approaches in detail. There is some research to show that matching instructional and learning styles does promote learning (e.g. Wesche, 1981). There is also a rich literature dealing with the need for learners to be autonomous, so that they can formulate their own aims, choose their own materials and learning methods and carry out self-evaluation of their progress (e.g. Holec, 1980). Such a learner is equipped not only to learn during the course of instruction but also to carry on learning when it is over. We must acknowledge, as teachers, our responsibility to make the learner responsible for her own learning and not encourage teacher-dependency.

It seems to me that interesting as these two approaches are, they will never provide the real answer to diversity in learning styles for most teachers. It is simply not practical for most teachers to try to diagnose the learning styles of their learners, divide them into groups and provide different instructional treatments to match each group.

Learner training directed at making learners more autonomous is more feasible and, probably, more useful, but it is unlikely that most teaching contexts will have sufficient resources to cater for totally self-directed learning. If we want to accommodate diversity, then, we must seek out different answers.

I think the real answer is to be found in two very general approaches to teaching:

(1) Teachers need to negotiate the learning tasks with the learners. The nature of the negotiation may be relatively formalised in the sense that teachers can actively seek the opinions of learners about what kinds of learning and evaluation activities they would like to participate in. Alternatively, it can take place in a more informal manner, as when a teacher reacts to the different ways in which individual learners respond to tasks selected by the teacher. This informal kind of negotiation serves as the main way in which teachers try to accommodate variation in learning styles. Good teachers have always been sensitive to what works and what does not work with particular learners. They seek to ensure that there is sufficient variety in the kinds of tasks learners are asked to undertake to satisfy all the learners at least some of the time.

(2) Teachers need to adapt the way they communicate to suit individual learners. The teacher who seeks 'a meeting of minds' with her learners does so principally by the way she communicates with them — both collectively and individually. Accommodation to the needs and preferences of individual learners needs to be seen as part of the overall process of communicating with them. To succeed, teachers have to be able to assess not only what each learner is capable of in communication but also his or her personal preferences. To force a learner to produce when she prefers to function as an 'active listener' is potentially damaging. So too would be to prevent the risk-taking learner from playing a prominent role as a speaker. Some learners find teachers' questions threatening; others welcome them. Some learners want to be corrected; others do not. It is through interacting

with learners that the process of negotiating an individualised curriculum really takes place. A learner-centred curriculum is not something that is planned (although planning can help), but something that unravels through classroom communication.

It is by negotiating the choice of learning task and by showing sensitivity to individual learners in the way she communicates with them that the teacher can foster a positive affective climate in the classroom. A humanistic classroom is not one where certain rather special kinds of activities take place, but one where learners are valued and nurtured as individuals. A learner is more likely to be active if she feels she has some say in what happens in the classroom and if, day by day, her personal learning style is respected in communication with the teacher.

The idea of an individualised approach to language pedagogy has, I think, always been threatening to teachers — because they have not been able to see how it could work in practical terms. In fact, the good teacher has always provided individualised instruction by negotiating formally or informally what is done and by adjusting the way in which it is done in how she communicates with different learners.

Conclusion

In a sense, then, helping learners to grow and catering for diversity calls for the same set of basic skills from the teacher. In particular, the teacher needs to be a good communicator. The truth of this observation becomes more and more apparent to me as I observe lessons in different parts of the world. Teachers vary enormously in their abilities to communicate effectively in the classroom. Some are expert, able to provide the kinds of interactional conditions that help learning to grow and to adapt how they communicate with individual learners to cater for diversity among them. Other teachers are less expert.

Language pedagogy has been traditionally seen in terms of 'approaches', 'methods' and 'techniques' (Anthony, 1963). It is true that teachers need to know what to do in the classroom, so these concepts are useful. But ultimately, stimulating growth and catering for diversity is not a question of any of these, but of how well the teacher can communicate with her learners.

11. Contextual Variability in Second Language Acquisition and the Relevancy of Language Teaching

Introduction

The purpose of this paper is to address the question: 'How can we take account of what is known about the nature of contextual variability in second language acquisition (SLA) in language teaching?' In general, theories of L2 acquisition have paid scant regard to the variability of interlanguage systems (Beebe & Zuengler, 1983), while language teaching has tended to treat learning as the acquisition of a homogeneous competence enshrined as a grammar of target language norms. My concern, then, is to argue both for a model of L2 acquisition that gives due recognition to language-learner language variability and for an approach to language teaching based on the acquisition of a heterogeneous competence.

The question that motivates this paper has arisen as a result of research that shows the effects of language pedagogy to be far from straightforward. Two examples of this research will serve to illustrate this point. Schumann (1978b) attempted to give instruction in English negatives to Alberto, a Spanish speaking subject learning English in the United States. His reason for giving this instruction was to discover whether the apparent 'pidginisation' of Alberto's English could be overcome. Prior to the instructional experiment, Alberto's negatives were primarily of the 'no + V' type. The instruction covered a seven-month period, during which both elicited and spontaneous negative utterances were collected. The elicited utterances showed a marked development (64% correct as opposed to 24% before instruction). The spontaneous utterances, however, showed no significant change (20% correct as opposed to 22% before instruction). Schumann concluded that the instruction influenced production only in test-like situations, while normal communication remained unaffected. The second study was carried out by Perkins & Larsen-Freeman (1975). They investigated the effects of two months' instruction on 12 Venezuelan undergraduates in the United States. Two tasks were used to collect data: (1) a translation task, and (2) an oral description task based on a non-dialogue film. On (1) the morpheme orders before and after instruction differed significantly but on (2) there was no significant difference. The researchers concluded that where spontaneous oral performance was concerned the instruction did not influence development.

To explain their results, then, these researchers drew a distinction between the kind of careful language elicited, for instance, by translation tasks and the kind of spontaneous language use associated with unplanned oral production. They noted that the instruction they provided influenced the former but not the latter. The results are intuitively appealing, given that, as teachers, we are familiar with the problem of 'backsliding', where students perform a particular structure accurately in the context of controlled language practice but fail to do so in free practice or in communication outside the classroom. The problem is an important one because it raises one of the central questions of language pedagogy, namely the relationship between what Brumfit (1984) has called 'accuracy' and 'fluency' activities.

One answer to this question can be found in Krashen's (1981a) Monitor Model of SLA. This rests on the now well-known distinction between 'acquisition' and 'learning'. Krashen postulates specific conditions for the use of 'learnt' knowledge (i.e. there must be sufficient time and the learner must be focused on form) and argues that if these conditions are not met the learner will be able to call on only 'acquired' knowledge. Thus in spontaneous communication 'learnt' knowledge is not available for monitoring. Krashen argues that acquired and learnt knowledge are entirely separate. Thus he sees no relationship between the development that arises from 'accuracy' and 'fluency' teaching, as each contributes to a distinct kind of competence. But such a position is not acceptable to many teachers who operate a methodology based on distinguishing 'skill getting' and 'skill using' (Rivers & Temperley, 1978), and who see, therefore, 'accuracy' training as a preparation for eventual 'fluency'. Yet Krashen's views on the relevancy of instruction are compatible with the results of the research undertaken by Schumann and Perkins & Larsen-Freeman.

The question we need to consider is whether Krashen's explanation is the only one and whether it is the best one. In this paper I want to explore how an alternative theoretical framework for SLA, based on the notion of contextual variability, can account for the research findings. In particular I want to argue that such a framework can provide a principled basis for interrelating 'accuracy' and 'fluency' work.

The paper falls into two principal parts. In the first part I review some research into contextual variability in SLA and develop a framework for a 'variability perspective' on SLA. In the second part of the paper I explore the relevance of this 'variability perspective' for three areas of language pedagogy — syllabus design, language teaching materials and classroom practice. In the conclusion I return to a consideration of the relationship between 'accuracy' and 'fluency' teaching.

Some Major Issues: A Look at the Research

Earlier I stated that theories of L2 acquisition have ignored interlanguage variability. This is not entirely correct, however. There have been a number of studies of contextual variability in L2 acquisition and at least one major theoretical statement (Tarone, 1983). A good starting point, then, is to briefly survey the major research findings.

SLA researchers have been aware for some time that data collected using different instruments reveal different linguistic properties. Lococo (1976) for instance, found major differences in the percentage of errors in prepositions, adjectives and determiners produced by university students enrolled in an elementary Spanish course, according to the kind of task used to collect the data. Similar results have been reported by Larsen-Freeman (1976) and Bahns & Wode (1980). In particular, differences occur as a result of whether the data reflect spontaneous language performance or elicited language.

Given that the performance data of L2 learners differ according to task, the question arises as to whether these differences are systematic or haphazard. Tarone makes a strong case for systematicity. She reviews a number of studies of variability in L2 acquisition and argues that they provide clear evidence of style-shifting. That is, L2 learners can be credited with a variable capacity and draw on particular variants according to the degree of attention they are paying to linguistic form. Style shifting occurs along a continuum ranging from a 'careful' to a 'vernacular' (or 'casual') style. The careful style is most evident in grammatical intuition data and the vernacular style in spontaneous oral communication.

There are a number of further points to make about style shifting in L2 acquisition. First, it needs to be emphasised that the evidence shows that L2 learners possess a number of styles, not just two, as in the acquisition/learning dichotomy. This suggests that the Monitor Model may not constitute an adequate account of the nature of interlanguage systems. Contextual variability is not an either–or phenomenon; it is a continuous phenomenon.

Second, the research provides strong evidence to suggest that when tasks are ordered according to the degree of attention to linguistic form they require, accuracy levels in the use of specific linguistic forms vary continuously, with the highest levels evident in the learner's careful style and the lowest levels in the vernacular style. It has been suggested that it is the careful style that is most permeable to the influence of target language forms.

Third, it has been shown that the careful style is also the style that is most influenced by the learner's first language (L1). Beebe (1980b), for instance, found that Thai learners used /r/ variably depending on whether they were conversing or listing words. But the nature of the variability was complex. When /r/ occurred finally the customary pattern of style shifting was observed. That is, the learners performed more accurately in their careful style than in their vernacular style. However, initial /r/ showed the opposite effect, with the vernacular style displaying more accuracy than the careful style. The reason for this, Beebe suggests, was that the learners were transferring a prestige /r/ variant, which differed from target language /r/, in this position when they were focused on form. Schmidt (1977) reports the same effect for the *th*-variable in Arabic learners of English. Thus the careful style is also permeable to the influence of the L1 when the native language forms have prestige value in the L1.

Fourth, whereas the pattern of style shifting in interlanguage phonology appears to be fairly predictable, style shifting in interlanguage grammar appears to be more complex, subject to the interplay of additional factors. Tarone (1985) found that the type of discourse affected the levels of accuracy of certain morphological structures and could produce a different effect than the expected one. Tarone found that the learners in her study used the third person singular verb morpheme -*s* as expected (i.e. with greatest accuracy in the careful style and lowest accuracy in a casual style). However, the pattern of use for two other structures — direct object pronoun and articles — was the opposite. Tarone explains this by postulating that the task used to tap the vernacular style also required the production of cohesive discourse. Thus the learners' use of direct object pronouns and articles (but not of the third person singular morpheme) was motivated by the need to make their discourse textually cohesive and this need overrode the normal pattern of style shifting. Fakhri (1984) also found that discourse factors influenced the use of linguistic forms. In this case it was not the type of discourse that counted but pragmatic considerations. Her subject made variable use of the pro-drop rule according to her perceived need to keep the reference clear. These studies indicate that contextual variability in grammar is a complex affair, influenced not only by style shifting but also by discourse and pragmatic factors.

Another factor that can influence the general pattern of style shifting in interlanguage grammar is the nature of the linguistic rule. Ellis (1987b) found that not all structures manifest style shifting or manifest it to the same degree. Apart from the fact that some structures may have been thoroughly acquired in the sense that they are used categorically in all styles, other structures, which are still in the process of being acquired may not be subject to style shifting. Ellis found that whereas an easily learnt structure such as regular past tense style shifted in a highly regular fashion, a structure such as irregular past tense, which is not easily learnt, did not style shift at all. The absence or presence of style shifting, therefore, appears to be dependent on the nature of the forms in question.

So far, my review of the major issues concerning variability in interlanguage has considered the systematic variability that arises from style shifting. However, contextual variability also occurs as a function of linguistic context. That is, systematic variation arises as a result of internal as well as external factors. Dickerson (1975), for instance, found that Japanese learners of English varied in their use of /z/ according to the linguistic environment of the sound. The precise phonetic quality of /z/ changed according to the adjacent consonants and vowels. L2 acquisition can be characterised as the gradual movement towards categoricality as the learner masters the use of variants in one linguistic context after another.

What is the relationship between external factors responsible for style shifting and internal factors responsible for incremental learning across different linguistic contexts? Downes (1984), writing about sociolinguistic variation in natural languages, proposes that stylistic variability is primary. He argues that there is a prior probability of a rule applying determined by extralinguistic factors. This leads to style shifting. Probabilities can then be assigned to various internal linguistic environments. There has, however, to the best of my knowledge, been no study investigating whether this is the case in interlanguage.

Finally, we need to acknowledge that not all variability is systematic (i.e. describable in terms of intra- and extralinguistic factors). If interlanguage is to be treated as a natural language (Adjemian, 1976) we can expect considerable non-systematic variability. As Downes puts it, 'heterogeneity is the normal state of language'. Systematic variability only arises when speakers make selections from the 'pervasive fluctuation'. Thus systematic variability is a reflection of linguistic *change*. Non systematic variability is present before change is initiated and serves as the resource for change. It is this view of variability that Ellis (1985) proposes as a basis for understanding the role of variability in SLA. Because of the permeability of interlanguage systems new forms are constantly entering but in the first place are used together with existing forms in free variation to perform the same range of language functions. At some later point the learner tries to maximise his linguistic resources by eliminating free variation. At this point we will observe systematic variability according to the situational and linguistic contexts of use. At a still later stage, systematic variability may for some learners, at least, give way to the categorical use of chosen variants (which may or may not be identical with target language norms). This process of development is shown diagramatically in Figure 11.1. It should be noted, however, that this is not intended as a model of overall interlanguage development (i.e. the stages do not correspond to stages in the vertical development of L2 acquisition taken as a whole). Rather it shows how new interlanguage forms, which may appear at different development points, evolve.

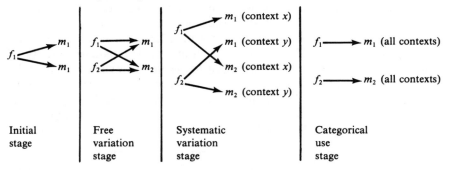

f = form
m = meaning
'context' refers to both situational and linguistic contexts

FIGURE 11.1   *The changing pattern of variability in SLA*

This review of the major issues involved in viewing interlanguage as a variable system points to the pervasivensss of different kinds of variability in language-learner language and also suggests the significance of variation as a mechanism for change in the process of L2 acquisition. At this point it is useful to step back from the research and formulate an overall framework for considering variability in L2 acquisition. This I now attempt in the form of a series of propositions, based both on the foregoing research and sociolinguistic theory.

A General Framework for Variability in L2 Acquisition

The following propositions are an attempt to define a framework for viewing L2 acquisition as a variable phenomenon. They should be viewed as hypotheses rather than absolute facts. They are our 'best bets' from what we currently know about variability in L2 acquisition.

(1) All interlanguage systems are heterogeneous. At any single stage of development, including the terminal stage, at least some forms will exist in free variation.

(2) Systematic variability occurs when the learner selects specific forms and begins to use them in accordance with extralinguistic and intralinguistic factors. This variability will be evident in all levels of interlanguage (phonology, lexis and grammar).

(3) Stylistic variability is a reflection of the degree of explicitness/implicitness with which knowledge of linguistic variants is represented in the learner's interlanguage. The learner operates a stylistic continuum such that different variants are manifested with different frequencies in different styles. These styles range from the careful to the vernacular and arise as a product of the degree to which the learner is focused on form.

(4) New linguistic forms can enter the learner's interlanguage in any style, but the careful style is especially prone to invasion. In contrast the vernacular style is relatively stable. One of the principal ways in which change takes place in interlanguage is through the spread of selected variants from the careful style towards the vernacular style.

(5) When new linguistic forms enter the learner's interlanguage they will not do so in all linguistic environments at once. Environments can be ordered according to their 'weight', with learning occurring first in 'heavy' environments (in which it is psychologically easy for the learner to acquire and use a new form) and then proceeding to increasingly 'light' environments.

(6) Changes in interlanguage are reflected in the incremental progress towards categoricality across styles and across linguistic environments. Learners will differ in how far along the path to categoricality they travel. In some learners prestige 'variants' (e.g. those corresponding to target language norms) will not reach their more casual styles.

(7) The process of change in interlanguage is powered primarily by normative pressures. These can be of two kinds. The learner may be motivated to 'belong' to the target language community and will endeavour, therefore, to acquire those patterns of variability that characterise the target dialect of his contact group. This type or normative pressure can be labelled 'social'. Alternatively the normative pressures can derive from the

authority and status inherent in institutional structures. These will be influential either when group structure is weak so that 'social' pressures are minimised or when the context of learning does not involve contact with the target language community, as, for instance, in classroom learning. The particular type of institutional normative pressure present in the foreign language classroom can be characterised as 'pedagogic'. Learning continues as long as the learner acknowledges either 'social' or 'pedagogic' normative pressures; it ceases when the learner is no longer open to such pressures. In this case the learner's interlanguage 'fossilises' in whatever state of variability it has reached at that point.

(8) Change can also occur as a result of structural pressures that arise in an interlanguage system through the introduction of new variants. The learner is led to maximise the efficiency of his system in order to communicate effectively. This induces a chain reaction effect on existing resources once these are augmented. Whereas the normative pressures referred to above can be viewed as 'external', the kind of structural pressure that occurs as a result of these normative pressures, can be seen as 'internal'. The constant flux of interlanguage systems is the result of this internal pressure.

These eight propositions comprise what I call a 'variability perspective' on L2 acquisition. It is now time to consider the relevancy of language teaching in the light of this perspective.

The Relevancy of Language Teaching

It is possible to identify a clear thread in many of the current attempts to apply models of L2 acquisition to language teaching. It is this. Language teaching should attempt to create in the classroom conditions which exist in 'natural' language learning (Hughes, 1983). In its strongest form this has led to the claim that formal language instruction involving the presentation and practice of target language rules has no place in successful language learning. In other words, for language teaching to be relevant it must only provide opportunities for authentic communication. In this part of the paper I want to dispute this claim. I shall endeavour to show that the 'variability perspective' outlined above provides a principled basis in L2 acquisition theory for 'accuracy' work as well as 'fluency' work. I shall consider three areas of language pedagogy — syllabus design, language teaching materials and classroom methodology — and argue in each case for a balanced approach incorporating both 'accuracy' and 'fluency'.

Syllabus design

A syllabus for language teaching will consist of a statement of the content that is to be taught. This content can be specified in two different ways. It can consist of an itemisation of *linguistic* features. These may be presented either directly as a list of language forms or indirectly as a list of functions and semantico-grammatical categories together with their linguistic exponents. Both a structural and a notional syllabus provide a linguistic content, differing only in how the linguistic material for learning is organised. Thus they are both *product* syllabuses, because they are both characterised by a content consisting of the linguistic products to be learnt. The alternative to this kind of syllabus is a *process* syllabus (also referred to as a procedural or task based syllabus). In a process syllabus no attempt is made to specify the linguistic features to be taught. Instead the content of the syllabus is specified as a list of activities or tasks to be performed by the learners under the guidance of the teacher. A process syllabus, in fact, will not have the appearance of a language syllabus at all, but will resemble the syllabus of a content subject such as science or geography. An example of a process syllabus is that used in the Communicational Teaching Project (see Johnson, 1982). Examples of the kind of content found in this syllabus are 'making the plan of a house', 'choosing routes from a map', etc.

There are two major questions we need to ask about these two methods of specifying the content of a syllabus. (1) Is it possible to make a principled choice between them, i.e. to argue that one is more likely to lead to successful classroom learning than the other? (2) If no principled choice is possible, how can the two methods be jointly used to produce an integrated syllabus involving both product and process elements? I shall address these questions from the variability perspective.

The assumption that underlies a process syllabus is that 'form is best learnt when the learner's attention is on meaning' (Prabhu, 1982; cited in Brumfit, 1984). We find a similar claim in Krashen & Terrell (1983): 'Language is best taught when it is used to transmit messages not when it is explicitly taught for conscious learning'. Also Breen (1983) argues for 'greater concern with the capacity for communication . . . with a focus upon means rather than predetermined objectives'. The justification for these claims comes from L2 acquisition theory, in particular Krashen's Monitor Model. The learner is credited with an in-built syllabus of his own which dictates the route of acquisition and which cannot be altered by pedagogic attempts to structure the linguistic content of learning from the outside. All that is required is the opportunity to engage in meaningful communication. But the theory of L2 acquisition that protagonists of a process syllabus draw upon takes no account of variability and its role in acquisition. Instead it views the learner's competence as homogeneous and learning as a series of more or less discrete stages.

A variability model of L2 acquisition lends greater support to a product syllabus. Recall that it is the learner's careful style that is most permeable. Recall also that new rules arise as the result of normative pressures, one source of which is the authority of institutional structures (i.e. in the case of the classroom, the teacher). The careful style is characterised by close attention to form. Here, then, are grounds for arguing that the process of change in interlanguage can be directed by supplying the learner with the norms of the target language, presented as a series of items to be carefully learnt. This is exactly what is intended by a product syllabus. The learner is systematically introduced to the formal structures of the target language which are given normative status by authority of the syllabus. A variability perspective, therefore, provides a warrant for a product syllabus. Such a syllabus can serve two functions. First, it can provide a basis for developing the learner's careful style (which in the case of learners who have no need or wish to engage in spontaneous language use will be sufficient in itself). Second, it can serve as a basis for fostering variable structures in the learner's interlanguage by introducing new variants, which, later on, given the right conditions, can spread through the stylistic continuum and so become available for use in more casual styles.

Our knowledge of the nature of variability in L2 acquisition, however, suggests that not all grammatical structures are candidates for style shifting and, the corollary of this, not all structures can enter into the learner's careful style as explicit knowledge. Structures that are regular are easy to formulate, thus easy to teach and easy to learn. Faerch & Kasper (forthcoming), for instance, found that a Danish learner of L2 English and L2 German found it easier to apply conscious knowledge in a translation task (which tapped the careful style) for German than for English. They speculate that this was because this kind of knowledge was more comprehensive in this subject's German interlanguage because German has many low-level rules that are obligatory, frequent, easy to formulate and thus easy to teach. It may be, therefore, that we need to restrict the items in a product syllabus to those that are learnable as explicit knowledge. Pica (1985) lends support to such a view. Her research shows that whereas instruction appears to be successful in the case of structures where there is form-function transparency (e.g. plural -s), it has no effect on structures which are complex (e.g. article a). We need to know more about those structures that can be influenced by instruction. We also need to discover more about what structures exhibit variability, because it is in precisely these areas that instruction should help most (Hyltenstam, 1985).

With these provisos, a variability model of L2 acquisition provides a solid rationale for a product syllabus.

It also provides a rationale for a process syllabus. The spread of knowledge along the stylistic continuum requires the opportunity to engage in a range of language styles, including the vernacular. This is precisely what a process syllabus aims to provide. It presents the learner with a series of tasks the main purpose of which is to motivate communication. We can hypothesise that this fosters interlanguage development in a number of ways. First, the learner will be motivated to eliminate free variation in order to increase the efficiency of his communication. Thus free variation will give way to systematic variation. Second, he will have the opportunity of 'trying out' the variants of his careful style in more casual styles. Third, he will be encouraged to explore new linguistic environments for existing variants, i.e. learn how to use them in increasingly 'light' linguistic contexts. The process by which new forms advance along the stylistic continuum is a complex one. It is doubtful whether this process can be structured from the outside. Therefore, a process syllabus has value because it provides the learner with the 'space' for his variable system to grow and to reshape. A process syllabus is the best bet for encouraging the movement towards categoricality.

Swan (1985) comments 'learning a language is not the same as using a language'. I believe that learning is very closely related to using but that nevertheless the point that Swan is getting at is correct. Swan, as I understand him, wants to make a distinction between the 'learning' that occurs as a result of teaching directed by a product syllabus with 'using' what has been learnt in natural communication. In the context of variability theory the same idea can be expressed more neatly; learning to perform in a careful style is not the same as learning how to perform in a vernacular style. It is, however, as Swan argues, a good start. The point I wish to emphasise is that different kinds of use result in different kinds of learning.

The variability perspective, then, lends support to both a product and a process syllabus. The question arises as to how they can be combined into a single integrated syllabus. One possibility is to arrange a tight integration, where specific 'products' are linked to the performance of specific tasks in the process component of the syllabus. This will produce a 'spiral syllabus' of the kind proposed by Brumfit (1980) — see Figure 11.2 (a). Although this arrangement is appealing, it is not, I think, feasible. This is because it is impossible for syllabus designers to predict which linguistic forms introduced as explicit knowledge will actually be called upon when the learner is required to perform in casual styles. It is the learner himself who must determine how his variable system will develop. The 'spiral syllabus', therefore, seems less appropriate than the 'parallel syllabus', in which there are two separate strands, one for 'products' and the other for tasks, each graded and sequenced separately. In such a syllabus the principal decision will be to decide what proportions of teaching time to allocate to the product and process strands. This decision will need to be informed by a number of factors, including the general goal of the syllabus (e.g. whether to develop a full stylistic range in the learner or whether to focus on developing a mono-stylistic competence, careful or vernacular) and the age of the learner (e.g. young children may not have developed the cognitive capacity to acquire a careful style and so would benefit from a syllabus heavily weighted in favour of the process component).

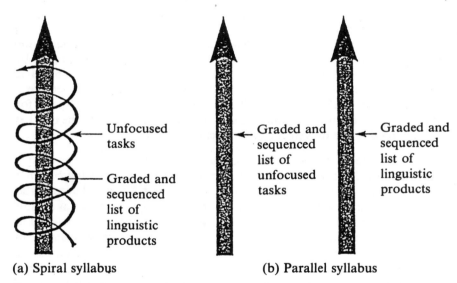

← Unfocused tasks

← Graded and sequenced list of linguistic products

← Graded and sequenced list of unfocused tasks

← Graded and sequenced list of linguistic products

(a) Spiral syllabus   (b) Parallel syllabus

FIGURE 11.2   *Two ways of 'integrating' product and process in syllabus design*

Language teaching materials

One way of viewing language teaching materials is as devices for implementing a syllabus. It follows, then, from what has already been argued, that we require materials of two basic kinds. First, materials are needed to introduce the learner to the norms of the chosen target language variety, that is, to present and practise specific linguistic items derived from the product component of the syllabus. We can refer to these as 'focused materials'.

Second, materials are needed to enable the learner to develop his variable interlanguage system. These will facilitate the dispersal of variants throughout the stylistic continuum. This kind of materials will consist of 'unfocused activities' based on the process component of the syllabus.

Where focused materials are concerned, one decision to make is how to deal with meaning. In structural materials the focus will be placed on linguistic forms and meaning will be handled through contextualisation. In functional and notional materials the focus will be placed on meaning and linguistic form will be handled by selecting exponents of specific functions and notions. I do not wish to enter into the pros and cons of these two approaches to focused materials. Probably, as Swan (1985) argues, we need both. Essentially, however, both approaches serve the same basic purpose. That is, their relevancy lies in the effects they achieve in developing the learner's careful style. They will enable the learner to consciously manipulate specific linguistic items for conveying specific meanings, when he is focused on form. There should, however, be no expectancy that focused materials of either type will in themselves foster the ability to use these items in spontaneous language use (i.e. the vernacular style). Their role in language pedagogy should be seen as that of laying a foundation of knowledge upon which the learner can himself act in the subsequent process of building a variable interlanguage.

A variability perspective on L2 acquisition does suggest one way in which focused materials can be refined. Traditionally language drills have been developed to practise selected formal features (and their meanings) with little regard for the linguistic environment in which these features are embedded. We might try to take acount of the way the learner acquires new forms by systematically presenting them in different linguistic contexts, sequenced according to how 'heavy' or 'light' they are. This is likely to call for a cyclical approach in which items are initially presented in 'heavy' environments and then later reintroduced in 'lighter' environments. At the moment SLA research does not provide us with sufficient information to reliably determine how linguistic environments should be weighted, but there is nothing to stop the materials writer doing as he has always done and base his decisions on his own intuitions, informed by the general principle of incremental learning over different linguistic environments for which a sufficient warrant already exists in SLA research.

Unfocused activities are designed to stimulate what is often referred to as 'authentic communication' in the classroom. They are characterised by the following (based on Ellis, 1982):

(1) A non-linguistic outcome (e.g. drawing a picture, making a model, solving a problem)

(2) A concern for message rather than channel.
(3) A gap of some kind (opinion, information, personal feelings) which has to be bridged.
(4) A need to negotiate meanings in order to achieve the outcome.
(5) Learner control over the resources (verbal or non-verbal) that are used.

When the learner performs in unfocused activities he will not, in the first instance, be able to access forms in his careful style. Thus, analysed knowledge learnt through drills will not be readily available. He will be forced back on those processes involved in using and internalising a vernacular style. However, we can hypothesise that the communicative pressure that arises from using language in this way induces a 'pull' effect and so leads to the stylistic spread of new forms. The extent to which this takes place will be influenced by the extent to which the learner accepts the social norms implicit in the 'correct' target language forms. For unfocused materials to do their job the learner must be seen to be 'striving toward a norm', for it is this that 'will pull the learner's whole repertoire in the direction of variation similar to that found in the native speaker's use of the language' (Littlewood, 1981a: 155). However, this striving should consist of a general orientation to the learning task rather than as a conscious attempt to apply target language norms in specific activities. The latter would simply result in further practice of the learner's careful style.

So far this discussion of language teaching materials has been based on the apparent dichotomy of focused and unfocused materials. However, these constitute a continuum rather than a dichotomy. Many pedagogic activities are intermediate. That is, they will meet some but not all of the five criteria listed above. It is tempting, therefore, to see a parallel between the stylistic continuum of interlanguage and the focused/unfocused continuum of language teaching materials. At one end there will be drills which influence the learner's careful style while at the other end there will be communication activities that influence the vernacular style. In between there will be a variety of activities corresponding to the range of styles between the poles of the continuum. We might go further and speculate that by sequencing activities according to their degree of focus, we can lead the learner along the stylistic continuum. In such a course, we would start with focused activities and then gradually introduce more and more unfocused activities. In this way the materials would reflect and support the process by which a variable interlanguage develops. Such a proposal is far from revolutionary. Arguably, it corresponds to well tried pedagogic practice.

The most important lesson to be learnt from a variability perspective on L2 acquisition is that the value of language teaching materials is relative.

Different kinds of materials foster different kinds of learning. Potentially all materials are relevant. Irrelevancy occurs when the teacher or the learner seeks to achieve one kind of learning through the exploitation of materials which are only capable of fostering a different kind of learning.

Classroom methodology

Dickerson (1975) makes a number of general comments about the applications of a variability perspective on L2 acquisition to classroom practice. She writes:

> The knowledge that the learner operates a variable interlanguage system should be of practical value to the language teacher in such areas as teacher attitude, teacher expectations and the evaluation of student practice.

Dickerson argues that the teacher should expect variability in her students' performance and should cease to be surprised that 'backsliding' occurs. Also the teacher should recognise that change is bound to be gradual. No matter how skilfully the teacher handles the presentation and practice of new items these will not be immediately assimilated into the learner's system. Therefore the teacher should be prepared to acknowledge degrees of attainment. That is, she should not measure all learner productions against the norms of the target language but give credit for productions that display progress even though they are still 'deviant' in terms of the native speaker's grammar. Finally, Dickerson suggests that, because learner performance varies according to task, the teacher should avoid making comparisons between different kinds of task. The learner's progress needs to be measured with reference to performance in each style considered separately.

Perhaps the major aspect of classroom practice which a variability perspective can shed light on is classroom interaction. Any learning that takes place in the classroom arises in the course of interaction — between the teacher and the students, in pairs or groups of students or between students and texts. Interaction, then, is 'the fundamental fact of language pedagogy' (Allwright, 1984). In this view language teaching materials are not so much devices for implementing the syllabus as tools for generating classroom interaction. What does a variability perspective have to say about the relationship between classroom interaction and language learning?

The classroom has the potential for affording a range of interactional types (see Ellis, 1984a). These can derive from pedagogic activities (i.e. from the implementation of different kinds of language teaching materials). They can also derive from classroom management and organisation activities, providing that these are conducted in the target language. Also, if the target language functions as the medium of communication between students (as is likely to be the case in mixed ESL classes) there will also be interactions of a social nature. These various kinds of interaction can be classified according to whether they afford 'planned' or 'unplanned' discourse. The former is discourse that lacks forethought and that has not been organised prior to actual performance. It is most clearly evident in spontaneous oral communication. Planned discourse is discourse that has been organised before it is performed. This organisation can occur at different levels — the overall framework of the discourse, the construction of sentence plans and the motor programme for performing the discourse. The two discourse types constitute the poles of an interactional continuum and they arise under different conditions of use. In unplanned discourse we find interchangeability of roles between the participants, informality, spontaneity and reciprocity. In planned discourse we find fixed roles, formality, rigidity and lack of reciprocity (cf. Lakoff, undated).

Now, the argument I want to advance is that different types of classroom interaction contribute to the advancement of the learner's variable interlanguage system in different ways. The stylistic continuum is both the product and the reflection of participating in different types of discourse ranged along the planned/unplanned continuum. Participation in the kind of planned discourse that results from teacher-directed language drills leads to the acquisition of target language norms in the learner's careful style. Such discourse is likely to be characterised by the familiar three-phase pattern (initiate – response – feedback) described by Sinclair & Coulthard (1975) and also by overt error correction. Its purpose is to enforce pedagogic norms. Participation in the more freely-structured discourse that results from unfocused activities requires the performance of a greater range of speech acts and induces the negotiation of meanings required for the development of a vernacular style. Thus, learning is linked to language use with different kinds of learning arising out of different kinds of language use. The development of a variable interlanguage rests on the availability of opportunities to take part in different kinds of classroom interaction.

We can conclude, therefore, that the relevancy of language teaching is, in the final analysis, to be found in ensuring a match between the interactional opportunities afforded the learner and the kind of competence the teaching is designed to create. As Ellis (1984c) comments:

> Because different kinds of knowledge and different processes of language use are involved in different discourse types, it cannot be expected that the acquisition of one style will facilitate the use of another style.

Conclusion

I began this paper by referring to research that showed that although formal instruction appears to have a beneficial effect on the language performance that is elicited by using instruments such as translation tasks, it does not appear to have any effect on spontaneous use. I noted that Krashen's Monitor Model provides an apparent explanation in terms of the distinction between 'acquisition' and 'learning'. I would like to conclude this paper by querying whether Krashen's explanation is the best one.

First, it should be clear that a variability model of L2 acquisition, such as that outlined in this paper, is also capable of explaining why formal instruction benefits only elicited performance. We can assume that the instruction provided by Schumann and Perkins & Larson-Freeman was of the kind that affected the development of the learner's careful repertoire. That is, that it consisted largely of focused activities leading to planned discourse. This repertoire would be available when the learners performed their careful style but would not be available for spontaneous language use in the vernacular style. Thus the effects of instruction would be observed when the learners' careful style was elicited but not when the data collection instrument required the vernacular style. This is exactly what the results of the two studies show.

Thus Krashen's Monitor Model and the Variability Model are both able to explain the research results. How, then, can we choose between them? One way is by taking a look at some further research into the effects of instruction on L2 acquisition. Long (1983c) has reviewed most of the available research dealing with this issue. His conclusion is as follows:

> Put rather crudely instruction is good for you, regardless of your proficiency level, of the wider linguistic environment in which you receive it, and of the type of test you are going to perform on.

In other words, instruction helps to speed up the rate of learning even if it does not effect the pattern of learning. Long argues that these findings are not easily accommodated by the Monitor Model unless the importance of 'learning' is upgraded. Now, this is precisely what a variability model does by suggesting that (1) formal instruction can benefit the development of the learner's careful style and (2) knowledge initially available in the learner's careful style can be 'pulled' into other more casual styles, providing that certain conditions are met. Classroom learners will outperform naturalistic learners on tasks that tap the careful style. They will also outperform them on tasks that tap other styles providing they have the opportunity to extend explicit knowledge towards and into the vernacular style. This opportunity can exist in the classroom when unplanned discourse occurs. For ESL learners (who were the subjects of most of the research Long looked at) this opportunity is also likely to exist outside the classroom. To put it another way, when learners are subject to pedagogical and social normative pressures, their interlanguages will be more permeable to change and thus will develop more rapidly.

The Monitor Model is a homogeneous competence model. Krashen sees no connection between 'acquisition' and 'learning'; monitoring is a feature of performance, not competence. Krashen has used the Monitor Model, which I believe to be fundamentally wrong, to argue the case for a language pedagogy directed at supplying comprehensible input through focusing on meaning in natural communication. In this scheme of things the formal teaching of the linguistic code is relegated to a position of almost zero importance. As Faerch (1985) points out the blanket rejection of formal language teaching is both arrogant and contrary to the successful experience of many teachers, who have used traditional grammar teaching methods. Nor, I have tried to argue, is the blanket rejection of grammar teaching warranted if account is taken of interlanguage as a variable system. A variability perspective treats the learner's competence as heterogeneous. Applied to language pedagogy, it stresses the dual contribution of formal and informal instruction, of accuracy and fluency. These can be fostered by a parallel syllabus incorporating both product and process elements leading to materials that vary in the extent to which they are 'focused' on language form and, through these, to a range of discourse types from the planned to the unplanned in the classroom itself. Not only is such a model of L2 acquisition better equipped to deal with the known facts of SLA, but the approach to language pedagogy which it supports is compatible with the experiences of countless successful teachers.

I would like to end with a few words of caution. The proposals for language teaching that I have put forward on the basis of a variability perspective for L2 acquisition are intended to stimulate thought — in particular regarding the relationship between 'accuracy' and 'fluency' activities. I am aware that our current knowledge of L2 acquisition — and this includes our knowledge of variability — is still sparse. Arguably it does not provide an adequate basis for making explicit recommendations. Hyltenstam (1985) suggests that SLA research is applicable to pedagogy on two levels: (1) a very specific and narrow level (i.e where detailed proposals about syllabus design and teaching methodology are made), and (2) a more general level (i.e. where the teacher's general knowledge about L2 acquisition influences his daily practice in different ways). Hyltenstam argues that the results of SLA research are still too fragmentary to justify (1). It seems to me, though, inevitable that we should seek to apply our increasing understanding about how SLA takes place to language pedagogy, and that, there is nothing wrong with specific and direct proposals, providing that these are treated in the same way as other specific proposals based, for instance, on linguistic enquiry. That is, they should be viewed tentatively, as *suggestions* rather than directions. It is in this spirit that I have advanced arguments for a pedagogical approach based on what we currently know about SLA variability.

12. Grammar Teaching — Practice or Consciousness-Raising?

Introduction

There are two major questions that we need to consider with regard to grammar teaching in second language (L2) pedagogy. These are:

(1) Should we teach grammar at all?
(2) If we should teach grammar, how should we teach it?

The first question has been answered in the negative by some applied linguists. Krashen (1982), for instance, has argued that formal instruction in grammar will not contribute to the development of 'acquired' knowledge — the knowledge needed to participate in authentic communication. Prabhu (1987) has tried to show, with some success, that classroom learners can acquire an L2 grammar naturalistically by participating in meaning-focused tasks. Others, however, including myself, have argued that grammar teaching does aid L2 acquisition, although not necessarily in the way in which teachers often think it does. My principal contention is that formal grammar teaching has a delayed rather than instant effect.

The focus of this article is the second question. I am going to assume that we should teach grammar (see Ellis (1990) for the reasons why) and turn my attention to how we should set about doing so. Specifically, I want to consider two approaches, which I shall refer to as 'practice' and 'consciousness-raising'. I shall begin by defining these. I will then briefly consider the case for practice and argue that the available evidence suggests that it may not be as effective as is generally believed. I will then present a number of arguments in support of consciousness-raising and conclude with an example of a 'CR-task'.

Defining Practice and Consciousness-raising

For most teachers the main idea of grammar teaching is to help the learners internalise the structures taught in such a way that they can used in everyday communication. To this end, the learners are provided with opportunities to *practise* the structures, first under controlled conditions, and then under more normal communicative conditions. Ur (1988: 7) describes the practice stage of a grammar lesson in these terms:

> The practice stage consists of a series of exercises . . . whose aim is to cause the learners to *absorb* the structure thoroughly; or to put it another way, to *transfer what they know from short-term to long-term memory*.

It is common to distinguish a number of different types of practice activities — mechanical practice, contextualised practice and communicative practice. Mechanical practice consists of various types of rigidly controlled activities such as substitution exercises. Contextualised practice is still controlled, but involves an attempt to encourage learners to relate form to meaning by showing how structures are used in real-life situations. Communicative practice entails various kinds of 'gap' activities which require the learners to engage in authentic communication while at the same time 'keeping an eye, as it were, on the structures that are being manipulated in the process' (Ur, 1988: 9).

Irrespective of whether the practice is controlled, contextualised or communicative, it will have the following characteristics:

(1) There is some attempt to *isolate* a specific grammatical feature for focused attention.
(2) The learners are required to *produce* sentences containing the targeted feature.
(3) The learners will be provided with opportunities for *repetition* of the targeted feature.
(4) There is an expectancy that the learners will perform the grammatical feature *correctly*. In general, therefore, practice activities are 'success oriented' (Ur, 1988: 13).
(5) The learners receive *feedback* on whether their performance of the grammatical structure is correct or not. This feedback may be immediate or delayed.

These five characteristics provide a definition of what most methodologists mean by 'practice'. It should be noticed that each characteristic constitutes an assumption about how grammar is learnt. By and large, though, these assumptions go unchallenged and have become part of the mythology of language teaching.

Consciousness-raising, as I use the term, involves an attempt to equip the learner with an understanding of a specific grammatical feature — to develop declarative rather than procedural knowledge of it. The main characteristics of consciousness-raising activities are these:

(1) There is an attempt to *isolate* a specific linguistic feature for focused attention.
(2) The learners are provided with *data* which illustrate the targeted feature and they may also be supplied with an *explicit rule* describing or explaining the feature.
(3) The learners are expected to utilise *intellectual effort* to understand the targeted feature.
(4) Misunderstanding or incomplete understanding of the grammatical structure by the learners leads to *clarification* in the form of further data and description/explanation.
(5) Learners may be required (although this is not obligatory) to articulate the rule describing the grammatical structure.

It should be clear from this list that the main purpose of consciousness-raising is to develop *explicit knowledge* of grammar. I want to emphasise, however, that this is not the same as *metalingual knowledge*. It is perfectly possible to develop an explicit understanding of how a grammatical structure works without learning much in the way of grammatical terminology. Grammar can be explained, and, therefore, understood in everyday language. It may be, however, that access to some metalanguage will facilitate the development of explicit knowledge.

A comparison of the characteristics of consciousness-raising with those listed for practice shows that the main difference is that consciousness-raising does not involve the learner in *repeated production*. This is because the aim of this kind of grammar teaching is not to enable the learner to perform a structure correctly but simply to help her to 'know about it'. This is how Rutherford & Sharwood-Smith (1985) put it:

> CR is considered as a potential facilitator for the acquisition of linguistic competence and has nothing directly to do with the use of that competence for the achievement of specific communicative objectives, or with the achievement of fluency.

Whereas practice is primarily behavioural, consciousness-raising is essentially concept-forming in orientation.

The two types of grammar work, however, are not mutually exclusive. Thus, grammar teaching can involve a combination of practice and consciousness-raising and, indeed, traditionally does so. Thus, many methodologists recommend that practice work is preceded by a presentation stage, to ensure that the learners have a clear idea about what the targeted structure consists of. This presentation stage may involve an inductive or deductive treatment of the structure. Also, practice work can be rounded off with a formal explanation of the structure. Even strict audiolingualists like Brooks (1960) recognised the value of formal explanations of patterns as 'summaries' once the practice activities had been completed. Indeed, it is arguable that no grammar teaching can take place without some consciousness-raising occurring. Even if the practice work is directed at the implicit learning of the structure and no formal explanation is provided, learners (particularly, adults) are likely to try to construct some kind of explicit representation of the rule.

Nevertheless, the distinction is a real one and it is an important one. Whereas practice-work cannot take place without some degree of consciousness-raising (even if this is incidental), the obverse is not the case; consciousness-raising can occur without practice. Thus, it is perfectly possible to teach grammar in the sense of helping learners to understand and explain grammatical phenomena without having them engage in activities that require repeated production of the structures concerned. One way this has occurred is by presenting learners with rules for memorisation — teaching about grammar. This is what occurred in the grammar-translation method. Such an approach has been discredited on a number of grounds and it is not my intention to advocate its reintroduction. There are other ways of raising consciousness that are compatible with contemporary educational principles, however. Before considering these I want to consider to what extent the faith which methodologists have in practice is justified.

Does Practice Work?

There have been a number of empirical studies that have investigated whether practice contributes to L2 acquisition (cf. Ellis (1988b) and this collection, for a review). These studies are of two kinds — those that seek to relate the *amount* of practice achieved by individual learners with general increases in *proficiency* (e.g. Seliger, 1977; Day, 1984) and those which have examined whether practising a specific linguistic structure results in its acquisition (e.g. Ellis, 1984c).

The results of both types of research are not encouraging for supporters of practice. Correlational studies (i.e. the first kind referred to above) have produced mixed results. Some studies have found a relationship between amount of practice and gains in proficiency, but other studies have failed to do so. Even when a study does show a strong relationship, it does not warrant claiming that practice *causes* learning. In order to say something about cause and effect we have to interpret a correlational relationship. It is perfectly possible to argue that it is the learners' proficiency that influences practice, rather than vice versa. Teachers may direct more practice opportunities at those learners who they think are able to supply correct answers — thus, the more proficient receive more practice. Indeed, one of the requirements of practice — that it is success-oriented — would lead us to predict that this will happen. The detailed analysis of classroom interactions that result from practice activities supports such an interpretation.

Studies which have investigated whether practising a specific structure results in its acquisition provide evidence to suggest that practice does not result in the autonomous ability to use the structure. In other words, practising a grammatical structure under controlled conditions does not seem to enable the learner to use the structure freely. I carried out a study (Ellis, 1984c; and this volume) to see whether practising 'when' questions enabled learners to acquire this structure. It did not. More recently Ellis & Rathbone (1987) investigated whether practising a difficult word order rule with learners of L2 German resulted in its acquisition. Again, it did not. There are also doubts whether learners are able to transfer knowledge from controlled to communicative practice. Once learners move into a meaning-focused activity they seem to fall back on their own resources and ignore the linguistic material they have practised previously in form-focused activity.

There are, of course, problems with such studies as these, and it would be unwise to claim that they conclusively demonstrate that practice does not work. It may be that the practice was of the wrong kind, that it was poorly executed, or that there was not enough of it. It may be that practice only works with some kinds of learners. Nevertheless, the studies cast doubts on the claims which methodologists make about practice.

There are also strong theoretical grounds for questioning the effectiveness of practice. Pienemann (1985) has proposed that some structures are *developmental* in the sense that they are acquired in a defined sequence. It is impossible for the learner to acquire a developmental structure until the psycholinguistic processing operations associated with easier structures in the acquisitional sequence have been acquired.

According to Pienemann's *teachability hypothesis* a structure cannot be successfully taught (in the sense, that it will be used correctly and spontaneously in communication) unless the learner is developmentally ready to acquire it. In other words, the teaching syllabus has to match the learner's developmental syllabus. For practice to work, then, the teacher will have to find out what stage of development the learners have reached. Although it is technically possible for the teacher to do this, it is impractical in most teaching situations.

Of course, it does not follow from these arguments that practice is without any value at all. Practice probably does help where pronunciation is concerned — it gives learners opportunities to get their tongues around new words and phrases. Also, practice may be quite effective in helping learners to remember new lexical material, including formulaic chunks such as 'How do you do?', 'Can I have a . . .?' and 'I don't understand.' Some learners — extroverts who enjoy speaking in the classroom, for example — may respond positively to practice activities. For these reasons, practice will always have a place in the classroom. It needs to be recognised, however, that practice will often not lead to immediate procedural knowledge of grammatical rules, irrespective of its quantity and quality.

To sum up, there are strong grounds — empirical and theoretical — which lead us to doubt the efficacy of practice. 'Practice' is essentially a *pedagogic* construct. It assumes that the acquisition of grammatical structures involves a gradual automatisation of production, from controlled to automatic and it ignores the very real constraints that exist on the ability of the teacher to influence what goes on inside the learner's head from the outside. Practice may have limited *psycholinguistic* validity.

The Case for Consciousness-raising

We have seen that the goal of practice activities is to develop the kind of automatic control of grammatical structures that will enable learners to use them productively and spontaneously. We have also seen that there are reasons to believe that this may not be achievable. The problem lies in assuming that we can teach grammar for use in communication. If we lower our sights and instead aim to develop the learner's awareness of what is correct but without any expectancy that we can bring the learner to the point where she can use this knowledge in normal communication, then the main theoretical objections raised against practice disappear. Consciousness-raising is predicated on this lesser goal.

Practice is directed at the acquisition of *implicit* knowledge of a grammatical structure — the kind of tacit knowledge needed to use the structure effortlessly for communication. Consciousness-raising is directed at the formation of *explicit* knowledge — the kind of intellectual knowledge which we are able to gather about any subject, if we so choose. Of course, the construction of explicit representations of grammatical structures is of limited use in itself. It may help the learner to perform successfully in certain kinds of discrete-item language tests. It may also help the learner to improve her performance in planning her discourse, as when we monitor our output in order to improve it for public perusal. But, crucially, it will not be of much use in the normal, everyday uses of language. Explicit knowledge is not much use when it comes to communicating. For this, we need implicit knowledge.

We need to ask, therefore, whether the more limited goal of consciousness-raising — to teach explicit knowledge — has any value. Ultimately, consciousness-raising can only be justified if it can be shown that it contributes to the learner's ability to communicate. I want to argue that, although consciousness-raising does not contribute directly to the acquisition of implicit knowledge, it does so indirectly. In other words, consciousness-raising *facilitates* the acquisition of the grammatical knowledge needed for communication.

The acquisition of implicit knowledge involves three processes:

(1) noticing (i.e. the learner becomes conscious of the presence of a linguistic feature in the input, whereas previously she had ignored it).
(2) comparing (i.e. the learner compares the linguistic feature noticed in the input with her own mental grammar, registering to what extent there is a 'gap' between the input and her grammar).
(3) integrating (i.e. the learner integrates a representation of the new linguistic feature into her mental grammar).

The first two processes involve conscious attention to language; the third process takes place at a very 'deep' level of which the learner is generally not aware. Noticing and comparing can take place at any time; they are not developmentally regulated. But integration of new linguistic material into the store of implicit knowledge is subject to the kinds of psycholinguistic constraints discussed above.

How then does consciousness-raising contribute to the acquisition of implicit knowledge? I would like to suggest that it does so in two major ways:

(1) It contributes to the processes of noticing and comparing and, therefore, prepares the grounds for the integration of new linguistic material. However, it will not bring about integration. This process is controlled by the learner and will take place only when the learner is developmentally ready.

(2) It results in explicit knowledge. Thus, even if the learner is unable to integrate the new feature as implicit knowledge, she can construct an alternative explicit representation which can be stored separately and subsequently accessed when the learner is developmentally primed to handle it. Furthermore, explicit knowledge serves to help the learner to continue to notice the feature in the input, thereby facilitating its subsequent acquisition.

Consciousness-raising, then, is unlikely to result in immediate acquisition. More likely, it will have a *delayed* effect.

There are also educational reasons that can be advanced for grammar teaching as consciousness-raising. The inclusion of foreign languages in the school curriculum is not motivated entirely by the desire to foster communication between speakers of different languages, although this has become the most prominent aim in recent years. It has, and always has had, a more gneral goal — that of fostering intellectual development. 'Grammar' embodies a corpus of knowledge the study of which can be expected to contribute to students' cognitive skills. It constitutes a serious content and, as such, contrasts with the trivial content of many modern text books.

It is not my intention, however, to advocate a return to 'teaching about grammar' or, at least, not in the form that this was carried out in the past. The arguments that I have presented in favour of consciousness-raising do not justify giving lectures on grammar. Such a transmission-oriented approach runs contrary to progressive educational principles. What I have in mind is a task-based approach that emphasises discovery learning by asking learners to solve problems about grammar. I would like to conclude with an example of this approach.

An example of a consciousness-raising task

Consciousness-raising tasks can be *inductive* or *deductive*. In the case of the former, the learner is provided with data and asked to construct an explicit rule to describe the grammatical feature which the data illustrate. In the case of the latter, the learner is supplied with a rule which they then use in order to carry out some task. We do not know, as yet, which type results in the more efficient learning of explicit knowledge — probably both will prove useful.

Table 12.1 provides a simple example of an inductive task designed to raise learners' awareness about the grammatical differences between 'for' and 'since'. This problem has been designed with a number of points in mind. First, the intention is to focus on a known source of difficulty; learners frequently fail to distinguish 'for' and 'since'. Second, the data provided must

TABLE 12.1   *An example of a CR problem-solving task.*

1. Here is some information about when three people joined the company they now work for and how long they have been working there.

Name	Date joined	Length of time
Ms Regan	1945	45 yrs
Mr Bush	1970	20 yrs
Ms Thatcher	1989	9 mths
Mr Baker	1990 (Feb)	10 days

2. Study these sentences about these people. When is 'for' used and when is 'since' used?

    a. Ms Regan has been working for her company *for* most of her life.
    b. Mr Bush has been working for his company *since* 1970.
    c. Ms Thatcher has been working for her company *for* nine months.
    d. Mr Baker has been working for his company *since* February.

3. Which of the following sentences are ungrammatical? Why?

    a. Ms Regan has been working for her company for 1945.
    b. Mr Bush has been working for his company for twenty years.
    c. Ms Thatcher has been working for her company since 1989.
    d. Mr Baker has been working for his company since 10 days.

4. Try and make up a rule to explain when 'for' and 'since' are used.

5. Make up one sentence about when you started to learn English and one sentence about how long you have been studying English. Use 'for' and 'since'.

be adequate to enable the learners to discover the rule that governs the usage of these prepositions in time expressions. In the case of this task, the data includes both grammatical and ungrammatical sentences. Third, the task requires minimal production on the part of the learners; instead, emphasis is placed in developing an 'idea' of when the two forms are used. Fourth, there is an opportunity to apply the rule in the construction of personalised statements. This is not intended to 'practise' the rule but to promote its storage as explicit knowledge; production, therefore, is restricted to two sentences and there is no insistence on automatic processing. Such tasks as these can be designed with varying formats. They can make use of situational information, diagram, charts, tables etc. They can also be used in both lockstep teaching (i.e. when the teacher works through a problem with the whole class) or in small group work.

Conclusion

In this paper I have tried to argue the case for grammar teaching as consciousness-raising. In one respect this does not constitute a radical departure from what teachers have always done. Many teachers have felt the need to provide formal explanations of grammatical points. But in another respect it does represent a real alternative in that it removes from grammar teaching the need to provide learners with repeated opportunities to produce the target structure. So much effort has gone into to devising ingenious ways of eliciting and shaping learners responses, more often or not to little avail as learners do not acquire the structures they have practised. Consciousness-raising constitutes an approach to grammar-teaching which is compatible with current thinking about how learners acquire L2 grammar. It also constitutes an approach that accords with progressive views about education as a process of discovery through problem-solving tasks.

There are, of course, limitations to consciousness-raising. It may not be appropriate for young learners. Some learners (e.g. those who like to learn by 'doing' rather than 'studying') may dislike it. It can only be used with beginners if the learners' first language is used as the medium for solving the tasks. However, the alternative in such situations is not practice. Rather, it is to provide opportunities for meaning-focused language use, for communicating in the L2, initially perhaps in the form of listening tasks. All learners, even those who are suited to a consciousness-raising approach, will need plenty of such opportunities. Consciousness-raising is not an alternative to communication activities, but a supplement.

Section 7
Conclusion

The goal of SLA is to describe and explain how L2 acquisition takes place. The goal of language pedagogy is to arrange the learning experiences of L2 learners in such a way that they will learn with maximal efficiency. Clearly, the design and implementation of instructional programmes will benefit from attending to what SLA has discovered about L2 acquisition. SLA may also derive benefit from studying how different instructional programmes affect learning outcomes.

The essential question which both SLA and language pedagogy need to address is this: 'To what extent and in what ways do different kinds of input affect L2 acquisition?' For the SLA researcher, the classroom provides a convenient 'laboratory' for examining this question. For the language teacher, the practice of teaching serves as a means of evaluating on a day-by-day basis various proposals for organising the input to which the learner is to be exposed.

It would be pleasing to report that the combined efforts of SLA classroom researchers and teachers have resulted in a clear picture of how input affects acquisition. But, in fact, they are far from achieving this. Teachers are often dissatisfied with the products of SLA research, feeling that they do not provide them with the answers to their pressing problems. SLA researchers remain suspicious of the instant solutions which language pedagogy at times seems ready to adopt.

The task of establishing links between the input the learner is exposed to (the process) and the acquisition of new linguistic knowledge (the product) has proved an extremely difficult one. One reason for this is that there is no agreement among SLA researchers about the process-product relationship at the theoretical level. On the one hand there are researchers like Hatch (1978b; 1983) who see interaction as contributing directly to acquisition by helping the learner to produce new structures. On the other hand there are researchers like White (1987; 1990) who argue that the input seriously underdetermines acquisition and that learners must make use of innate knowledge in the form of a Universal Grammar in order to go beyond the input.

Another reason for the failure of process-product studies is the difficulty of establishing precisely what constitutes input to particular learners. This is especially true of the classroom context. Even in formal language lessons, where the focus is on teaching a specific linguistic feature in lockstep fashion, there can be no guarantee that all the learners are attending equally to the input the teacher supplies. In an informal lesson, designed to provide learners with opportunities to communicate naturally, there is even less certainty about what constitutes 'input'. Lightbown (1990: 82) catalogues the problems that the process-product classroom researcher faces:

> ... the impossibility of identifying comparable control groups or ensuring random selection for treatment groups; the influence of unmeasured variables such as momentary motivation and attentiveness; the problem of knowing what happens in the classroom environment when no observer is present; the fact that in second language situations learning continues outside the classroom.

It is, therefore, perhaps not so surprising that so little has been discovered about how instructional input affects acquisition.

One of the most carefully-designed process-product studies of recent years is that of Allen *et al.* (1990). The researchers took as their starting point Stern's (1981) distinction between 'experiential' and 'analytical' approaches to language teaching. In the case of the former, the input to the learner derives from interactions which are focused on the exchange of messages and, therefore, are likely to have the characteristics of real conversation. In the case of the latter, the focus is placed on specific aspects of the L2 (phonological, grammar of functions) and the input occurs in the context of contrived practice activities. Such research, as I argued in the 'Introduction' to this volume, is potentially of special value to teachers because it is based on a distinction taken from language pedagogy rather than on one taken from SLA research. The results obtained by this study were disappointing, however — recalling similar disappointments with the comparative method studies of the 1960s (e.g. Smith, 1970). There were very few significant differences in learning outcomes between classes of learners taught experientially and those taught analytically. This study then, despite the care that went into its design, was unable to demonstrate that one kind of instructional input had a different effect on learning than another kind.

Even studies which have set out to investigate the effects of formal instruction directed at specific grammatical features have produced indeterminate results. We have already seen the mixed results of studies which have investigated the effects of practice (see 'The Role of Practice in Classroom Language Learning', chapter 5). These have been unable to show any consistent relationship between practice opportunities and learning. In some cases, experimental studies have shown a general improvement in the performance of targeted features but the effects of instruction may not last, as accuracy levels in the use of the features atrophy with time (e.g. Lightbown *et al.*, 1980). Studies which fail to show any definite effect for instruction (as was the case in the two studies reported in Section Two) are always open to the criticism that it is not formal instruction *per se* that is failing but rather the particular type of formal instruction used in the study or simply the lack of sufficient practice opportunities.

It is easy, therefore, to view the contribution of SLA to language pedagogy as nugatory. Yet although few definite answers to pedagogic questions are possible on the basis of available SLA studies (even those conducted with specific pedagogical issues in mind), it would be mistaken to dismiss the overall contribution which such studies have made. This contribution takes the form not of 'solutions' but of 'illuminations'. As a result of the research and theory-development which has taken place to date, we have obtained a number of insights which together with insights drawn from other fields of enquiry can help to inform pedagogic decision-taking. We should not, then, talk of 'applying' SLA research to language pedagogy but rather of 'evaluating' instructional options in the light of what is known about L2 acquisition.

What, then, have we discovered about SLA that can help us evaluate proposals for teaching an L2? Tentatively, I would like to suggest the following:

(1) Classroom learners, like naturalistic learners, have the capacity to acquire a new language 'naturally' as a result of participating in classroom communication. Instruction that fails to provide opportunities for natural communication will deprive the learner of a major source of input and inhibit acquisition.

(2) Although there is uncertainty regarding what constitutes an 'acquisition-rich' environment, there are grounds for believing that classroom learners benefit from interaction in which the choice and development of topic rests with them. They also benefit from listening to other learners trying to communicate and to the feedback these learners receive on their efforts.

(3) Learner output will be variable according to a number of linguistic, social and psychological factors. In many instances, correct production in careful language use will not be matched by correct production in casual language use. Instruction, ideally, needs to provide for different kinds of language use in order to ensure full acquisition of new linguistic features.

(4) There are constraints of a psycholinguistic nature that govern whether

attempts to teach new linguistic features are successful. Formal instruction will not always work, therefore. However, formal instruction directed at raising learners' consciousness about specific features may well facilitate their subsequent acquisition. In general, there is ample support in the SLA literature for grammar teaching.

(5) Learners differ in a variety of ways (such as their preferred learning style) with the result that a particular instructional approach that works well for one student may not work so well for another.

There is, I believe, a general consensus regarding these conclusions among SLA researchers with an interest in language pedagogy. Clearly, though, these conclusions are pitched at a very high level of generality and ideally we would wish to see much more precise information available about what constitutes an 'acquisition-rich' environment, how instruction can take account of variability in learner-language, what psycholinguistic constraints affect the success of formal instruction and how learner-instruction matching can best be achieved. But either such information is not yet available or alternatively the information that is available is controversial.

These conclusions provide a basis for determining which *approach* to language teaching should be adopted. They suggest that some kind of combination of an experiential and analytic approach are required, so that learners have an opportunity to both learn through communicating and through studying the language. However, they do not cast much light on how experiential and analytical teaching should be incorporated into the overall curriculum. My own proposal — based on variability theory — that they should be kept as separate modules (see 'Contextual variability in second language acquisition and the relevancy of language teaching', chapter 11) is controversial.[1] Also, these conclusions, because of their generality, do not help very much in providing fine-grained answers regarding such issues as the selection and grading of teaching content or the choice of methodological procedures.

Thus, although we do not need to be unduly negative about the contribution of SLA studies to language pedagogy, we do need to be aware of their limitations. SLA is of some value in deciding on *approach* but of very little value in clarifying which *techniques* (Anthony, 1963) to use. It is perhaps because teachers are often (and justifiably) concerned with techniques rather than principles, that they look disparingly on the efforts of SLA researchers. But, the choice of technique depends on the approach which has been adopted. There are assumptions about learning that underlie every classroom technique. The value of SLA is in helping teachers to make these assumptions more explicit by forcing them to answer the question 'If I do x, is it likely to help my students learn?' As I have argued elsewhere (Ellis, 1985; 1990), teachers who hold an *explicit* theory of L2 acquisition are in a better position to evaluate their own teaching, and therefore to change it, than are teachers who hold only vague, *implicit* ideas about learning.

There is, however, an obvious need to consider what kinds of SLA studies are most likely to take us forward — to move us beyond the general conclusions listed above. If I trace the direction that my own research efforts have followed, I can see that I have gradually shifted the focus of my attention from trying to describe the learning opportunities that learners experience in classrooms and to understand how these contribute to acquisition towards trying to investigate whether specific instructional practices work. This has led me from exploratory research of an ethnographic nature to hypothesis-testing research of an experimental or pseudo-experimental nature. This general trend is reflected more generally in SLA (as illustrated by the Allen *et al.* study referred to earlier). The bulk of the studies conducted today are quantitative and cross-sectional in nature, involving the investigation of fairly specific hypotheses. The time may have come for us to reverse this trend and once again conduct more qualitative studies of individual classrooms and learners, using the insights provided by SLA as a basis for deciding which aspects to focus on.

One of the major problems of an experimental approach is that it it is based on the assumption that we know how to characterise input or how instructional approaches differ. But as Allwright (1988: 8) has argued 'any *a priori* characterisation of learning and teaching environments is bound to be suspect for fundamental research purposes'. Even a thoughtful study such as that of Allen *et al.* took as given the validity of the experiential/analytical distinction. Yet it is precisely such a distinction — which was derived not directly from the observation of classroom events but indirectly from a review of the literature — that needs to be validated (and operationalised) through the careful study of instructional environments. Allwright goes on to warn that even if experimental research does find significant differences in learning outcomes between two 'treatments' these will not be properly understood if it is simply assumed that the learning differences derive from the treatment differences. Allwright's central point is that it is just as important (perhaps even more important) to understand whether instructional approaches which are held to be different are actually different and if so in what ways they are different, as it is to find out whether they result in different learning outcomes. Only in this way will SLA/pedagogic research provide the teacher with the kind of detailed information needed to enlighten classroom practice.

If we accept Allwright's arguments that 'the characterization of teaching and learning environments is something that must *emerge from* research rather than something that can be *imposed upon* research', then the question arises as to how we can accomplish this. It is here that the often mentioned idea of *triangulation* becomes so important, for we cannot assume that the researcher's understanding of what is taking place is also the teacher's, nor can we assume that what the teacher is teaching is what the learner is learning. In particular, it is important to take the learners' perspective in order to discover what it is in the input that they attend to. Nor can it be assumed that an instructional event is responded to identically by all the learners in the classroom. We need to investigate how *individual* learners construct learning experiences out of the instructional events to which they all have access.

All this calls for careful, painstaking work, involving a variety of qualitative research techniques — classroom observation by means of interaction analysis schedules, the detailed analysis of classroom discourse, interviews, questionnaires, think-aloud tasks etc. In addition, thought needs to be given to how we can establish links between input and acquisition. In this respect, it is important to acknowledge the variation in individual learners' responses. One way in which this might be achieved is through the use of uptake charts (Slimani, 1989), where each learner fills in a questionnaire indicating what has been learnt during the previous lesson. The items recorded on the charts can then be traced back to their occurrence in the lesson in order to uncover what features of the input/interaction made the learners notice them. Such a procedure allows for the qualitative study of the relationship between instruction and acquisition. It is not without its problems, however — in particular, there is uncertainty regarding whether 'uptake', as reported by learners, constitutes a valid and reliable measure of acquisition.

Perhaps the most effective way of obtaining precise information about how learners respond to instruction and what they learn from it is through longitudinal case studies of individual learners. This was the approach that I initially chose to adopt (cf. Ellis, 1982a). It provides extremely rich data about the classroom and the way individual learners behave as well as affording a detailed picture about how their L2 knowledge and skills develop over time. There have been surprisingly few cases studies of classroom learners, however — mainly because of the time-consuming nature of such research. Yet, arguably, it is such an approach that is now needed to help us understand both what constitutes a 'learning opportunity' and what is learnt from it.

To conclude, SLA studies will continue to inform language pedagogy through the application of theoretical positions and empirical findings. In this respect, SLA occupies the same position as other disciplines (linguistics, sociology and education) which contribute to the development of instructional practice and any move to give it some kind of privileged status must be resisted. Also, and perhaps more importantly, SLA research will increasingly be carried out inside the classroom, adding to our understanding of the relationship between instruction and learning. I have argued that at the present time such research needs to adopt qualitative, ethnographic procedures in order to account for how instructional events are enacted and how individual learners respond to them.

A final observation — the relationship between SLA research and language pedagogy has been largely non-reciprocal. Teachers and teacher educators have 'consumed' the information and ideas provided by SLA researchers. But SLA researchers have, in general shown scant regard for the constructs that inform language pedagogy. This is disappointing as much can be learnt by seeking answers to questions of pedagogic significance. As I argued in the introduction, there is a strong case for an 'educational approach' to SLA, not just because such an approach may be of more direct benefit to language pedagogy but also because it may throw light on SLA itself. One way in which both SLA researchers and teachers may benefit is through collaborating as partners in research which is of interest to both their concerns. As Handscombe (1990) argues, a significant contribution to the improvement of L2 teaching is most likely to take place if researchers and teachers learn how to value each others' knowledge and skills.

Notes

1. Methodologists generally advocate integrating analytic and experiential approaches. They suggest two ways in which this can take place. First, specific linguistic features can be taught as a *preparation* for a subsequent communicative task. Second, grammar teaching can precede by providing opportunities for 'free' communicative practice after controlled practice. My argument against both proposals is that transfer from analytic to experiential activities is severely constrained with the result that in many cases it will not take place. It is inefficient, therefore, to base pedagogic proposals on the assumption that such transfer will take place.

References

ABRAHAM, R. and VANN, R. 1987, Strategies of two language learners: A case study. In A. WENDEN and T. RUBIN (eds) *Learner Strategies in Language Learning*. London: Prentice Hall International.

ADJEMIAN, C. 1976, On the nature of interlanguage systems. *Language Learning* 26, 297–320.

ALLEN, P., FRÖHLICH, M. and SPADA, N. 1984, The communicative orientation of language teaching: An observation scheme. In J. HANDSCOMBE, R. OREM and B. TAYLOR (eds) *On TESOL '83: The Question of Control*. Washington DC: TESOL.

ALLEN, P., HARLEY, B. and SWAIN, M. 1989, Analytic and experiential aspects of second language teaching. *RELC Journal* 20, 1–19.

ALLEN, P., SWAIN, M., HARLEY, B. and CUMMINS, J. 1990, Aspects of classroom treatment: Towards a more comprehensive view of second language education. In B. HARLEY, P. ALLEN, J. CUMMINS and M. SWAIN (eds) *The Development of Bilingual Proficiency*. Cambridge: Cambridge University Press.

ALLWRIGHT, R. 1975, Problems in the study of the language teacher's treatment of error. In M. BURT and H. DULAY (eds) *On TESOL '75*. Washington DC: TESOL.

— 1980, Turns, topics and tasks: Patterns of participation in language learning. In D. LARSEN-FREEMAN (ed.) *Discourse Analysis in Second Language Acquisition Research*. Rowley, Mass.: Newbury House.

— 1984, The importance of interaction in classroom language learning. *Applied Linguistics* 3, 156–71.

ALLWRIGHT, R. 1988, The characterization of teaching and learning environments: Problems and perspectives. Paper given at Conference on Empirical Research into Foreign Language Teaching Methods, Bellagio, Italy.

ANTHONY, M. 1963, Approach, method and technique. *English Language Teaching* 17, 63–7.

ARTHUR, B., WEINER, R., CULVER, M., YOUNG J. and THOMAS, D. 1980, The register of impersonal discourse to foreigners: Verbal adjustments to foreign accent. In D. LARSEN-FREEMAN (ed.) *Discourse Analysis in Second Language Acquisition Research*. Rowley, Mass., Newbury House.

ASHER, J. 1977, *Learning Another Language Through Actions: The Complete Teacher's Guidebook*. Los Gatos, California: Sky Oaks Publication.

AUFDERSTRASSE, H., BOCK, H., GERDES, M. and MULLER, H. 1983, *Themen*. München: Max Hueber Verlag.

AUSUBEL, D. 1971, Some psychological aspects of the structure of knowledge. In P. JOHNSON (ed.) *Learning: Theory and Practice*. New York: Thomas Y Crowell.

BAHNS, J. and WODE, H. 1980, Form and function in L2 acquisition. In S. FELIX (ed.) *Second Language Development*. Tubingen: Gunter Narr.

BAILEY, C. 1973, *Variation and Linguistic Theory*. Arlington, VA: Center for Applied Linguistics.

BAILEY, N., MADDEN, C. and KRASHEN, S. 1974, Is there a 'natural sequence' in adult second language learning? *Language Learning* 24, 235–44.

BARNES, D. 1976, *From Communication to Curriculum*. Harmondsworth: Penguin.

BEEBE, L. 1980s, Measuring the use of communication strategies. In R. SCARCELLA and S. KRASHEN (eds) *Research in Second Language Acquisition*. Rowley, Mass.: Newbury House.

— 1980b, Sociolinguistic variation and style shifting in second language acquisition. *Language Learning* 30, 433–47.

BEEBE, L. and ZUENGLER, J. 1983, Accomodation theory: An explanation for style shifting in second language dialects. In N. WOLFSON and E. JUDD (eds) *Sociolinguistics and Language Acquisition*. Rowley, Mass.: Newbury House.

BIALYSTOK, E. 1982, On the relationship between knowing and using linguistic forms. *Applied Linguistics* 3, 181–206.

— 1983, Inferencing: Testing the 'hypothesis-testing' hypothesis. In H. SELIGER and M. LONG (eds) *Classroom Oriented Research in Second Language Acquisition*. Rowley, Mass.: Newbury House.

— 1985, The compatibility of teaching and learning strategies. *Applied Linguistics* 6, 255–62.

BIALYSTOK, E. and FRÖHLICH, M. 1977, Aspects of second language learning in classroom settings. *Working Papers on Bilingualism* 13, 2–26.

— 1978, Variables of classroom achievement in second language learning. *Modern Language Journal* 62, 327–35.

BIALYSTOK, M. and SHARWOOD-SMITH, M. 1985, Interlanguage is not a state of mind: An evaluation of the construct for second language acquisition. *Applied Linguistics* 6, 101–17.

BICKERTON, D. 1973, The structure of polylectal grammars. In R. SHUY (ed.) *Proceedings of the Twenty-Third Annual Round Table*. Washington DC: Georgetown University Press.

— 1975, *Dynamics of a Creole System*. Cambridge: Cambridge University Press.

— 1981, Discussion of Andersen 1981. In R. ANDERSEN (ed.) *New Dimensions in Second Language Acquisition Research*. Rowley, Mass.: Newbury House.

BIRCKBICHLER, D. and OMMAGIO, A. 1978, Diagnosing and responding to individual learner needs. *Modern Language Journal* 62, 336–44.

BLEY-VROMAN, R. 1988, The fundamental character of foreign language learning. In W. RUTHERFORD and M. SHARWOOD-SMITH (eds) *Grammar and Second Language Teaching*. Rowley, Mass.: Newbury House.

BLOOM, L. 1970, *Language Development: Form and Function in Merging Grammars*. Cambridge, Mass.: MIT Press.

BLUM-KULKA, S., HOUSE, J. and KASPER, G. (eds) 1989, *Cross-cultural Pragmatics: Requests and Apologies*. Norwood, NJ.: Ablex.

BREEN, M. 1983, Prepared comments on Keith Johnson's 'Syllabus design: Possible future trends'. In K. JOHNSON and D. PORTER (eds) *Perspectives in Communicative Language Teaching*. London: Academic Press.

— 1987, Learner contribution to task design. In C CANDLIN and D. MURPHY (eds) *Language Learning Tasks*. Prentice Hall International and Lancaster University.

BROCK, C. 1986, The effects of referential questions on ESL classroom discourse. *TESOL Quarterly* 20, 47–59.

BROOKS, N. 1960, *Language and Language Learning*. New York: Harcourt Brace and World.

BROWN, R. 1968, The development of WH questions in child speech. *Journal of Verbal Learning and Behavior* 7, 279–90.

— 1973, *A First Language: The Early Stages*. Cambridge, Mass.: Harvard University Press.

BROWN, P. and FRASER, C. 1979, Speech as a marker of situation. In K. SCHERER and H. GILES (eds) *Social Markers in Speech*. Cambridge: Cambridge University Press.

BROWN, P. and LEVINSON, S. 1978, Universals of language use: Politeness phenomena. In E. GOODY (ed.) *Questions and Politeness*. Cambridge: Cambridge University Press.

BRUMFIT, C. 1979, 'Communicative' language teaching: An educational perspective. In C. BRUMFIT and K. JOHNSON (eds) *The Communicative Approach to Language Teaching*. Oxford: Oxford University Press.

— 1980, *Problems and Principles in Language Teaching*. Oxford: Pergamon.

— 1984, *Communicative Methodology in Language Teaching*. Cambridge: Cambridge University Press.

BRUMFIT, C. and JOHNSON, K. (eds) 1979, *The Communicative Approach to Language Teaching*. Oxford: Oxford University Press.

BRUNER, J., GOODNEW, J. and AUSTIN, G. 1977, *A Study of Thinking*. Huntington, NY: Krieger.

BYGATE, M. 1988, Units of oral expression and language learning in small group interaction. *Applied Linguistics* 9, 59–82.

BYRNE, D. 1986, *Teaching Oral English* (2nd edn). London: Longman.

CANALE, M. 1983, From communicative competence to communicative language pedagogy. In J. RICHARDS and R. SCHMIDT (eds) *Language and Communication*. London: Longman.

CANALE, M. and SWAIN, M. 1980, Theoretical bases of communicative approaches to second language teaching and testing. *Applied Linguistics* 1, 1–47.

CANCINO, H., ROSANSKY, E. and SCHUMANN, J. 1978, The acquisition of English negatives and interrogatives by Spanish native speakers. In E. HATCH (ed.) *Second Language Acquisition*. Rowley, Mass.: Newbury House.

CAROLL, J. and SAPON, S. 1959, *Modern Language Aptitude Test (MLAT)*. New York: Psychological Corporation.

CAZDEN, C., CANCINO, H., ROSANSKY, E. and SCHUMANN, J. 1975, Second language acquisition sequences in children, adolescents and adults, Final Report. IS Department of Health, Education and Welfare.

CHAPELLE, C. and ROBERTS, C. 1986, Ambiguity tolerance and field independence as predictors of proficiency in English as a second language. *Language Learning* 36, 27–45.

CHAUDRON, C. 1988, *Second Language Classrooms*. Cambridge: Cambridge University Press.

CHOMSKY, N. 1965, *Aspects of the Theory of Syntax*. Mass.: MIT Press.

— 1980, On cognitive structures and their development: A reply to Piaget. In M. PIATELLI-PALMARINI (ed.) *Language and Learning*. London: Routledge and Kegan Paul.

— 1981, *Lectures on Government and Binding*. Dordrecht: Fortris.

CLAHSEN, H. 1980, Psycholinguistic aspects of second language acquisition. In S. FELIX (ed.) *Second Language Development*. Tübingen; Gunter Narr.

— 1984, The acquisition of German word order: A test case for cognitive approaches to L2 development. In R. ANDERSEN (ed.) *Second Languages: A Cross-linguistic Perspective.* Rowley, Mass.: Newbury House.

— 1985, Profiling second language development: A procedure for assessing L2 proficiency. In K. HYLTENSTAM and M. PIENEMANN (eds) *Modelling and Assessing Second Language Acquisition.* Clevedon, Avon: Multilingual Matters.

CLAHSEN, H. and MUYSKEN, P. 1986, The availability of universal grammar to adult and child learners: A study of the acquisition of German word order. *Second Language Research* 2, 93–119.

COENEN, J. and VAN HOUT, R. 1987, Word order phenomena in second language acquisition of Dutch. *Linguistics in the Netherlands* 83–92.

CORDER. S.P. 1967, The significance of learners' errors. *International Review of Applied Linguistics* 5: 161–9.

— 1976, The study of interlanguage. In *Proceedings of the Fourth International Congress of Applied Linguistics.* Münich: Hochschulverlag. Also in Corder (1981).

— 1977, Language continua and the interlanguage hypothesis. In *Proceedings of the Fifth Neuchatel Colloquium.* University of Neuchatel. Also in Corder, S. (1981).

— 1981, *Error Analysis and Interlanguage.* Oxford: Oxford University Press.

CROSS, T. 1977, Mothers' speech adjustments: The contribution of selected child listener variables. In C. SNOW and C. FERGUSON (eds) *Talking to Children.* Cambridge: Cambridge University Press.

CRYSTAL, D. and DAVY, D. 1969, *Investigating English Style.* London: Longman.

DANIEL, I. 1983, On first-year German forgien language learning: A comparison of language behavior in response to two instructional methods. Unpublished Ph.D. dissertation, University of Southern California.

DAY, R. 1984, Student participation in the ESL classroom. *Language Learning* 34, 69–89.

DE JONG, J.H.A.L. and STEVENSON, D.K. 1990, *Individualizing the Assessment of Language Abilities.* Clevedon: Multilingual Matters.

DECHERT, H. 1984, Individual variation in language. In H. DECHERT, D. MÖHLE and M. RAUPACH (eds) *Second Language Productions.* Tübingen: Gunter Narr Verlag.

DECHERT, H., MÖHLE, D. and RAUPACH, M. (eds) 1984, *Second Language Productions.* Tübingen: Gunter Narr Verlag.

DICKERSON, L. 1975, The learner's interlanguage as a system of variable rules. *TESOL Quarterly* 9: 401–7.

DICKERSON, L. and DICKERSON, W. 1977, Interlanguage phonology: Current research and future directions. In P. CORDER and S. ROULET (eds) *The Notions of Simplification, Interlanguages and Pidgins, Proceedings of the Sixth Neuchatel Colloqium.* University of Neuchatel.

DOUGHTY, C. and PICA, T. 1986, Information gap tasks: Do they facilitate second language acquisition? *TESOL Quarterly* 20, 305–25.

DOWNES, W. 1984, *Language and Society.* London: Fontana.

DUFF, P. 1986, Another look at interlanguage talk. In R. DAY (ed.) *Talking to Learn: Conversation in Second Language Acquisition.* Rowley, Mass.: Newbury House.

DULAY, H. and BURT, M. 1973, Should we teach children syntax? *Language Learning* 23, 245–58.

— 1974a, You can't learn without goofing. In J. RICHARDS (ed.) *Error Analysis.* London: Longman.

— 1974b, Natural sequences in child second language acquisition. *Language Learning* 24, 37–53.

DULAY, H., BURT, M. and KRASHEN, S. 1982, *Language Two.* New York: Oxford University Press.

DUPLESSIS, H., SOLIN, D., TRAVIS, L. and WHITE, L. 1987, UG or not UG, that is the question: A reply to Clahsen and Muysken. *Second Language Research* 3, 56–67.

ECKMAN, F., BELL, L. and NELSON, D. 1988, On the generalization of relative clause instruction in the acquisition of English as a second language. *Applied Linguistics* 9, 1–20.

EDMONDSON, W. 1985, Discourse worlds in the classroom and in foreign language learning. *Studies in Second Language Acquisition* 7, 159–68.

EISENSTEIN, M., BAILEY, N. and MADDEN, C. 1982, It takes two: Contrasting tasks and contrasting structures. *TESOL Quarterly* 16, 381–93.

ELLIS, R. 1980, Classroom interaction and its relation to second language learning. *RELC Journal* 11, 29–48.

— 1982a, Discourse processes in classroom second language development. Unpublished Ph.D. thesis, University of London.

— 1982b, Informal and formal approaches to communicative language teaching. *ELTJ* 36, 73–81.

— 1984a, *Classroom Second Language Development.* Oxford: Pergamon.

— 1984b, Can syntax be taught? A study of the effects of formal instruction on the acquisition of WH questions by children. *Applied Linguistics* 5, 138–55. Also published in this collection.

— 1984c, The role of instruction in second language acquisition. In D. SINGLETON and D. LITTLE (eds) *Language Learning in Formal and Informal Contexts.* IRAAL.

— 1984d, Formulaic speech in early classroom second language development. In J. HANDSCOMBE, R. OREM and B. TAYLOR, (eds) *On TESOL '83: The Question of Control.* Washington DC: TESOL.

— 1985, *Understanding Second Language Acquisition.* Oxford: Oxford University Press.

— (ed.) 1987a, *Second Language Acquisition in Context.* London: Prentice Hall International.

— 1987b, Interlanguage variability in narrative discourse: Style shifting in the use of the past tense. *Studies in Second Language Acquisition* 9, 1 2–20.

— 1988a, Investigating language teaching: The case for an educational perspective. *System* 16, 1–11.

— 1988b, The role of practice in classroom language learning. *Teanga* 8, 1–25. Also in this collection.

— 1989a, Sources of intra-learner variability in language use and their relationship to second language acquisition. In S. GASS, C. MADDEN, D. PRESTON and L. SELINKER (eds) *Variation in Second Language Acquisition: Psycholinguistic Issues.* Clevedon: Multilingual Matters.

— 1989b, Are classroom and naturalistic acquisition the same? A study of the classroom acquisition of German word order rules. *Studies in Second Language Acquisition* 11, 305–28. Also in this collection.

— 1990, *Instructed Second Language Acquisition.* Oxford: Basil Blackwell.

ELLIS, R. and RATHBONE, M. 1987, *The Acquisition of German in a Classroom Context.* London: Ealing College of Higher Education.

ELLIS, R. and WELLS, G. 1980, Enabling factors in adult–child discourse. *First Language* 1, 46–82.

ELY, C. 1986, An analysis of discomfort, risktaking, sociability and motivation in the L2 classroom. *Language Learning* 36, 1–25.

FAERCH, C. 1980, Describing interlanguage through interaction: Problems of systematicity and permeability. *Working Papers on Bilingualism* 19, 59–78.
— 1985, Metatalk in FL classroom discourse. *Studies in Second Language Acquisition* 7, 184–99.
FAERCH, C. and KASPER, G. 1980, Processes in foreign language learning and communication. *Interlanguage Studies Bulletin* 5, 47–118.
FAKHRI, A. 1984, The use of communicative strategies in narrative discourse. A case study of a learner of Moroccan Arabic as a second language. *Language Learning* 34, 15–37.
FATHMAN, A. 1975, The relationship between age and second language productive ability. *Language Learning* 25, 245–53.
— 1978, ESL and EFL learning: Similar or dissimilar? In C. BLATCHFORD and J. SCHACTER (eds) *On TESOL '78: Policies, Programs and Practices* (pp. 213–23). Washington DC: TESOL.
FELIX, S. 1977, Kreative and reprodukitive Kompetenz in Zweitensprachenwerb. In H. HUNTFIELD (ed.) *Neue Perspectiven der Fremdsprachendidaktik.* Kronberg.
— 1981, The effect of formal instruction on second language acquisition. *Language Learning* 31, 87–112.
FLYNN, S. 1987, *A Parameter-setting Model of L2 Acquisition.* Dortrecht: Reidel.
FRAWLEY, W. and LANTOLG, J. 1985, Second language discourse: A Vygotskyan perspective. *Applied Linguistics* 6, 19–44.
GAIES, S. 1977, The nature of linguistic input in formal second language learning: Linguistic and communicative strategies. In H. BROWN, C. YORIO and R. CRYMES (eds) *On TESOL '77.* Washington DC: TESOL.
GARDNER, R. 1980, On the validity of affective variables in second language acquisition: conceptual, contextual and statistical considerations. *Language Learning* 30, 255–70.
GASS, S. 1982, From theory to practice. In W. RUTHERFORD and M. HINES (eds) *On TESOL '81.* Washington DC: TESOL.
GASS, S. and MADDEN, C. (eds) 1985, *Input in Second Language Acquisition.* Rowley, Mass.: Newbury House.
GASS, S. and SELINKER, L. (eds) 1983, *Language Transfer in Language Learning.* Rowley, Mass.: Newbury House.
GATBONTON, E. 1978, Patterned phonetic variability in second language speech: A gradual diffusion model. *Canadian Modern Language Review* 34, 335–47.
GIVON, R. 1979, *On Understanding Grammar.* New York: Academic Press.
GODFREY, D. 1980, A discourse analysis of tense in monologues. In D. LARSEN-FREEMAN (ed.) *Discourse Analysis in Second Language Acquisition Research.* Rowley, Mass.: Newbury House.
GOWER, R. and WALTERS, S. 1983, *Teaching Practice Handbook.* London: Heinemann Educational.
GREGG, K. 1984, Krashen's Monitor and Occam's Razor. *Applied Linguistics* 5, 79–100.
— 1990, The variable competence model of second language acquisition and why it isn't. *Applied Linguistics* 11, 364–83.
GREGORC, A. 1979, *Learning/Teaching Styles: Their Nature and Effects in Students' Learning Styles.* Reston, Va.: National Association of Secondary School Principals.

HÅKANSSON, G. 1986, Quantitative studies of teacher talk. In G. KASPER (ed.)

Learning, Teaching and Communication in the Foreign Language Classroom. Aarhus: Aarhus University Press.

HAKUTA, K. 1974, A case study of a Japanese child learning English as a second language. *Language Learning* 26, 321–51.

HANDSCOMBE, J. 1990, The complementary roles of researchers and practitioners in second language education. In B. HARLEY, P. ALLEN, J. CUMMINS and M. SWAIN (eds) *The Development of Bilingual Proficiency.* Cambridge: Cambridge University Press.

HANSEN, J. and STANSFIELD, C. 1981, The relation of field dependent-independent cognitive styles to foreign language achievement. *Language Learning* 31, 349–67.

HARLEY, B. 1989, Functional grammar in French immersion: A classroom experiment. *Applied Linguistics* 10, 331–59.

HARLEY, B., ALLEN, P., CUMMINS, J. and SWAIN, M. (eds) 1990, *The Development of Bilingual Proficiency.* Cambridge: Cambridge University Press.

HARMER, J. 1984, *The Practice of English Teaching.* London: Longman.

HARTNETT, D. 1985, Cognitive style and second language learning. In M. CELCE-MURCIA (ed.) *Beyond Basics: Issues and Research in TESOL.* Rowley, Mass.: Newbury House.

HATCH, E. 1974, Second language learning — universals. *Working Papers on Bilingualism* 3, 1–18.

— 1978a, Discourse analysis and second language acquisition. In E. HATCH (ed.) *Second Language Acquisition.* Rowley, Mass.: Newbury house.

— 1978b, Acquisition of syntax in a second language. In J. RICHARDS (ed.) *Understanding Second and Foreign Language Learning.* Rowley, Mass.: Newbury House.

— 1983, *Psycholinguistics: A Second Language Perspective.* Rowley, Mass.: Newbury House.

— 1986, The experience model and language teaching. In R. DAY (ed.) *Talking to Learn: Conversation in Second Language Acquisition.* Rowley, Mass.: Newbury House.

HATCH, E. and FARHADY, H. 1982, *Research Design and Statistics for Applied Linguistics.* Rowley, Mass.: Newbury House.

HATCH, E., SHAPIRA, R. and GOUGH, J. 1978, 'Foreigner-talk' discourse. *ITL Review of Applied Linguistics* 39/40, 39–59.

HAYCRAFT, J. 1978, *An Introduction to Language Teaching.* London: Longman.

HEATON, J. 1975, *Beginning Composition Through Pictures.* London: Longman.

HENZL, V. 1979, Foreigner talk in the classroom. *International Review of Applied Linguistics* 17, 159–67.

HOLEC, H. 1980, Learner training: Meeting needs in self-directed learning. In H. ALTMAN and C. JAMES (eds) *Foreign Language Teaching: Meeting Individual Needs.* Oxford: Pergamon.

HOSENFELD, C. 1976, Learning about language: Discovering our students' strategies. *Foreign Language Annals* 9, 117–29.

HUBBARD, P., JONES, H., THORNTON, B. and WHEELER, R. 1983, *A Training Course for TEFL.* Oxford: Oxford University Press.

HUEBNER, T. 1979, Order-of-acquisition vs. dynamic paradigm: A comparison of method in interlanguage research. *TESOL Quarterly* 13, 21–8.

— 1981, Creative construction and the case of the misguided pattern. In J. FISHER, M. CLARKE and J. SCHACHTER (eds) *On TESOL '80: Building Bridges.* Washington DC: TESOL.

HUGHES, A. 1983, Second language learning and communicative language teaching. In K. JOHNSON and D. PORTER (eds) *Perspectives in Communicative Teaching*. New York: Academic Press.

HULSTIJN, J. and HULSTIJN, W. 1984, Grammatical errors as a function of processing constraints and explicit knowledge. *Language Learning* 34, 23–43.

HYLTENSTAM, K. 1984, The use of typological markedness as predictor in second language acquisition: The case of pronominal copies in relative clauses. In R. ANDERSEN (ed.) *Second Languages*. Rowley, Mass.: Newbury House.

— 1985, Learners' variable output and language teaching. In K. HYLTENSTAM and M. PIENEMANN (eds) *Modelling and Assessing Second Language Acquisition*. Clevedon, Avon: Multilingual Matters.

IOUP, G. and WEINBERGER, S. (eds) 1987, *Interlanguage Phonology*. Rowley, Mass.: Newbury House.

JOHNSON, K. 1982, *Communicative Syllabus Design and Methodology*. Oxford: Pergamon.

JOHNSON, S. 1990, Teacher questions in the academic language-content classroom. Unpublished paper, Temple University Japan.

JOHNSTON, M. 1987, Second language acquisition research: A classroom perspective. In M. JOHNSTON and M. PIENEMANN *Second Language Acquisition Research: A Classroom Perspective*. NSW: Adult Migrant Education Service.

— undated, L2 acquisition research: A classroom perspective. In M. Johnston and M. Pienemann (eds) *Second Language Acquisition: A Classroom Perspective*. Sydney: Adult Migrant Education Service.

JORDENS, P. 1988, The acquisition of word order in L2 Dutch and German. Unpublished manuscript, Vrje Universiteit, Amsterdam.

KANEKO, M. 1990, L1 use in foreign language classrooms. Unpublished paper, Temple University, Japan.

KASPER, G. (ed.) 1986, *Learning, Teaching and Communication in the Foreign Language Classroom*. Aarhus: Aarhus University Press.

KEEFE, J. 1979, Learning style: An overview. In J. KEEFE (ed.) *Student Learning Styles: Diagnosing and Prescribing Programs*. Reston, VA: National Secondary School Principals.

KELLERMAN, E. 1985, If at first you *do* succeed . . . . In S. GASS and C. MADDEN (eds) *Input in Second Language Acquisition*. Rowley, Mass.: Newbury House.

KITAZAWA, M. 1990, Is Pica and Doughty's system of interaction classification applicable to a Japanese language classroom? Unpublished paper, Temple University Japan.

KLEIFGEN, J. 1985, Skilled variation in a kindergarten teacher's use of foreigner talk. In S. GASS and C. MADDEN (eds) *Input in Second Language Acquisition*. Rowley, Mass.: Newbury House.

KLEIN, W. and PERDUE, C. 1988, *Second Language Acquisition by Adult Migrants*, Final Report (Vol.4). Strasburg: ESF.

KOLB, D. 1976, *Learning Style Inventory*. Boston: McBer.

KRAMSCH, C. 1985, Classroom interaction and discourse options. *Studies in Second Language Acquisition* 7, 169–83.

KRASHEN, S. 1977, The Monitor Model for adult second language performance. In M.

BURT, H. DULAY and M. FINOCCHIARO (eds) *Viewpoints on English as a Second Language*. New York: Regents.
— 1981a, *Second Language Acquisition and Second Language Learning*. Oxford: Pergamon.
— 1981b, Consciousness-raising and the second language acquirer: A response to Sharwood-Smith. Unpublished paper, University of Southern California.
— 1982, *Principles and Practice in Second Language Acquisition*. Oxford: Pergamon.
— 1985, *The Input Hypothesis*. London; Longman.
KRASHEN, S. and TERRELL, T. 1983, *The Natural Method: Language Acquisition in the Classroom*. Oxford: Pergamon.
KRASHEN, S., JONES, C., ZELINKSI, C., USPRICH, C. 1978, How important is instruction? *ELT Journal* 32, 257–61.
KRASHEN, S., SFERLAZZA, V., FELDMAN, L. and FATHMAN, A. 1976, Adult performance on the SLOPE test: More evidence for a natural sequence in adult second language acquisition. *Language Learning* 26, 145–51.

LABOV, W. 1963, The social motivation of sound change. *Word* 19, 273–309.
— 1970, The study of language in its social context. *Studium Generale* 23, 3–87.
LADO, R. 1964, *Language Teaching: A Scientific Approach*. New York: McGraw Hill.
LAKOFF, R. undated, Expository writing and the oral dyad as points on a communicative continuum. Mimeograph, University of California.
LARSEN-FREEMAN, D. 1976, An explanation for the morpheme accuracy order of learners of English as a second language. *Language Learning* 26, 125–35.
LEOPOLD, W. 1939, *Speech Development of a Bilingual Child: A Linguist's Record*, Vol. 1. Evanston Ill.: Northwestern University Press.
LIGHTBOWN, P. 1983, Exploring relationships between developmental and instructional sequences in L2 acquisition. In H. SELIGER and M. LONG (eds) *Classroom Oriented Research in Second Language Acquisition*. Rowley, Mass.: Newbury House.
— 1984, The relationship between theory and method in second language acquisition research. In A. DAVIES, C. CRIPER and A. HOWATT (eds) *Interlanguage*. Edinburgh: Edinburgh University Press.
— 1985a, Great expectations: Second-language acquisition research and classroom teaching. *Applied Linguistics* 6, 173–89.
— 1985b, Can language acquisition be altered by instruction? In K. HYLTENSTAM and M. PIENEMANN (eds) *Modelling and Assessing Second Language Acquisition*. Cleveland, Avon: Multilingual Matters.
— 1990, Process-product research on second language learning in classrooms. In B. HARLEY, P. ALLEN, J. CUMMINS and M. SWAIN (eds) *The Development of Bilingual Proficiency*. Cambridge: Cambridge University Press.
LIGHTBOWN, P., SPADA, N. and WALLACE, R. 1980, Some effects of instruction on child and adolescent ESL learners. In R. SCARCELLA and S. KRASHEN (eds) *Research in Second Language Acquisition*. Rowley, Mass.: Newbury House.
LITTLEWOOD, W. 1981a, *Communicative Language Teaching*. Cambridge: Cambridge University Press.
— 1981b, Language variation and second language acquisition theory. *Applied Linguistics* 2, 150–8.
LOCOCO, V. 1976, A comparison of three methods for the collection of L2 data: Free composition, translation and picture description. *Working Papers on Bilingualism* 8, 59–86.

LONG, M. 1977, Teacher feedback on learner error: Mapping cognitions. In H. BROWN, C. YORIO and R. CRYMES (eds) *On TESOL '77*. Washington DC: TESOL.
— 1981, Input, interaction and second language acquisition. In H. WINITZ (ed.) *Native Language and Foreign Language Acquisition*, Annals of the New York Academy of Sciences 379.
— 1983a, Native speaker/non-native speaker conversation in the second language classroom. In M. CLARKE and J. HANDSCOMBE (eds) *On TESOL '82: Pacific Perspectives on Language Learning and Teaching*. Washington DC: TESOL.
— 1983b, Native speaker/non-native speaker conversation and the negotiation of meaning. *Applied Linguistics* 4, 126–41.
— 1983c, Does second language instruction make a difference? A review of the research. *TESOL Quarterly* 17, 359–82.
— 1985a, Input and second language acquisition theory. In S. GASS and C. MADDEN (eds) *Input in Second Language Acquisition*. Rowley, Mass.: Newbury House.
— 1985b, A role for instruction in second language acquisition: Task-based language training. In K. HYLTENSTAM and M. PIENEMANN (eds) *Modelling and Assessing Second Language Acquisition*. Clevedon, Avon; Multilingual Matters.
— 1988a, Instructed interlanguage development. In L. BEEBE (ed.) *Issues in Second Language Acquisition: Multiple Perspectives*. Rowley, Mass.: Newbury House.
— 1988b, Maturational constraints on language development. Mimeograph, University of Hawaii.
LONG, M., BROCK, C., CROOKES, G., DEICKE, C., POTTER, L. and ZHANG, S. 1984, The effect of teachers' questioning patterns and wait-time on pupil participation in public high school in Hawaii for students of limited English proficiency. *Technical Report No. 1*. Honolulu: Center for Second Language Classroom Research, University of Hawaii at Manoa.
LONG, M. and SATO, C. 1983, Classroom foreigner talk discourse: Forms and functions of teachers' questions. In H. SELIGER and M. LONG (eds) *Classroom Oriented Research in Second Language Acquisition*. Rowley, Mass.: Newbury House.
LÖRSCHER, W. 1986, Conversational structures in the foreign language classroom. In G. KASPER (ed.) *Learning, Teaching and Communication in the Foreign Language Classroom*. Aarhus: Aarhus University Press.
LOSCHKY, L. 1989, The effects of negotiated interaction and premodified input on second language comprehension and retention. Unpublished MA thesis, University of Hawaii at Manoa.

McDONOUGH, S. 1987, *Psychology in Foreign Language Teaching* (2nd edn). London: Allen and Unwin.
McTEAR, M. 1975, Structure and categories of foreign language teaching sequences. In R. ALLWRIGHT (ed.) *Working Papers: Language Teaching Classroom Research*. University of Essex, Department of Language and Linguistics.
MAKINO, T. 1980, Acquisition order of English morphemes by Japanese secondary school students. *Journal of Hokkaido*, University of Education, Section IV (Humanities), 30, 101–48.
MEISEL, J. 1983, Strategies of second language acquisition: More than one kind of simplification. In R. ANDERSEN (ed.), *Pidginization and Creolization as Language Acquisition*. Rowley, Mass.: Newbury House.
— 1984, Strategies of second language acquisition: More than one kind of simplification. In R. Andersen (ed.) *Pidginization and Creolization as Language Acquisition*. Rowley, Mass.: Newbury House.

MEISEL, J., CLAHSEN, H. and PIENEMANN, M. 1981, On determining developmental stages in natural second language acquisition. *Studies in Second Language Acquisition* 3, 109–35.

MIDORIKAWA, H. 1990, The effects of questions on Japanese EFL discourse. Unpublished paper, Temple University Japan.

MITCHELL, R. 1988, *Communicative Language Teaching in Practice*. London: CILT.

NAIMAN, N., FRÖHLICH, M., STERN, H. and TODESCO, A. 1978, *The Good Language Learner*, Research in Education No. 7. Toronto, Ontario: Institute for Studies in Education.

NEMSER, W. 1971, Approximate systems of foreign language learners. *IRAL* 9, 115–23.

NEWMARK, L. 1966, How not to interfere in language learning. *International Journal of American Linguistics* 32, 77–83.

NICHOLAS, H. 1986, The acquisition of language as the acquisition of variation. *Australian Working Papers in Language Development* 1, 1–30.

NUNAN, D. 1988, *The Learner-centred Curriculum*. Cambridge: Cambridge University Press.

OCHS, E. 1979, Planned and unplanned discourse. In T. GIVON (ed.) *Syntax and Semantics Vol.12: Discourse and Semantics*. New York: Academic Press.

ODLIN, T. 1989, *Language Transfer*. Cambridge: Cambridge University Press.

PASK, G. 1976, Styles and strategies of learning. *British Journal of Educational Psychology* 22, 217–53.

PERDUE, C. (ed.) 1984, *Second Language Acquisition by Adult Immigrants: A Field Manual*. Rowley, Mass.: Newbury House.

PERKINS, K. and LARSEN-FREEMAN, D. 1975, The effect of formal language instruction on the order of morpheme acquisition. *Language Learning* 25, 237–43.

PICA, T. 1983, Adult acquisition of English as a second language under different conditions of exposure. *Language Learning* 33, 465–97.

— 1985, Instruction on second-language acquisition. *Applied Linguistics* 6, 214–22.

— 1987, Second-language acquisition, social interaction, and the classroom. *Applied Linguistics* 8, 3–21.

— 1990, The textual outcomes of NS–NNS negotiation: What do they reveal about second language learning? Paper given at Conference on Text and Context, Cornell University, Ithaca, New York.

PICA, T. and DOUGHTY, C. 1985, The role of group work in classroom second language acquisition. *Studies in Second Language Acquisition* 7, 233–49.

PICA, T. and LONG, M. 1986, The linguistic and conversational performance of experienced and inexperienced teachers. In R. DAY (ed.) *Talking to Learn: Conversation in Second Language Acquisition*. Rowley, Mass.: Newbury House.

PICA, T. YOUNG, R. and DOUGHTY, C. 1987, The impact of interaction on comprehension. *TESOL Quarterly* 21, 737–58.

PIENEMANN, M. 1980, The second language acquisition of immigrant children. In S. FELIX (ed.) *Second Language Development*. Tübingen: Gunter Narr.

— 1984, Psychological constraints on the teachability of languages. *Studies in Second Language Acquisition* 6, 186–214.

— 1985, Learnability and syllabus construction. In K. HYLTENSTAM and M. PIENEMANN (eds) *Modelling and Assessing Second Language Acquisition*. Clevedon, Avon: Multilingual Matters.

— 1986, Is language teachable? Psycholinguistic experiments and hypotheses. *Australian Working Papers in Language Development* 1, 3.

PIMSLEUR, P. 1966, *Pimsleur Language Aptitude Battery (PLBAT)*. New York: Harcourt Brace Jovanovich.

POLITZER, R. 1970, Some reflections on 'good' and 'bad' language teaching behaviors. *Language Learning* 20, 31–43.

POULISSE, N. 1989, *The Use of Compensatory Strategies by Dutch Learners of English*. Sneldruk, The Netherlands: Enschede.

PRABHU, N. 1982, The communicational teaching project. Unpublished paper, South India, Madras: The British Council.

— 1985, Coping with the unknown in language pedagogy. In R. QUIRK and H. WIDDOWSON (eds) *English in the World: Teaching and Learning the Language and Literatures*. Cambridge: Cambridge University Press.

— 1987, *Second Language Pedagogy*. Oxford: Oxford University Press.

PRESTON, D. 1989, *Sociolinguistics and Second Language Acquisition*. Oxford: Basil Blackwell.

RAVEM, R. 1968, Language acquisition in a second language environment. *International Review of Applied Linguistics* 6, 175–85.

REID, J. 1987, Learning style preferences of ESL students. *TESOL Quarterly* 20, 87–111.

REISS, M. 1981, Helping the unsuccessful language learner. *Modern Language Journal* 65, 121–8.

— 1985, The good language learner: Another look. *The Canadian Modern Language Review* 41, 511–23.

REYNOLDS, P. 1971, *A Primer in Theory Construction*. Indianapolis: Bobbs-Merrill.

RICHARDS, J. 1971, A non-contrastive approach to error analysis. *English Language Teaching* 25, 204–19.

RICHARDS, J. and ROGERS, T. 1986, *Approaches and Methods in Language Teaching: A Description and Analysis*. Cambridge: Cambridge University Press.

RILEY, P. 1977, Discourse networks in classroom interaction: Some problems in communicative language teaching. *Melangues Pedagogiques*, University of Nancy: CRAPEL.

RIVERS, W. and TEMPERLEY, M. 1978, *A Practical Guide to the Teaching of English*. Oxford: Oxford University Press.

ROBSON, C. 1973, *Experiment, Design and Statistics in Psychology*. London: Penguin.

ROSANSKY, E. 1976, Methods and morphemes in second language acquisition research. *Language Learning* 26, 409–25.

RUBIN, J. 1975, What the good language learner can teach us. *TESOL Quarterly* 9, 41–51.

RUTHERFORD, W. and SHARWOOD-SMITH, M. 1985, Consciousness-raising and universal grammar. *Applied Linguistics* 6, 274–81.

SACHS, H., SCHEGLOFF, E. and JEFFERSON, G. 1974, A simplest systematics for the organization of turn taking in conversation. *Language* 50, 696–735.

SAJAVAARA, K. 1981, The nature of first language transfer: English as L2 in a foreign language setting. Paper presented at the first European–North American Workshop in Second Language Acquisition Research, Lake Arrowhead, California.

SAMPSON, G. 1982, Converging evidence for a dialectal model of function and form in second language learning. *Applied Linguistics* 3, 1–28.

SATO, C. 1984, Phonological processes in second language acquisition: Another look at interlanguage syllable structure. *Language Learning* 34, 43–57.

— 1985, Task variation in interlanguage phonology. In S. GASS and C. MADDEN (eds) *Input in Second Language Acquisition*. Rowley, Mass.: Newbury House.

— 1986, Conversation and interlanguage development: Rethinking the connection. In R. DAY (ed.) *Talking to Learn: Conversation in Second Language Acquisition*. Rowley, Mass.: Newbury House.

SCARCELLA, R. and HIGA, C. 1981, Input, negotiation and age differences in second language acquisition. *Language Learning* 31, 409–37.

SCHACHTER, J. 1986, In search of systematicity in interlanguage production. *Studies in Second Language Acquisition* 8, 119–134.

SCHAPERS, R., LUSCHER, R. and GLÜCK, M. 1980, *Grundkurs Deutsch*. Munchen: Verlag fur Deutsch.

SCHERER, A. and WERTHEIMER, M. 1964, *A Psycholinguistic Experiment in Foreign Language Teaching*. New York: McGraw Hill.

SCHMIDT, R. 1977, Sociolinguistic variation and language transfer in phonology. *Working Papers on Bilingualism* 12, 79–95.

— 1983, Interaction, acculturation and the acquisition of communicative competence. In N. WOLFSON and E. JUDD (eds) *Sociolinguistics and Second Language Acquisition*. Rowley, Mass.: Newbury House.

— 1990, The role of consciousness in second language learning. *Applied Linguistics* 11, 17–46.

SCHUMANN, J. 1978a, *The Pidginization Process: A Model for Second Language Acquisition*. Rowley, Mass.: Newbury House.

— 1978b, Second language acquisition: The pidginization hypothesis. In E. HATCH (ed.) *Second Language Acquisition*. Rowley, Mass.: Newbury House.

SCHWARTZ, J. 1980, The negotiation for meaning: Repair in conversations between second language learners of English. In D. LARSEN-FREEMAN (ed.) *Discourse Analysis in Second Language Acquisition*. Rowley, Mass.: Newbury House.

SCOLLON, R. 1976, *Conversations with a One Year Old*. University of Hawaii, Honolulu.

SCOVEL, T. The effect of affect on foreign language learning: A review of the anxiety research. *Language Learning* 28, 129–42.

SELIGER, H. 1977, Does practice make perfect? A study of interaction patterns and L2 competence. *Language Learning* 27, 263–75.

— 1979, On the nature and function of language rules in language teaching. *TESOL Quarterly* 13, 359–69.

— 1980, Utterance planning and correction behavior: Its function in the grammar construction process for second language learners. In H. DECHERT and M. RAUPACH (eds) *Towards a Cross-linguistic Assessment of Speech Production*, Kasseler Arbeiten zur Sprache und Literatur 7. Frankfurt am Main: Peter D. Lang.

— 1984, Processing universals in second language acquisition. In F. ECKMAN, L. BELL and D. NELSON (eds) *Universals of Second Language Acquisition*. Rowley, Mass.: Newbury House.

SELINKER, L. 1972, Interlanguage. *International Review of Applied Linguistics* 10, 209–30.

SELINKER, L. and DOUGLAS, D. 1985, Wrestling with context in interlanguage theory. *Applied Linguistics* 6, 190–204.

SHARWOOD-SMITH, M. 1981, Consciousness-raising and the second language learner. *Applied Linguistics* 2, 159–69.

— 1986, Comprehension versus acquisition: Two ways of processing input. *Applied Linguistics* 7, 239–56.

SIEGEL, S. 1956, *Nonparametric Statistics for the Behavioral Sciences*. New York: McGraw-Hill.

SINCLAIR, J. and COULTHARD, M. 1975, *Towards an Analysis of Discourse*. Oxford: Oxford University Press.

SKEHAN, P. 1982, Memory and motivation in language aptitude testing. Unpublished Ph.D. dissertation, University of London.

— 1989, *Individual Differences in Second-Language Learning*. London: Edward Arnold.

SLIMANI, A. 1987, The teaching–learning relationship: Learning opportunities and learning outcomes, an Algerian case study. Unpublished Ph.D. thesis, University of Lancaster.

— 1989, The role of topicalization in classroom language learning. *System* 17, 223–34.

SLOBIN, D. 1973, Cognitive prerequisites for the development of grammar. In C. FERGUSON and D. SLOBIN (eds) *Studies of Child Language Development*. New York, Holt: Rinehart and Winston.

SMITH, P. (Jr) 1970, *A Comparison of the Cognitive and Audiolingual Approaches to Foreign Language Instruction: The Pennsylvania Foreign Language Project*. Philadelphia, PA: Center for Curriculum Development.

SPADA, N. 1987, Relationships between instructional differences and learning outcomes: A process-product study of communicative language teaching. *Applied Linguistics* 8, 137–55.

STERN, H. 1975, What can we learn from the good language learner? *The Canadian Modern Language Review* 34, 304–18.

— 1981, Communicative language teaching and learning: Towards a synthesis. In J. ALATIS, H. ALTMAN and P. ALATIS (eds) *The Second Language Classroom: Directions for the 1980s*. New York: Oxford University Press.

— 1983, *Fundamental Concepts of Language Teaching*. Oxford: Oxford University Press.

STEVICK, E. 1980, *Teaching Languages: A Way and Ways*. Rowley, Mass.: Newbury House.

SWAIN, M. 1985, Communicative competence: Some roles of comprehensible input and comprehensible output in its development. In S. GASS and C. MADDEN (eds) *Input in Second Language Acquisition*. Rowley, Mass.: Newbury House.

SWAN, M. 1985, A critical look at the communicative approach. *ELTJ* 39/1 and 39/2.

TARONE, E. 1977, Conscious communication strategies in interlanguage: A progress report. In H. BROWN, C. YORIO and R. CRYMES (eds) *On TESOL '77*. Washington DC: TESOL.

— 1981, Some thoughts on the notion of communication strategy. *TESOL Quarterly* 15, 285–95.

— 1983, On the variability of interlanguage systems. *Applied Linguistics* 4, 143–63.

— 1985, Variability in interlanguage use: A study of style-shifting in morphology and syntax. *Language Learning* 35, 373–404.

— 1988, *Variation in Interlanguage*. London: Edward Arnold.

TURNER, D. 1979, The effect of instruction on second language learning and second language acquisition. In R. ANDERSEN (ed.) *The Acquisition and Use of Spanish as First and Second Languages*. Washington, DC: TESOL.

UR, P. 1988, *Grammar Practice Activities*. Cambridge: Cambridge University Press.

VAN LIER, L. 1988, *The Classroom and the Learner*. London: Longman.
DE VILLIERS, J. and DE VILLIERS, P. 1973, A cross-sectional study of the acquisition of grammatical morphemes in child speech. *Journal of Psycholinguistic Research* 2, 267–78.
VYGOTSKY, L. 1962, *Thought and Language*. Cambridge, Mass.: MIT Press.

WAGNER-GOUGH, J. 1975, *Comparative Studies in Second Language Learning*. CAL-ERIC/CLL Series on Language and Linguistics, 26.
WEINERT, R. 1987, Processes in classroom second language development: The acquisition of negation in German. In R. ELLIS (ed.) *Second Language Acquisition in Context*. London: Prentice Hall International.
WELLS, G. 1980, Apprenticeship in meaning. In K. NELSON (ed.) *Children's Language*, Vol. 2. New York: Gardner Press.
— 1981, *Learning Through Interaction*. Cambridge: Cambridge University Press.
— 1985, *Language Development in the Pre-School Years*. Cambridge: Cambridge University Press.
— 1986, *The Meaning Makers: Children Learning and Using Language to Learn*. London: Hodder and Stoughton.
WENDEN, A. 1986, What do second language learners know about their language learning: A second look at retrospective accounts. *Applied Linguistics* 7, 186–205.
WENDEN, A. and RUBIN, J. (eds) *Learner Strategies in Language Learning*. Englewood Cliffs, NY: Prentice-Hall.
WESCHE, M. 1981, Language aptitude measures in streaming, matching students with methods and diagnosis of learning problems. In K. DILLER (ed.) *Individual Differences and Universals in Language Learning*. Rowley, Mass.: Newbury House.
WESCHE, M. and READY, D. 1985, Foreigner talk in the university classroom. In S. GASS and C. MADDEN (eds) *Input in Second Language Acquisition*. Rowley, Mass.: Newbury House.
WESTMORELAND, R. 1983, L2 German acquisition by instructed adults. Unpublished manuscript, University of Hawaii at Manoa.
WHITE, L. 1987, Against comprehensible input: The Input Hypothesis and the development of second-language competence. *Applied Linguistics* 8, 95–110.
— 1989, The principle of adjacency in second language acquisition: Do L2 learners observe the subset principle? In S. GASS and J. SCHACHTER (eds) *Linguistic Perspectives on Second Language Acquisition*. Cambridge: Cambridge University Press.
— 1990, Second language acquisition and universal grammar. *Studies in Second Language Acquisition* 12, 120–34.
WIDDOWSON, H. 1975, The significance of simplification. *Studies in Second Language Acquisition* 1, 11–20.
— 1978, *Teaching Language as Communication*. Oxford: Oxford University.
WILLING, K. 1987, *Learning Styles in Adult Migrant Education*. National Curriculum Resource Centre, Adult Migrant Education Program Australia.
— 1988, Learning styles in adult migrant education. National Curriculum Resource Centre, Adult Migrant Education Programm, Australia.
WITKIN, H., OLTMAN, P., RASKIN, E. and KARP, S. 1971, *A Manual for the Embedded Figures Test*. Palo Alto, California Consulting Psychologists Press.

WODE, H. 1976, Developmental sequences in naturalistic L2 acquisition. *Working Papers on Bilingualism* 11, 1–13.

— 1980, *Learning a Second Language: An Integrated View of Language Acquisition.* Tübingen: Gunter Narr.

WONG FILLMORE, L. 1985, When does teacher talk work as input? In S. GASS and C. MADDEN (eds) *Input in Second Language Acquisition.* Rowley, Mass.: Newbury House.

YOSHIDA, M. 1978, The acquisition of English vocabulary by a Japanese-speaking child. In E.HATCH (ed.) *Second Language Acquisition.* Rowley, Mass.: Newbury House.

ZOBL, H. 1983, Markedness and the projection problem. *Language Learning* 33, 293–313.

— 1985, Grammars in search of input and intake. In S. GASS and C. MADDEN (eds) *Input in Second Language Acquisition.* Rowley, Mass.: Newbury House.

Index